Guide to College Writing

9th edition

"I meant…"
"But it says…"

Emily Dial-Driver
Rogers State University

Kendall Hunt
publishing company

Acknowledgements:
With special thanks to Jeana Driver, Grant Driver Jr., David Schramme, Alan Lawless, Guylene Hull, Claudia McBride, Linda Putnam, Julia Sheppard, Polly H. Dial, Ellen D. Fitzpatrick, Gary Moeller, Phil Sample, Shelly Borgstrom, Cassie Hughes, Sally Emmons-Featherston, Doug Martin, Robin Pryor, Victor Gischler, Jim Ford, Diana Lurz, Hugh Foley, Judy Hubble, Susan Rainey, Laura Gray, Chip Rogers, Bryce Brimer, Nat Hardy, Jesse Stallings, Brandon Jones, Laura Smith, Renée Turk, Frances Morris, and the students of composition.

Cover image © Thomas M Perkins, 2009. Used under license from Shutterstock, Inc.

Kendall Hunt
publishing company

www.kendallhunt.com
Send all inquiries to:
4050 Westmark Drive
Dubuque, IA 52004-1840

Copyright ©2009 by Emily Dial-Driver.

ISBN 978-0-7575-7006-3

All rights reserved. No part of this publication may be reproduced, stored in a retrieval system, or transmitted, in any form or by any means, electronic, mechanical, photocopying, recording, or otherwise, without the prior written permission of the copyright owner.

Printed in the United States of America
10 9 8 7 6 5 4 3

Contents

Using This Book	1
Learning Writing	2
Why Bother?	2
Taking Notes	2
Annotating Texts	3
Journals	4
Writing Process	4
Pre-Writing	5
Free-Writing	5
Brainstorming	6
Mapping	7
Journalists' Questions	8
Reading for Writing	8
Planning	9
Writing for a Purpose	9
Writing for an Audience	10
Organization	11
The College Essay	11
Formal Essay Organization	11
Writing Hints	13
Stylistic Hints	13
The Organization Plan Page	14
Outlines	19
Paragraphs	21
Development	21
Coherence and Unity	23
Patterns of Development for Paragraphs and Essays	27
Narration	27
Description	28
Example	28
Process	30
Comparison (and Contrast)	31
Analogy	32
Division and Classification	33

Analysis/Cause and Effect	35
Argumentation/Persuasion	36
Revision	37
Manuscript Preparation	38
Writing: The Recursive Process	40
Reading	41
Specialized Forms of Writing	47
Summarizing	47
Reports and Reviews	50
Making Evaluations	51
Reviews, Critiques, and Evaluations	52
Essay Tests	52
Electronic Communications	58
The Research Paper	59
Step One: Limited Topic	60
Step Two: Preliminary Bibliography	60
MLA Documentation	63
APA Documentation	68
Step Three: Notes	71
Assessing Sources	71
Plagiarism	72
Annotated Bibliography	77
Step Four: Plan and Outline	77
Step Five: First Draft	78
Using Quotations in the Paper	78
MLA Internal Documentation	79
Citing Literary Works in MLA	81
Special Punctuation for Quotations	82
Brackets and Ellipsis in MLA	82
Summary and Paraphrasing	85
Longer Quotations	85
APA Citation	86
Step Six: Revision	87
Step Seven: Final Draft	87
Checking the Paper	88

Reviewing Research Papers	89
Writing in Response to Literature	90
Analysis	94
Interpretation	99
Criticism	100
Film Analysis	102
Poetry Analysis	107
Glossary: Literary Terms	112
Business	117
Job Interviews	117
Business Letters	118
Résumés	121
Memoranda	126
Science Formats	127
Graphs	128
Library Discovery	129
Card Catalog	129
Articles from Magazines and Newspapers	132
Non-Print Resources	132
Special Help	133
Computer and Internet Sources	134
Librarians	134
Mechanics	135
Usage	135
Sentence Structure	136
Parallel Construction	137
Agreement	138
Verb/Subject	139
Pronoun	140
Capitalization	141
Numbers	144
Punctuation	145
End Marks	145
Commas	146
Colons	149
Semicolons	150
Apostrophes	150
Hyphens	151
Quotation Marks	152
Underlining	154
Parentheses	155
Brackets	155
Ellipsis	155
Dashes	156
Spelling	157
Spacing Punctuation Marks	159
Common Mistakes	161
Symbols for Graded/Marked Papers	162
Appendices	163
A: Student Models	163
Documented Essays	164
B: Principles of Reader Response and Review	185
Essay Response Form	185
Response Sheet for Essays	191
Response Sheet for Reports	193
Response Sheet for Paragraphs	193
Reader Response Form	195
Writer Reflection Form	197
General Rubric for Papers	199
Grade Sheets	203
Recognizing Logical Fallacies	209
C: Other Documentation Styles	211
Index	213

USING THIS BOOK

The *Guide to College Writing* is designed to be accessible, usable, and directive. It is not a philosophical statement about writing. It is a straightforward guide to writing easily-formatted, easily-read college essays. The principles are basic but can be applied to any level of complexity in writing. In addition, the *Guide* gives basic information on a number of other kinds of writing. The instructions are simple, written in a "first do this, then do that" style that should be easy to follow and easy to use.

The *Guide* is divided into sections. The majority of the text is devoted to the writing process and the development of the research paper, including using the library. Other sections include mechanics, business and science writing, and examples of various kinds of student writing.

Examples in the Appendix include papers with MLA style. The opening page of the Appendix has a key to those examples.

Examples in the main portion of the book that apply to all forms of documentation are boxed and unshaded:

Examples in the main portion of the book that are in MLA format are surrounded by a solid box and are shaded:

LEARNING WRITING

Why Bother?

"I just can't find anyone to do the job," says the employer.

The agency asks, "What's the problem?"

The employer replies, "Well, I guess the main problem is that I can't find anyone who can communicate in writing."

Yet another employer says plaintively, "Quit sending me applicants who can't express themselves on paper."

Almost every job requires some kind of writing. For example, you may think of police work as "cops and robbers," but police work is more than just action. Police have to write traffic accident reports, investigation reports, incident reports, prosecution reports, information reports, memos, letters, press releases, and so on. You would not survive in a quality police department if you could not write good, concise, complete, understandable reports. And most police work is not considered a desk job!

Another active job that requires writing is nursing. Aside from tending to patient needs, nurses compose both professional and business letters, design professional standards, write research reports and articles for professional journals and professional seminars, complete innumerable patient reports, and more.

So accept the fact that you are going to have to write. You are going to be held responsible for (and judged on) those "English things," such as spelling, sentence structure, and punctuation. In addition to being judged on mechanics, you will be judged on how your papers look. You have probably heard that "first impressions are important." This saying is true not only when meeting other people but also applies to how your paper looks when your boss, customer, or instructor sees it. If the paper is neat and looks as though you followed the rules for correct manuscript format, the first impression will be good; this could affect your grade!

> *Every job requires writing.*

Writing is not something you are born knowing how to do. It is a skill, like swimming, riding a bicycle, driving a car (or talking or reading), that you learn to do. Some people write more creatively than others, but anyone who wants to do so can learn to write well.

The best way to learn to write is to write. And in college—in all departments and in many different kinds of circumstances—you will be required to write. Writing is in your future!

Taking Notes

One of the ways that you write in college is by taking notes. Note taking helps you learn—by requiring you to listen, process, and paraphrase before writing. In addition, classroom note taking is the very best preparation for taking "field notes." The quality of the finished report, record, or study is based on the quality and quantity of raw information. The ability to take good notes is the way to get information of the quality and quantity that you need.

The style or manner of taking notes is not important. What is important is taking the notes. One method of taking notes is the outline method (see the section on outlines). Another is the "pearls of wisdom" method: you listen to the lecture and, every time you hear something that sounds important, you write it in your notebook. If information is written on the board, an overhead, or a PowerPoint slide, you should probably write it down!

Taking notes matters.

One way to take notes is to create a response log, which provides you with a review and study method. It also allows you to take an active part in learning, because the act of writing reinforces the concepts. Then the log becomes a visible, permanent record of the class and is handy for review.

Take notes on one-half of the front side of the paper only. Leave the other half blank. Later, when you are studying, cover the half with the class notes and use the other side, preferably the left side, to recall and recite the important information.

#5	26 May 09	Atomic Numbers	Dr. Lawless
Review main idea here Key detail review Review main idea here Key detail review Review main idea here Key detail review Review main idea here Key detail review		Class note main idea here Examples, important subpoints Class note main idea here Examples, important subpoints Class note main idea here Examples, important subpoints Class note main idea here Examples, important subpoints Vocabulary:	

ANNOTATING TEXT

The learning log system can also be used in response to print. You may interact with the text by annotating the margins. Annotating is marking, that is, marking the text with explanations or notes that relate to your own experience or information or to other information in the text. (Yes, you may still sell the book back at the end of the semester if there is writing in it. The next buyer may even be grateful.) Or you may choose to use the learning log method previously discussed, taking notes about the text selection on half of the page and responding to that section on the other half of the page.

Journals

Another way that you may be asked to write in college is to keep a journal. A journal records your work, your experiences, your impressions, and your thoughts. It helps you learn to write. It helps you learn about the subject on which you write—whether the subject is yourself, a course subject, or a topic in which you are interested.

A journal should be easily identifiable. Your name and the journal subject should appear prominently on the front cover or first page and on each following page. Each entry should be labeled by specific subject and date so that you or another reader can easily distinguish one entry from another.

Example (Journal Entry Heading)

- If you are keeping a journal for a physics class, you might write your name, class, number of the class, time of meeting, and semester in the upper right corner of the front cover or the inside of the front cover.
- The first entry might be labeled as follows:

#1　　　Aug 25, 2005　　　Discussion of Light Waves　　　Sally Student

---

Hints for Successful Journals:

1. Put the journal entries in the required type of notebook, spiral notebook, or folder.
2. Turn in the journal when it is due.
3. Complete the assignments, making each entry the suggested length.
4. Write legibly in ink on the front of the pages.
5. Be coherent; stick to the subject.
6. Show good writing skills.
7. Do not use the word *bored* or *boring*. To be bored shows a lack of inner resources, to which you should never admit.

THE WRITING PROCESS

Pre-Writing

Sometimes, when you are faced with a particular subject or a writing assignment, you may feel that you have little to say. But you have more ideas than you might think at first. The following techniques can help you generate those ideas.

Free Writing

Free writing is the technique of letting ideas flow from your head, maybe even from your subconscious, through your pen or through your fingers to a typewriter or computer keyboard. All you have to do is write. Begin by putting down the subject and just keep writing. Usually you can give yourself a time limit of five or ten minutes. Keep writing for the full time. Do not stop. If you run out of ideas, write "I cannot think of anything to say." The physical activity of continuing to write will help you generate ideas and prevent writer's block.

When you have finished free writing, you can look back over your paper and discover any relationships between ideas or thoughts. You can weed out the irrelevancies and concentrate on the meaty thoughts that you have generated. When you have chosen one idea or a group of ideas from one (or more) free writings, you can move on to one of the pre-writing techniques that involve more organization.

Example (Free Writing)

- The topic is music.
- For five minutes, you write and you generate this:

I have to write about music which I am listening to, and it's good stuff—only it's not regular music like country or rock or classical, and that's a weird term anyway because classical is only a period in music, like romantic or baroque, or that stuff that doesn't have music, just words like chants and then chants like the Buddhist monks, and they toured with the Dead. I like rock like the Dead. And it's weird that they are funding research into folk music like Pete Seeger and Joan Baez. I can't think of anything to say. I can't think . . . I don't like tribal, which can be cultural or about emotion, like New Age soothing stuff, or the nature stuff or wind chimes. Are they music? And what about just drums or hollow logs and even combinations, like rock and aboriginal? Where do people get recordings of tribal music and who buys that and who buys . . . ?

- You look at what you've written and find some topics on which you might be interested in writing. Those topics are in boldface print in the pre-writing that follows:

I have to write about music which I am listening to, and it's good stuff—only it's not regular music like **country or rock or classical**, and that's a weird term anyway **because classical is only a period in music, like romantic or baroque**, or that stuff that doesn't have music, just words like **chants** and then chants like **the Buddhist monks, and they toured with the Dead**. I like **rock like the Dead**. And it's weird that they are **funding research into folk music** like Pete Seeger and Joan Baez. I can't think of anything to say. I can't think. I don't like **tribal, which can be cultural or about emotion,** like **New Age** soothing stuff, or the **nature stuff** or **wind chimes. Are they music**? And what about just **drums or hollow logs** and even **combinations, like rock and aboriginal? Where do people get recordings** of tribal music and **who buys** that and who buys. . . .?

- You might decide that you need another free writing to generate more ideas about one of the topics in the first free writing, or you may decide to begin working with one of the topics that you have just discovered.

Brainstorming

Brainstorming means making a list of all of the ideas that occur to you about the subject. The list can be words or phrases related to the subject. Because a list is less structured than sentences, you will be able to explore ideas rapidly.

You may brainstorm by yourself and spark ideas from your own experiences. Or you may brainstorm in a group so that the group members can help each other generate ideas. If you brainstorm in a group, do not feel that you must accept the group members' ideas any more than they should feel that they have to use yours. Brainstorming is designed to bring you more, not fewer, ideas.

Probably the first brainstorming list will be a random one. Then you can relate and classify the ideas. This process generates your second list and maybe your third and fourth!

Example (Brainstorming)

Change (random list)

amt. money	work	insurance	food	play
lifestyles	computers	crime	malls	space
houses	cars	lawsuits	commitments	shopping
schooling	libraries	information	clothes	environment

Change (grouped list)

Lifestyles
  houses, types
  commitments
  clothes
  car
  food, restaurant--
      fast, convenient
  shopping--
      malls/catalogs
  insurance--
      lawsuits/crime

Work
  number of people in family
  computers
  amount of money--
      lifestyles
      work styles
  kind of job

Notice that the second list adds some ideas and that it leaves out a few as well.

Mapping

Mapping is like brainstorming, but it may be more creative and less restrictive for you than lines and lists. Start with putting the subject, circled, in the center of the paper. Draw a line from the subject circle to a major idea about your subject. Cluster any subordinate ideas relating to the major idea in circles at the ends of lines drawn from that major idea. Then draw another line from the subject circle to another major idea about the subject and cluster subordinate ideas around that major idea. Continue until you feel that you have finished.

Example (Mapping)

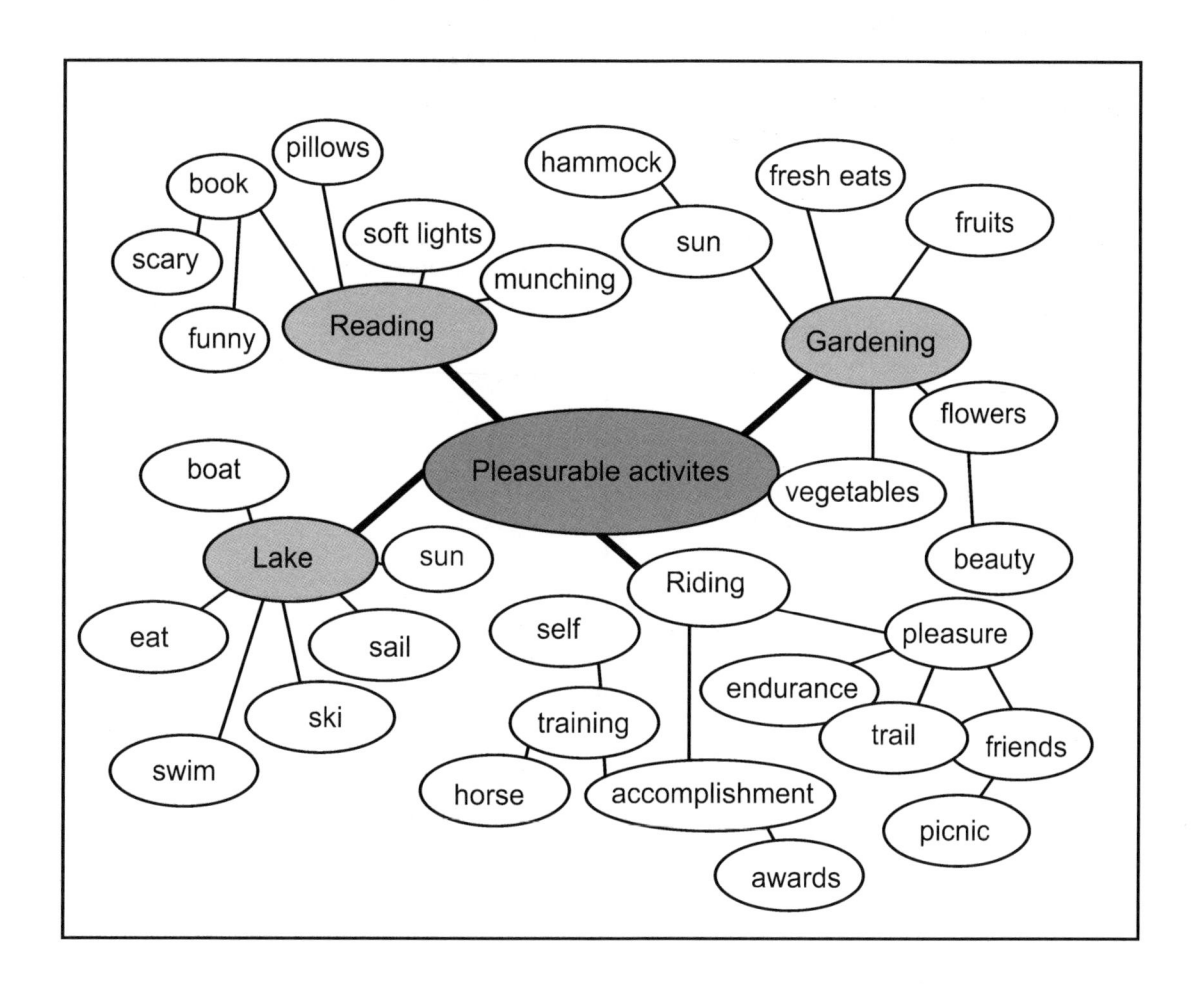

```
                pillows
         book          hammock    fresh eats
                soft lights                   fruits
   scary              sun
                munching
   funny   Reading              Gardening
                                            flowers
   boat
              Pleasurable activites    vegetables
                                              beauty
         Lake    sun
                        Riding            pleasure
   eat       sail         self
                                endurance
              ski    training         trail    friends
   swim
              horse    accomplishment
                                          picnic
                       awards
```

Journalists' Questions

Journalists ask these questions: who, what, when, where, why, and how. Asking yourself these questions forces you to investigate the subject from more than one perspective.

Example (Journalists' Questions)

The subject is **exercising**. Your lists might include these questions:	

Who exercises?
  people under a doctor's care
  fanatics and body builders
  people enrolled in classes
  people who paid good money
  desperate flabby people
  people who do physical jobs
  people who have physical hobbies
	What is exercising?
	  repetitive movement
	  aerobic
	  weight bearing
	  using weights
	  lifting boxes
	  picking cotton
	  jittering

When do people exercise?
  mornings
  after work
  at lunch hour
  evenings
  weekends
  only on vacation
  all day at work
  hobby time
	Where do people exercise?
	  at work
	  at home
	  at a spa
	  in a class
	  at a health club
	  in the park
	  at a mall

Why do people exercise?
  to feel good
  to punish themselves
  to follow doctor's advice
  to stay healthy
  to look good or look young
  to win a prize or award
  to make up for eating sundaes
  to do the job or hobby
  from a feeling of obligation
	How do people exercise?
	  running
	  walking
	  swimming
	  aerobics
	  weight lifting
	  doing the job
	  working on the hobby

Reading for Writing

After you have generated your own ideas, you might add outside support by reading critically and learning about the subject. However, do not depend only on using other people's words and ideas for your papers. Use your own words and ideas as well.

Sometimes the parameters of the assignment do not allow you to read about the subject. In that case, it is your thoughts and experiences that the instructor wants in the paper.

PLANNING

Writing for a Purpose

Writing must start with a purpose: to inform or explain, persuade, entertain, or explore.

Writing to inform means giving the audience information. Informative writing is straightforward; it does not appeal to emotion or to prejudice. Writing to explain is a kind of informative writing; explanatory writing may, however, be more personal than writing to inform.

Writing to persuade means persuading the reader to accept your point of view, perhaps about the validity or invalidity of an action. Persuasive writing may appeal to the audience's emotions but should not appeal to prejudice. In addition to emotional appeal, effective persuasion uses accurate information to convince the audience.

Entertaining writing amuses, frightens, depresses, uplifts, etc. It uses a combination of emotional and psychological devices to appeal to the audience.

Exploratory writing explores an idea, an emotion, or an experience of the writer for the benefit of the writer and of the audience. Writing to explore is probably the most difficult type of writing. As in other writing, word choice is vitally important because the emotional, logical, and psychological impacts on the audience are necessary ingredients of exploratory writing.

Some writing combines purposes. Some items that have been written mainly to inform the audience also include humor—to make the writing more interesting or more exciting. Most persuasive pieces are also informative, because people are unlikely to change their minds on the basis of just an appeal for the change. They need reasons, good solid reasons, and solid information on which to base their change of position. (At least we hope they need reasons!) And a persuasive piece may use humor to get across some of the information or some of the persuasion.

Jessica Mitford's article "Behind the Formaldehyde Curtain" is informative. The purpose of the article is to inform the reader about what goes on behind the "formaldehyde curtain" at a mortuary. But Mitford's selection of details and words make the subject entertaining, although it is still morbid to some.

The article "Self-Defense: Can You Protect Yourself and Avoid the Slammer?" by Arthur M. Miller is mainly informative but is also persuasive. The information about self-defense laws can persuade the reader to review opinions on self-defense and to consider the possible results of self-defense.

Thus, writing may contain purpose from each category. Nevertheless, when you are beginning to write, selection of a main purpose is necessary in order to decide just how to approach the subject. You would approach the subject of the Asiatic cockroach invasion of the United States one way if you wanted to inform your reader about what kind of roach this is and what problems society can anticipate. You would approach the subject differently if you wanted to persuade your reader that the Environmental Protection Agency (EPA) rules against some insecticides should be set aside so that Floridians, among others, could defend themselves against the invading roach. You would use another approach if you wanted to explain to or inform your reader about how to combat the roach. You would approach the subject still differently if you wanted to entertain your reader with stories of the roach who came to dinner and lunch and breakfast and . . .

Remember that, as a college student, you will mostly be writing to inform.

Writing for an Audience

Another important decision in writing is deciding to whom the writing will be addressed. The selection of the audience is vital to many of your decisions as you progress through the writing.

College writing is usually addressed to an audience that is as well informed on a subject as you were when you started writing. For instance, when you write a research paper in microbiology, the audience to which you write will probably be your classmates, who know as much about *staphylococcus* bacteria as you did when you began the paper.

> *Professors grade, but papers are written at classmate level.*

Even though an instructor or professor is going to read (and grade) your paper and even though you are always aware of that grader as you write, you do not actually write your paper to the audience of the grader. If you kept the grader in mind as the audience, you would have to write to the level of the grader. To inform the grader, a person who is purportedly an expert in the field in which you are taking a class, you would have to use a different vocabulary; include different sentence structure; take a different, more advanced approach; and furnish different, more complex, more esoteric information than you would have to use in addressing an audience of college students at your level. Choosing an audience of college students makes your chore easier.

If you do not choose a college audience, you may choose any specific audience: 4-year-old boys, second-year astronauts, gerontology majors, high school dropouts. Whatever audience you choose, you have some important decisions to make about how you write:

How much does the audience already know about the subject?
> What is the audience's age and education level?
> How much information can you give them?
> How much do they need?
> How much will they understand?

What kind of vocabulary will you use?
> Do any words you ordinarily use need defining for the audience?
> Is specialized vocabulary appropriate?

What preconceptions do you have to work against?
> Has the audience already made a decision on the issue?
> What do they already believe?
> What arguments can you use that will be persuasive?

Remember that, as a college student, you will mostly be writing to a college audience.

ORGANIZATION

THE COLLEGE ESSAY

An essay is a relatively brief piece of nonfiction prose that tries to make a point in an interesting way. Every essay emphasizes content by concentrating on subject, focus, and organization.

1. **An essay is fairly brief.** Some classic essays occupy only a few paragraphs, and in a composition course you may be asked to limit your first essays to between 350 and 750 words. The length of an essay generally falls between two and twenty-five typed, double-spaced pages. Below that minimum number of pages, the development typical of an essay is difficult. Above that maximum, people might be tempted to read the piece in installments.

2. **An essay is nonfiction.** An essayist tries to tell the truth about the world, an event, or a person or to speculate about possible changes in the world. If the essay contains a story or a description, the audience presumes that the details have not been made up.

3. **An essay makes a point.** An essay tells or explains something, expresses an attitude toward something, or supports or rejects something—an opinion, a person or place, a work of art, an institution, a movement. A poem, novel, or short story may also do these things, but it does them incidentally; a poem, novel, or short story appeals, above all, to the reader's imagination. An essay directly addresses a topic or specific subject, and its usual aim is to win sympathy with or agreement on the point (or thesis) that it is maintaining.

4. **An essay is meant to be engaging.** An essay should arouse curiosity, convince the reader that the main idea is worth bothering about, and move toward a satisfyingly conclusive finish. To be an effective essayist, you must be willing to strike some balances. You want to tell the truth but make people interested in reading it; write with conviction but consider whether your ideas and attitudes stand up under criticism; supply evidence but not become a bore about it; be purposeful but not follow such a predictable pattern that the reader's attention slackens.

Formal Essay Organization

Essays can be organized in any number of ways. You have seen examples of different kinds of organization in your reading—at school, in textbooks, in articles, in magazines, in lots of things. Essays can have an unstated main idea (or thesis); they can have very long or very short paragraphs, etc. However, the easiest essay to read and to write is the essay that is discussed here: the three-section essay.

The three-section essay (introduction, body, and conclusion) is a convenient, simple, easily-followed, simply-structured way to write about almost anything—but remember, it is not the only way.

The three-section essay is usually 500–1,500 words (and four, five, or more paragraphs), but it can be of any length, from a couple of pages to twenty-five pages. The principle is the same regardless of the length. The introduction becomes an introductory section, the body becomes a body section, and the conclusion becomes a conclusion section. If you are writing a ten-page paper, you will have, of course, more than five paragraphs. You might have three paragraphs of introduction that culminate in the statement of thesis; then have three body sections, each of which has five to seven paragraphs; and finally end with a two-paragraph conclusion. Still, the principle of the three-section essay remains.

Introduction

The introductory paragraph begins by capturing the reader's attention and ends by introducing the central idea of the paper. For a five-paragraph essay of two to five pages, a paragraph of introduction is generally five to thirteen sentences long.

> *Essays have thesis statements.*

The introduction may get the reader's attention in any number of ways, including using facts, quotation(s), a personal anecdote, or a story. The introduction may use one or more of these devices, depending on the length of the paper and the writer's decisions.

The paragraph moves from general statements about the topic to specific statements. The culminating specific statement in the introductory paragraph, the last sentence in the paragraph, is the thesis. The thesis statement announces the main idea of the paper and is usually the last sentence in the introductory section.

Body

Begin each body paragraph (which contains seven to thirteen sentences) with a topic sentence that is an expansion of one of the subject elements of the thesis. Thus, every topic sentence relates to and develops the thesis, and every sentence in the paragraph is related to and develops the topic sentence. (See the section on Paragraph Development.)

Conclusion

A paragraph (generally, five to thirteen sentences for a five-paragraph essay of two to five pages) is needed to unify the theme. The conclusion may summarize the main points, restate the thesis, or point out the significance of what you have said in the body of the paper. It may make a prediction or recommendation; it may refer to the introduction. What a conclusion may *not* do is introduce new material.

Writing Process • Organization

WRITING HINTS

1. *Plan.* (See the Organization Plan Page section.) Planning and organizing are, along with consideration of the audience, most important. It is vital to know where you are going on a trip before you start if you want to get there. It is also vital to know where you want your writing to go so you can decide how to arrive there. Make decisions on purpose, subject, audience, thesis, and subject elements before you start writing. Involve yourself in pre-writing activities such as brainstorming and mapping. (See the section on Pre-Writing.)

> *Write to an audience.*

2. *Choose a specific audience and write to that audience.* You may choose to write to someone who is reasonably familiar with the subject or who is as familiar with the subject as you were to start with. If you choose a different specific audience, keep your audience in mind constantly, throughout the writing process, and make decisions about vocabulary, style, explanation, and detail based on that audience. (See the section on Audience.)

Stylistic Hints

1. Italicize titles of books and television shows. Titles of episodes of television shows and of short stories and poems are set in quotation marks. (See the section on Punctuation for a complete explanation of italicizing.)
2. Avoid using the word *you* unless you are speaking to a specific audience—the way that I, the writer of this text, am speaking to you, the reader, and to you alone. To use the word *you* can be disconcerting or offensive to the reader. If you said, "The movie made you feel good" and some readers did not see the movie or did not enjoy the movie if they did see it, they might find the flow of reading disturbed. If you said, "You know that this is true" and readers did not wholly agree with you, they might not wish to read the remainder of the argument, and you would have lost the chance to inform or convince them.
3. Avoid using contractions, such as *can't* or *don't* or *I'm*.
4. Avoid making statements such as "This paper will show . . ." or "In this paper, I will . . ."
5. Avoid using the word *there* at the beginning of a sentence or the word *it* as the subject of a sentence.
6. Be very careful about using absolutes. If you say "Everyone is," you need to be sure that the word *everyone* really includes everyone—babies and people in hospitals and people with mental disorders, etc.
7. Take great care about punctuation, spelling, sentence structure, and other mechanics. Good mechanics make for good reading. Poor mechanics are obvious to informed readers and distract them from following your arguments or evidence. It is even possible that readers can take the opposite position from that which you encourage because they are irritated by poor mechanics or because they assume the writer is not credible or not informed.

8. Concentrate on using active voice rather than passive. Instead of saying "The beautiful blonde cocker spaniel was attacked by a ravening monster with green slimy fangs" (which is makes use of passive voice), say, in active voice, "A ravening monster with green slimy fangs attacked the beautiful blonde cocker spaniel." It is much more effective.
9. In writing about literature, use the present tense. Shakespeare's cast, with Romeo and Juliet, live today in Verona, despite having died at play's end many times.
10. Refer to authors by last names—unless you know them personally. Convention says they should be referred to by their last names and their last names only, not prefaced by an honorific such as Mr. or Ms.

THE ORGANIZATION PLAN PAGE

An organization plan page allows you to organize a topic efficiently by following these steps:

Step 1: General Topic

Begin with a general topic, which is usually the subject that is assigned to you by the college instructor or professor.

Step 2: Restricted Topic

Restrict or limit that topic in accordance with the parameters of the assignment. Those parameters include the audience, purpose, time, and length. The audience for a college paper is generally your classmates. It is true that the instructor or professor will grade the paper, but if you actually choose the professor as an audience, you have to do much more research in more depth than if you have your classmates as an audience. (See the section on Audience.)

As a purpose, you may choose to inform, persuade, entertain, or explore. Generally, in college, you will choose to inform.

The time and length are parameters that are generally assigned to you. A lecturer may say, "The paper is due in two weeks and it has to be between ten and fourteen pages long." How much time you have to do the paper and how long the paper has to be determine, to a large extent, how much information you need to gather and how much information you can use in the paper.

Step 3: Subject Elements

After you have determined the limited topic, you need to decide on two, three, or more supporting subjects for that limited topic. Those subjects become the basis for the supporting paragraphs in the paper. These specific subjects are called subject elements; they may also be called controlling elements, elements of control, subject segments, etc.

You should list the subject elements (or at least label them) in the order in which you plan to handle them. (See the section on Paragraph Organization.) Generally, you will use spatial order, chronological order, or order of importance. You have probably learned about these ways to organize previously, but a short review might help. Spatial order means that you organize the essay in the way that space is organized—left to right, up to down or down to up, clockwise, or counterclockwise. Chronological order means organizing the essay in order of time, generally from the first event to the last event. When you organize in order of importance, you usually organize the essay from the least important to the most important information, from the least amount to the greatest amount of information, or from the least persuasive to the most persuasive information. You want to leave the reader with the strongest possible image or argument so that the reader carries away your best idea.

Step 4: Title

The next step is choosing a working title. You are not stuck with this title; you can change it any time you want, but you may find the working title an aid in helping you focus on the topic.

Step 5: Thesis Statement

Now you can develop a thesis statement, a statement of the main point of the essay. The thesis may contain the subject elements to provide a focus for the paper and an aid to the reader. You may write a thesis statement that does not include the subject elements if you can clearly focus the thesis statement without the subject elements, but it is likely that you will need to use the subject elements in the thesis.

A thesis statement expresses the main idea of the essay. It is a statement—one sentence—that tells the reader what the remainder of the essay covers. The thesis delineates the central idea in the essay, clearly and completely. The thesis, because it gives the main idea in the essay, limits the essay's range and indicates the structure of the essay, generally by giving the subject elements to be covered in the essay. The thesis may state a topic and give an opinion on the topic that you intend to support or to prove.

A thesis statement does not use phrases such as "This paper will show," "I think," "I feel," or "In this paper, I will." A thesis statement does not ask a question or state a truism (a statement of the obvious, such as "People need education" or "Bears live in the woods").

A thesis statement should be clear and understandable. The reader needs guidance to understand the body of the paper; the thesis statement gives that guidance.

One way to form a thesis is to pose a question to yourself. If the subject you have chosen to write about is water pollution, you might ask yourself this question: What are the causes of water pollution? Examining the causes provides data for drawing a conclusion, which becomes the thesis. That is, examination of the causes of water pollution leads to this thesis statement: Water pollution is caused by chemical runoff, soil erosion, and excess biological waste. A discussion of these three ways (which are subject elements) provides the body of the paper. This statement of thesis contains a topic, an opinion, and the subject elements (also known as elements of control).

Examples of thesis statements appear in each of the essay examples in the section on essay development and in the Appendix.

Step 6: Topic Sentences

From the thesis statement and the subject elements, you can develop the topic sentences for the body paragraphs of your paper. Each subject element becomes a topic sentence. Remember to put the topic sentences in the order in which you plan to handle them in the paper.

As discussed in the section on paragraph development, the topic sentence directs and focuses the paragraph and should be clear and understandable. It should not be a question, should not state the obvious (such as "Radio is a medium of communication"), and should not use phrases such as "This paragraph will show," "In this paragraph I will," "I think," or "I feel."

Examples of topic sentences appear in each of the paragraph examples in the section on paragraph development and in the section on essay development sections.

Example (Organization Plan Page)

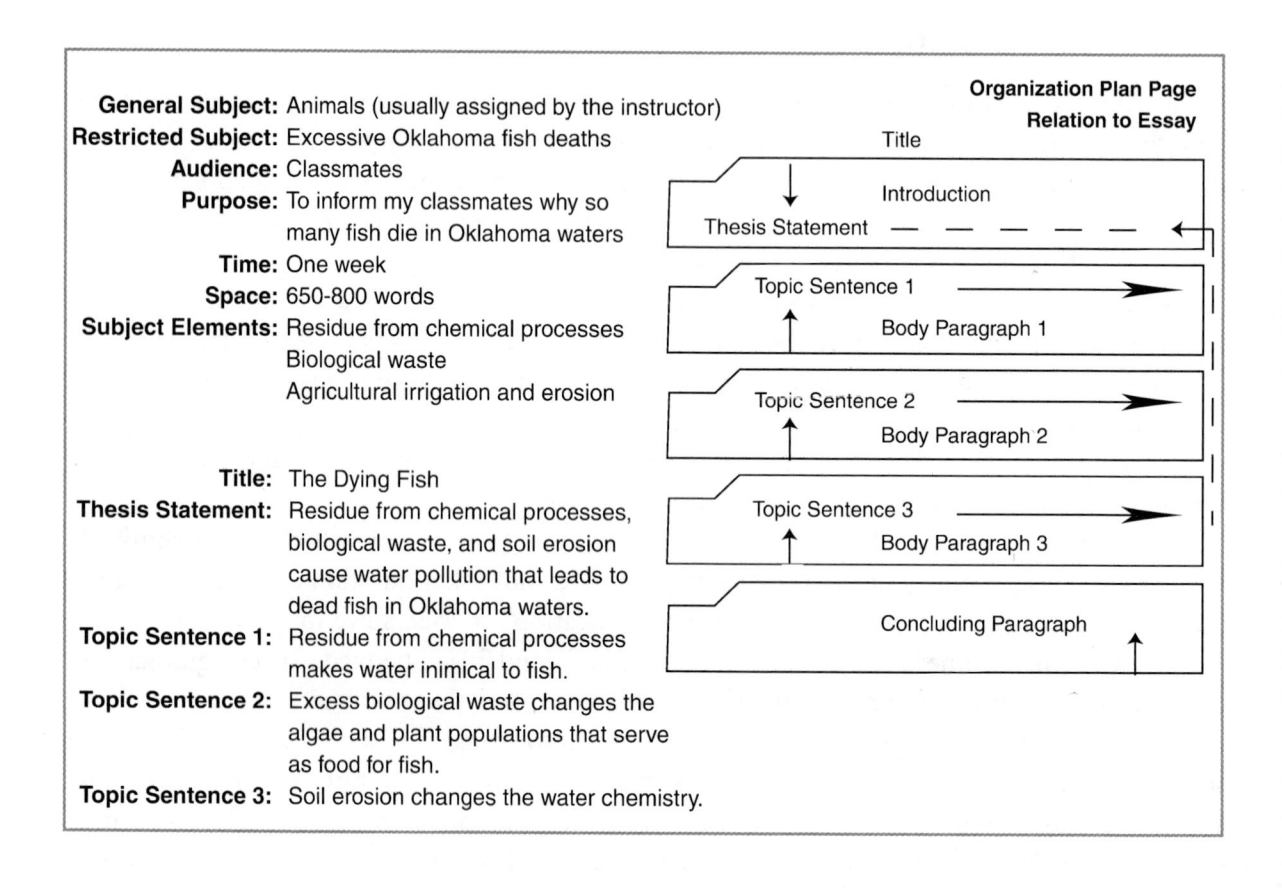

General Subject: Animals (usually assigned by the instructor)
Restricted Subject: Excessive Oklahoma fish deaths
Audience: Classmates
Purpose: To inform my classmates why so many fish die in Oklahoma waters
Time: One week
Space: 650-800 words
Subject Elements: Residue from chemical processes
Biological waste
Agricultural irrigation and erosion

Title: The Dying Fish
Thesis Statement: Residue from chemical processes, biological waste, and soil erosion cause water pollution that leads to dead fish in Oklahoma waters.
Topic Sentence 1: Residue from chemical processes makes water inimical to fish.
Topic Sentence 2: Excess biological waste changes the algae and plant populations that serve as food for fish.
Topic Sentence 3: Soil erosion changes the water chemistry.

Organization Plan Page
Relation to Essay

Title
Introduction
Thesis Statement
Topic Sentence 1
Body Paragraph 1
Topic Sentence 2
Body Paragraph 2
Topic Sentence 3
Body Paragraph 3
Concluding Paragraph

Longer essays follow the same basic plan as a simple five-paragraph essay: a clearly-defined thesis at the end of an introduction that catches the reader's attention and guides him or her to the main idea of the paper; body sections that support, develop, and explain the main idea of the paper; and a conclusion that ends the essay so that the reader feels closure. The following is an example of an organization plan page for a longer essay, followed by the relationship of the organization plan to the essay structure.

Example (Organization Plan Page)

General Subject:	Animals (usually assigned by the instructor)
Restricted Subject:	Excessive Oklahoma fish deaths
Audience:	Classmates
Purpose:	To inform my classmates why so many fish die in Oklahoma waters
Time:	One week
Space:	1000-2000 words
Subject Elements:	Residue from chemical processes
	Biological waste
	Agricultural irrigation and erosion
Title:	The Dying Fish
Thesis Statement:	Residue from chemical processes, biological waste, and soil erosion cause water pollution that leads to dead fish in Oklahoma waters.
Lead Topic Sentence 1:	Residue from chemical processes makes water inimical to fish.
Subsidiary Topic Sentence 1A:	Chemical residue leaches into lake water from ground water.
Subsidiary Topic Sentence 1B:	Residue from chemicals from agricultural and industrial use runs into waters.
Lead Topic Sentence 2:	Excess biological waste changes the algae and plant populations that serve as food sources for fish.
Subsidiary Topic Sentence 2A:	Biological waste can originate in factory farm operations.
Subsidiary Topic Sentence 2B:	Excess biological waste may originate in sewage systems.
Subsidiary Topic Sentence 2C:	Detritus from foliage may result in excess biological waste.
Lead Topic Sentence 3:	Soil erosion changes the water chemistry.
Subsidiary Topic Sentence 3A:	Prior to inclusion of soil, water chemistry is a result of several factors.
Subsidiary Topic Sentence 3B:	Erosion can result from defoliation of various kinds.
Subsidiary Topic Sentence 3C:	Soil in water becomes a different chemical mix.

The Dying Fish

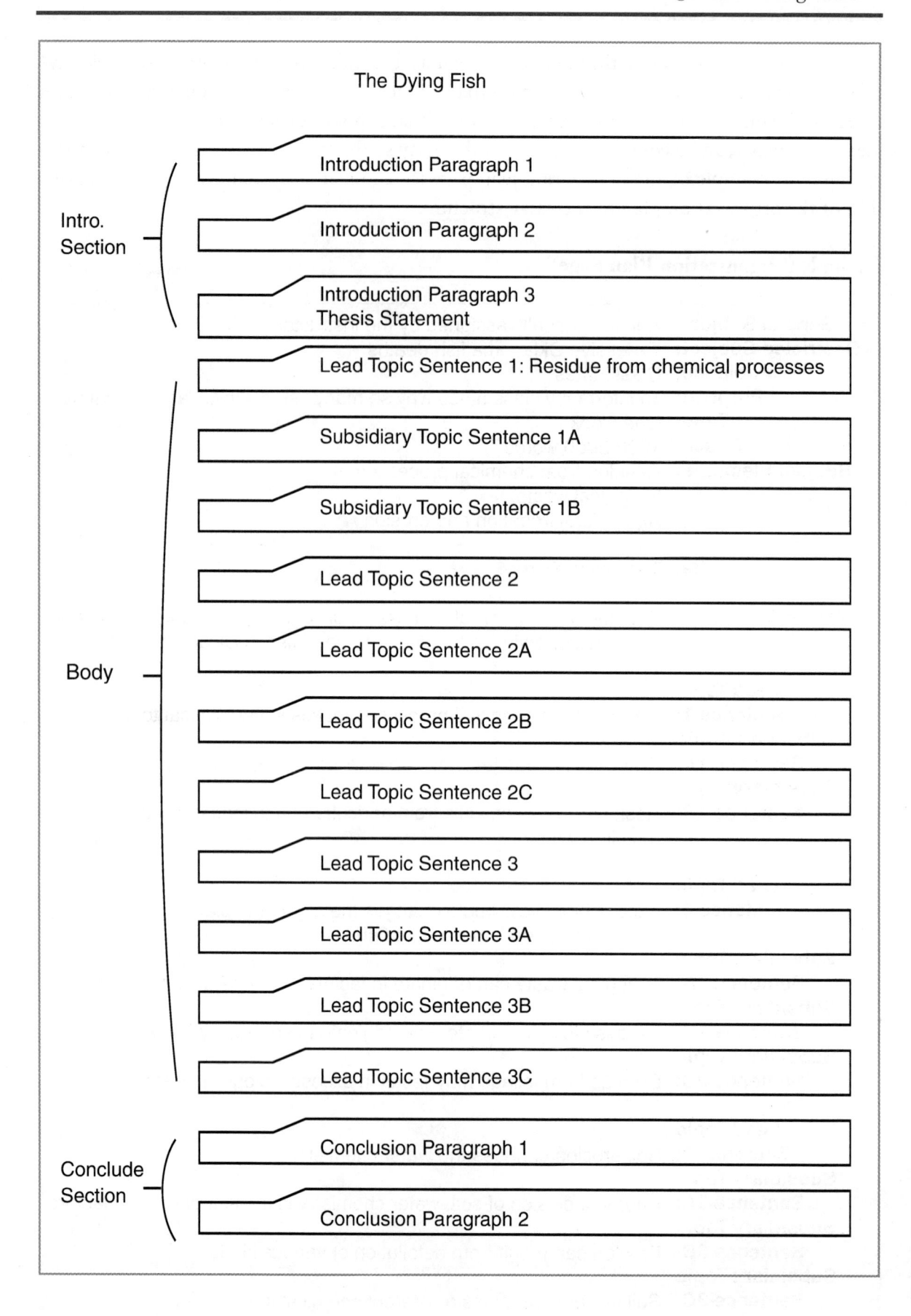

Intro. Section
- Introduction Paragraph 1
- Introduction Paragraph 2
- Introduction Paragraph 3
  Thesis Statement

Body
- Lead Topic Sentence 1: Residue from chemical processes
  - Subsidiary Topic Sentence 1A
  - Subsidiary Topic Sentence 1B
- Lead Topic Sentence 2
  - Lead Topic Sentence 2A
  - Lead Topic Sentence 2B
  - Lead Topic Sentence 2C
- Lead Topic Sentence 3
  - Lead Topic Sentence 3A
  - Lead Topic Sentence 3B
  - Lead Topic Sentence 3C

Conclude Section
- Conclusion Paragraph 1
- Conclusion Paragraph 2

OUTLINES

For a long paper, you might want to use the detail possible in an outline by incorporating one into the organization plan page. The specifics for writing a formal outline are included in the following example.

Example (Outline)

Topic: Outline

Audience: Classmates [Notation of audience, purpose, and thesis statement may be included either as part of this outline or as part of a formal organization plan page; the outline below would function in place of listing only the topic sentences.]

Purpose: To inform

Thesis Statement: Outlining follows specific rules of formatting and information.

I. An outline follows a particular format.
   A. An outline may use sentences, phrases, or words.
   B. The sequence of labeling is Roman numerals (I, II, etc.), then capital letters (A, B, etc.), then Arabic numbers (1, 2, etc.), and then lower case letters (a, b, etc.).
   C. Labels (letters or numbers) occur only in sets of two or more.
      1. Roman numeral I must be joined by II.
      2. Letter A must be accompanied by B, etc.

II. An outline covers the important points of the material.
   A. Each label type is of parallel importance.
      1. Main points appear with Roman numerals.
      2. Sub-points related to the Roman numeral heading appear as A, B, C, etc.
      3. Minor points related to the capital letter appear as 1, 2, etc.
   B. Clarity and precision are vital in entries.

NOTE:
1. Indent the outline parts as in the example.
2. Periods, not dashes, appear after the label numbers or letters.
3. Outlines may consist of sentences, topics, or words. The first word in each entry should be capitalized. If the outline is a sentence outline, it must contain only sentences; each sentence must end with the correct end mark. Topic and word outlines do not contain sentences and do not end with punctuation.
4. Each entry with a comparable label should be of parallel importance and phrasing. If the heading labeled I is a noun, II, III, etc., should be nouns. (Clarity is more important than parallelism, so you may sacrifice parallelism for accuracy.)

Alternative Ways to Write an Essay Outline

When you write an outline for an essay, you must include the statement of thesis. One way to do that appears in the previous section on the Organization Plan Page, or you might use one of the following alternatives.

Alternative 1

Topic: Outlining
Audience: Classmates
Purpose: To inform

I. **Introduction**
   A. Possibility: List the main strategies that you intend to use in writing the introduction.
   B. Note: Remember that the thesis statement actually appears at the end of the introductory section, even though you do not put the sentence in the outline until Roman numeral II.
II. **Thesis Statement**
   A. Topic sentence of first body paragraph
      1. Main point
         a. Supporting point
         b. Supporting point
         c. Supporting point
      2. Main point
   B. Topic sentence of second body paragraph
   C. Topic sentence of third body paragraph
III. **Conclusion**
   A. Possibility: List the strategy that you intend to use in the conclusion.
   B. Possibilities: Summarize the main points, restate the thesis (only in a long paper), or tell the significance of what you have said.

Alternative 2

Topic: Outlining
Audience: Classmates
Purpose: To inform

Thesis Statement: Write the thesis statement at the top of the page. Then make an outline.
I. Main point
   A. Supporting point
      1. Detail
      2. Detail
   B. Supporting point
II. Main point

PARAGRAPHS

A paragraph is a group of related thoughts that is generally longer than a sentence and shorter than a whole composition. A paragraph is a series of sentences developing one topic. This topic is usually introduced in the topic sentence of the paragraph. The topic is developed or illustrated in the remaining sentences of the paragraph. Sometimes a concluding sentence summarizes the topic of the paragraph or restates the topic sentence. Thus, a paragraph may have a structure something like this:

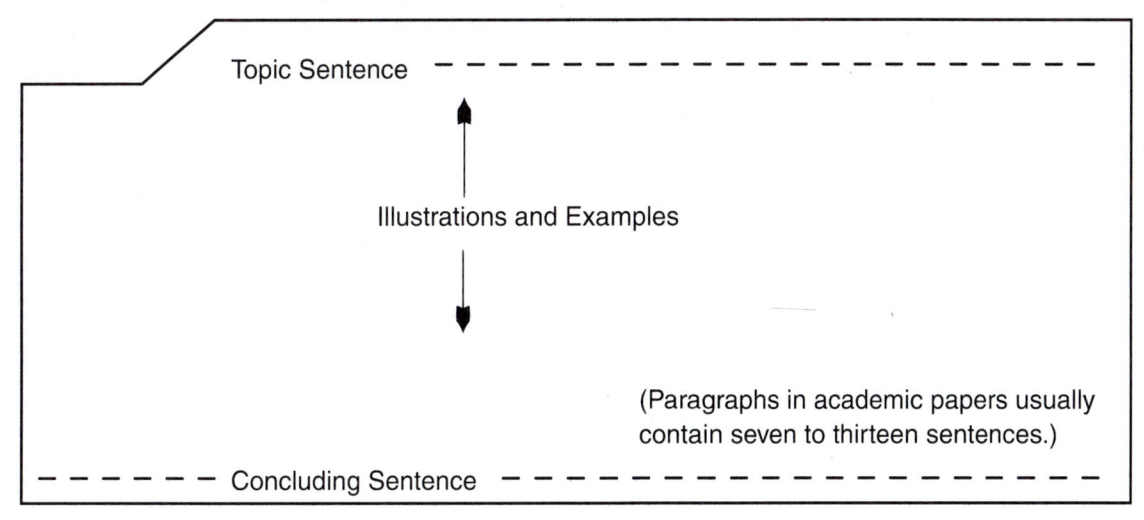

```
Topic Sentence – – – – – – – – – – – – – – – – – – – – – – –
               ↑
               |
    Illustrations and Examples
               |
               ↓
                              (Paragraphs in academic papers usually
                              contain seven to thirteen sentences.)
– – – – – – Concluding Sentence – – – – – – – – – – – – – – – – – –
```

A paragraph in an academic paper is generally seven to thirteen sentences in length.

Development

Paragraphs are not simply collections of sentences. Those sentences are related by topic. The topic is controlled by the topic sentence. Generally, in academic papers, the topic sentence appears as the first sentence in the paragraph.

To develop a paragraph, begin with a topic that you know about or can research and find out about. Then focus the topic into a controlling idea. How do you choose a controlling idea? First, you need to think about whether you have anything to say about the topic, whether you can elaborate on, or develop, the topic. You need to decide whether you can express the idea such that both you and the reader can determine what kind of information might appear in the paragraph. You need to consider whether the idea is both specific enough to handle in a single paragraph yet broad enough to need several sentences to support it.

Then, from the controlling idea, you create a topic sentence. A topic sentence should direct and focus the paragraph and should be clear and understandable. It should not be a question, should not state the obvious (such as "Radio is a medium of communication"), and should not use phrases such as "This paragraph will show," "In this paragraph I will," "I think," or "I feel."

To write a clear, understandable, directive, and focused topic sentence, you need to think about how you want to address your topic. For example, if you were really familiar with cars, you might want to write about the advantages of a standard shift. You decide that you have enough information to create at least a paragraph. You also know that you can narrow the topic so that you need only a paragraph in which to discuss the idea. You select the controlling idea that a standard shift is better than an automatic transmission. The topic sentence might read like this: Although automatic transmissions are convenient, standard transmissions are superior in three ways.

After you create a topic sentence, you have to think about support. You cannot just say standard transmissions are better than automatic transmissions; you have to tell the reader why you think they are better. To do that, you must create support for the topic sentence. The topic sentence is a general statement even though it is the focusing sentence. You must include specific statements supporting the topic sentence. For each specific statement of support, you probably also need details that develop and illustrate that statement.

You may think of these as a hierarchy of support. The topic sentence is the top of the hierarchy, the most important sentence, so to speak. The second step down is the specific statements of support, and the third step is the developing details. Based on this amount of support, you can conclude that paragraphs, in academic papers at any rate, usually contain seven to thirteen sentences, even though this may seem a relatively long paragraph to those who read only newspapers and magazines and are not familiar with academic, or scholarly, writing.

Example (Hierarchy of Support for a Paragraph)

> Topic sentence with focus and controlling idea
> > Specific supporting statement
> > > Detail 1
> > > Detail 2
> > Specific supporting statement
> > > Detail
> > Specific supporting statement
> > > Detail 1
> > > Detail 2
> > > Detail 3

Example (Hierarchy of Support for a Paragraph)

> - **PARAGRAPH**
>   Although automatic transmissions are convenient, standard transmissions are superior to automatic transmissions in three ways. First, standard transmissions are more enjoyable for some people to drive. The driver has a sense of power at his or her fingertips and is engaged with the driving experience. Second, engines are more responsive to standard transmissions. This allows more control over the car. Starts can be quicker; downward acceleration allows quick response in traffic. In mountainous terrain, the driver can shift to a lower gear to slow the car. Most important, standard transmissions are economical. Repair and maintenance are less expensive for a standard transmission than for an automatic transmission. A standard transmission also increases fuel economy. Cars with manual transmissions may get one to four miles per gallon better gas mileage than cars with automatic transmissions.

Writing Process • Organization

> • **LABELLED PARAGRAPH**
> **Topic sentence:** Although automatic transmissions are convenient, standard transmissions are superior to automatic transmissions in three ways. **Supporting statement 1:** First, standard transmissions are more enjoyable for some people to drive. **Detail 1:** The driver has a sense of power at his or her fingertips and is engaged with the driving experience. **Supporting statement 2:** Second, engines are more responsive to standard transmissions. **Detail 1:** This allows more control over the car. **Detail 2:** Starts can be quicker. **Detail 3:** Downward acceleration allows quick response in traffic. **Detail 4:** In mountainous terrain, the driver can shift to a lower gear to slow the car. **Supporting statement 3:** Most important, standard transmissions are economical. **Detail 1:** Repair and maintenance are less expensive for a standard transmission than for an automatic transmission. **Detail 2:** A standard transmission also increases fuel economy. **Extended detail 2:** Cars with manual transmissions may get one to four miles per gallon better gas mileage than cars with automatic transmissions.

Coherence and Unity

A paragraph is not simply a collection of sentences; a paragraph is not even a collection of sentences related by topic and under the control of a topic sentence. Paragraphs also have the attributes of coherence and unity.

Unity means oneness: all of the sentences in the paragraph work together as a whole. Thus, every sentence in a paragraph must develop and support the controlling idea of the paragraph.

Coherence means consistency and logical progression—making the paragraph fit together so that it makes good sense to the reader. The way to achieve coherence is through using organization, repetition, and transitions.

Generally, three kinds of organization or logical order occur: spatial order, chronological order, and order of importance.

When you use spatial order, you arrange the paragraph (use the support) in the way that space is arranged or ordered. For example, suppose you were describing a house arranged in the following way:

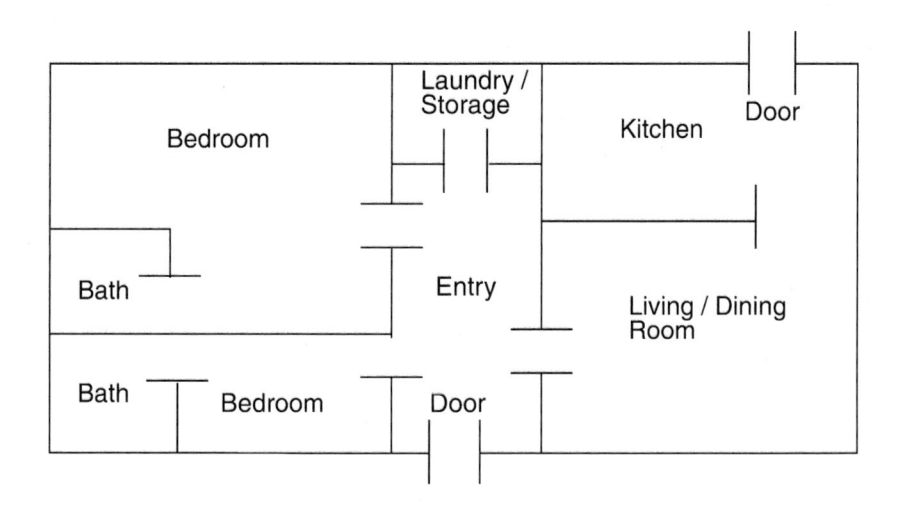

You would not want to describe the living or dining room, one bedroom, the kitchen, the bath, the entry, another bath, etc. It would be too confusing for the reader! Instead, you might want to describe the house by beginning in the entry, continuing into the living or dining room, the kitchen, the laundry room, the bedroom, the bath with that bedroom, the final bedroom, and then the bath with that bedroom. Of course, you might pick other ways to describe the house: by rooms oriented to each direction, or by going clockwise, for example. Whatever plan you choose to describe space, it should have a logical orientation to the space itself.

Example (Paragraph in Spatial Order)

My house, like Baba Yaga's, follows the sun. I do not mean that it literally turns using legs as Baba Yaga's house does, but it does have sunshine in every room. My front door faces directly south. My living room, which also contains an area for dining, is to the right as I enter the front door and has many windows on the south side so it is full of sun all winter long. I can walk through the living room to the kitchen, which has many windows on the north side, making the kitchen sunny all summer long. Directly to the west of the kitchen is a small storage area that contains my washer and dryer and has a set of windows on the north side as well. Directly to the west of the storage area is my extra bedroom. It has windows on the north and on the west, so it too is bright and sunny during the winter and summer. Attached to the extra bedroom is a small bathroom. Directly to the south of the small bathroom is my bathroom, which is inside my south-facing bedroom. My bedroom has floor to ceiling windows and is filled with light in all seasons. So, although my house does not have legs, all of the rooms follow the sun!

Organizing chronologically means organizing or arranging in the order that events happen. For example, you begin by telling what happened first, then what happened second, and so forth until the final event—the end.

Example (Paragraph Arranged in Chronological Order)

Organizing a film series using a committee can be a rewarding experience. The rewards accumulate with each step. First, the committee must decide on the theme of the series and on what films appropriately reflect the theme. Then the committee must decide exactly which films to order. The decision means discussing the films themselves, as well as film theory and history, and the discussion is enlightening and educational. More lessons follow. After the films are ordered, the committee has to prepare publicity, determine who will introduce or host the films, get information on the films to the hosts, and decide what kind of refreshments are appropriate. Each of these tasks requires learning to work with people in the committee, learning to negotiate with and work with people outside the committee and even outside the organization, and learning about the specifics associated with each task. Finally, the lessons continue with the showing of each film. The reaction of the viewers and the subsequent discussions, both formal and informal, reveal a range of ideas and opinions about each film. Each member of the committee learns much from the experience.

Organizing in order of importance generally means arranging in order of the least important to the most important or in order of the least emphasized to the most emphasized.

Example (Paragraph Arranged in Order of Importance)

> Training a dog requires three major attributes. A dog trainer must understand the reactions of dogs. What does it mean when a dog wags its tail, wrinkles its lips, or rolls over on its back? These may be mixed signals. A wagging tail can mean a greeting or a nervous reaction, a wrinkled lip can mean indecision about whether the dog is threatened or is threatening, and rolling onto the back may mean submission or a desire to have an itch scratched. In addition to understanding actions, a dog trainer must also be consistent. If a dog licks and the trainer scolds one time and praises another, the dog will be confused and consequently unruly. If the trainer rewards the dog with praise and goodies when the dog sits on command and does not scold the dog for doing the same thing, the dog learns that it is a good thing to sit when commanded "Sit." Finally, and most important, a trainer must be patient and loving. Dogs, like children and adults, make mistakes. Overreaction and brutality or screaming can cause a dog to lose confidence in the trainer and in self and, consequently, cause the dog to refuse to or be unable to learn. A trainer's consistent, calm relationship with the dog increases confidence and makes the learning process much easier.

Repetition is writing something again. Usually, repetition refers to repeating words. For example, in the paragraph on dog training the words *trainer* and *dog* are repeated. This repetition helps tie the paragraph together.

Transitions are words that function as cues. They serve as connections between sentences, connecting one sentence to a subsequent one. Order words, such as *first, second, next,* and *then,* are transition words. Other words are actually called transition words; they are connector words, such as *therefore, however, thus,* and *at any rate.* Transition words also tie the paragraph together, leading to increased coherency.

Example (Coherence, Using Repetition and Transition Words)

> In the following paragraph, repeated words appear in italics and transition words are underlined:
>
> *Training* a *dog* requires three major attributes. A *dog trainer* must understand the reactions of *dogs*. What does it mean when a *dog* wags a tail, wrinkles its lips, or rolls over on its back? These may be mixed signals. *A wagging tail* can mean a greeting or a nervous reaction, a *wrinkled lip* can mean indecision about whether the *dog* is threatened or is threatening, and *rolling onto the back* may mean submission or a desire to have an itch scratched. <u>In addition</u> to understanding actions, a *dog trainer* must also be consistent. If a *dog* licks and the *trainer* scolds one time and praises another, the *dog* will be confused and consequently unruly. If the *trainer* rewards the *dog* with praise and goodies when the *dog sits* on command and does not scold the *dog* for doing the same thing, the *dog* learns that it is a good thing to *sit* when commanded *"Sit."* <u>Finally, and most important,</u> a *trainer* must be patient and loving. *Dogs*, like children and adults, make mistakes. Overreaction and brutality or screaming can cause a *dog* to lose *confidence* in the *trainer* and in self and, consequently, cause the *dog* to refuse to or be unable to *learn*. A *trainer's* consistent, calm relationship with the *dog* increases *confidence* and makes the *learn*ing process much easier.

Transition Words:

to sequence
again
also
and
besides
even
finally
first, second,
　third
furthermore
in addition
indeed
last
moreover
next
one . . . another
still
then
too

**to conclude,
summarize, or repeat**
all in all
altogether
as a result
as has been said
consequently
in brief
in conclusion
in other words
in particular
in short
in simpler terms
in summary
on the whole
once again
that is
therefore
to conclude
to put it differently
to repeat
to summarize
thus

for timing
after
after a while
afterward
as long as
as soon as
at first
at last
at length
at that time
at the same time
before
during
earlier
eventually
finally
formerly
immediately
in the meantime
in the past
lately
later
meanwhile
next
now
presently
shortly
simultaneously
since
so far
soon
subsequently
then
thereafter
until
when

to narrow focus
after all
indeed
in fact
in other words
in particular
specifically
that is

**for comparison
(and contrast)**
also
but
by the same token
despite
even though
however
in comparison
in contrast
instead
likewise
meanwhile
nonetheless
on the contrary
on the one hand . . .
　on the other hand
similarly
still
the same way as
though
yet

to illustrate
after all
even
for example
for instance
indeed
in fact
namely
of course
specifically
such as
the following example
that is
thus
to illustrate

to show concession
admittedly
although
certainly
granted
naturally
of course

to show cause and effect
accordingly
as a result
because
consequently
for this purpose
for this reason
hence
otherwise
since
so
then
therefore
thereupon
thus
to this end
with this object

to show place
above
behind
below
elsewhere
far from here
here
nearby
on the other side
there
to the left
to the north
to the right
to the south

to limit
to state exception
but
however
nevertheless
nonetheless
notwithstanding
while

PATTERNS OF DEVELOPMENT FOR PARAGRAPHS AND ESSAYS

Essays and paragraphs must have coherence and unity (see the section on coherence and unity). Individual paragraphs must be coherent and unified, and the entire essay must have unity and continuity. All of the sentences in the paragraph must work together as a whole; in addition, each paragraph must contribute to the whole of the essay. Thus, every paragraph must develop and support the controlling idea of the essay, stated in the thesis statement.

The essay must also be consistent, with logical progression. It must make sense to the reader. Just as when you write paragraphs, an essay has coherence through organization, repetition, and transitions. When you plan the essay, you should consider the kind of organization—spatial order, chronological order, or order of importance—that you want. (See the section Organization Plan Page.)

Repetition is writing something again. Usually, when we talk about repetition we are referring to repeating words. Using transitions means using words that function as cues, as connections between sentences or paragraphs. Words such as *first*, *second*, *next*, *then*, *therefore*, *however*, *thus*, and *at any rate* are transition words. (See the previous transition word list.)

Just as you can have more than one purpose for writing, you can use different kinds of development in a paragraph or an essay. However, for the purpose of illustration, each pattern of development will be considered in isolation here.

Narration Development

Narration generally tells a story (or narrates an incident). It is usually chronological, told in order of time. Because it tells a story, narration can be seen as an extended, or elaborate, example. (See the section on example development.)

Example (Narration Paragraph)

> Going to a play is a traumatic experience for my family. Once we had tickets to see a production in a city about twenty-five miles away. We had plans for the entire evening. First, we would pick up some friends and go someplace to eat. After the play, we might stop at another place to have dessert. When we started for the play, everyone was ready, almost on time. We were running only fifteen minutes behind schedule. We picked up our friends–who had decided not to eat. So our family stopped at a fast-food place, intending to grab a bite on the way. After we got the food, the driver entered the exit ramp. Someone screamed from the back seat, "You are going the wrong way." He braked. The food slid. He grabbed. His tie and coat dipped into the catsup and baked beans. I grabbed for the coat and dragged the sleeve of my silk blouse through the gravy. We got onto the correct ramp and arrived, going the right way, at the theater, where we discovered that I had forgotten the tickets. The usher remembered us from a previous play (of course he would) and let us in to sit in freshly varnished–and still damp–seats. None of us remembers if the play was good because, during the first act, my son decided to throw up in a friend's hat. We left our friends and went home. They called a cab.

Description Development

Descriptive writing allows you to describe sensory experiences or to describe a person or people. Description emphasizes the senses—touch, taste, sight, smell, hearing.

Example (Description Paragraph)

> Morning is my favorite time of day. After the clock radio comes on with a soothing tune, I can stretch luxuriously in the warm, cozy bed and decide just to lie there and coast for a few more minutes. In just a moment ,I come more alive to the smell of fresh coffee, brewing in the automatically-timed coffee pot, and to the sound of bacon, frying in the automatically-timed microwave oven. Then I know it is time to put one foot at a time into my soft, fuzzy slippers and one arm into my woolly robe and slouch to the bathroom to turn on the shower. The shower fills the room with steam so that I have to wipe off the mirror squeakily with a fluffy towel so I can peer into my own clean face. Breakfast is cooking; I am warm and clean. What more could I want?

Example Development

In an example paragraph or essay, support comes from examples. The development may consist of a series of short examples, as in the following paragraph, or it may consist of one long example. In either case, the topic sentence (or, in the case of an essay, the thesis statement) is illustrated and supported by the examples.

Example (Example Paragraph)

> My sister is a notorious storyteller. I do not mean that she lies; she never lies. She just makes a story out of everything that happens to her. When she goes to the supermarket and has a good experience at the checkout stand, she makes a story out of it. When she drives her car and meets a lunatic driver, she tells us all about it in a detailed story. She has favorite stories that she tells over and over–like the time my brother slept with the frogs and the time my father fell out of the window. And she tells about the time I got bucked off the tiny pony–when I was six feet tall and twenty-seven years old. We do not really mind. We even ask her to tell her stories!

A formal definition has this form: The word to be defined is the general class to which the word belongs and the differentiating characteristics that make that word different from all of the other members of that class. The formula reads as follows:

Word = general class + differentiating characteristics.

Example (Formal Definition)

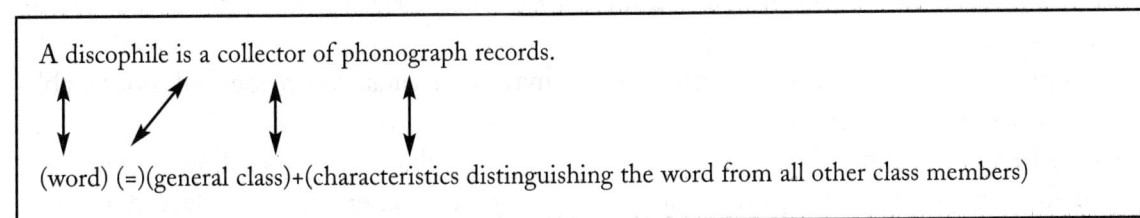

> A discophile is a collector of phonograph records.
>
> (word) (=)(general class)+(characteristics distinguishing the word from all other class members)

The topic sentence of a paragraph about a discophile may be the formal definition: A discophile is a collector of phonograph records. Then the paragraph would give examples of various discophiles and their habits.

Instead, the topic sentence may only introduce the term. For example, a topic sentence of the latter type may read like this one: The term discophile can mean different things in different fields. Then the paragraph might give examples of discophiles who collect records of radio shows or of one musical group or of one musical type or of one composer, etc.

Example (Definition Paragraph)

> One of the literary terms with which a reader should be familiar is that of conflict. Conflict means the strife between opposing forces in any work of literature. Usually, conflicts fall into one of five major categories. One category is person against person, as in most of the "good guy/bad guy" stories, such as John Collier's "Witch's Money," in which the townspeople are pitted against the newcomer artist. Person against society, the Harlequin against the time-ordered culture in which he lives, appears in Harlan Ellison's "'Repent, Harlequin,' Said the Tick-Tock Man." In W. Somerset Maugham's "Appointment in Samarra," we see person against fate (or God) because the servant comes up against his fate in the form of death. Person against nature is the conflict in Jack London's "To Build a Fire," when the prospector has to fight the cold and the snow to survive. And person against self, the madman trying to convince himself he is not mad, shows up in Edgar Allen Poe's "The TellTale Heart."

Definition development in an essay is also a kind of example development, because support is by example, but definition development includes defining a term or terms. The definition may appear in the thesis statement or in one or more of the topic sentences in the form of a formal definition, or the thesis statement may simply introduce the term to be defined.

Process Development

A process paragraph or essay tells how to do something. It is a series of explanatory steps telling the reader about how to complete some task successfully. Remember the following specific guidelines.

1. Remember the audience.
2. Be sure to introduce the subject early in the paragraph, ideally in the first sentence. Do not rely on the title of the piece to tell the reader what your subject is. Specify the task in the piece itself.
3. Describe all of the steps. Be sure not to skip anything because the reader will not be able to replicate what you are describing.
4. Describe the steps in order. Nothing is more irritating than trying to follow instructions and finding that you should have done a step earlier or later than you have done it—unless it is finding out that the step is missing entirely.
5. You may use the word *you*. This is the only time in formal writing that the term *you* is appropriate. It is possible to write a process paragraph or theme without using *you*, but using *you* is an option.

Example (Process Paragraph, Using Second Person)

> You should know how to change a flat tire. Ordinarily, you might just call a travel service, but what if you have a flat tire on a dark night on a deserted road and you have no cellular phone? What if there is no one else to whom to turn? You will have to change your own tire. First, make sure that the car will not roll. Set the emergency brake. Turn the wheel into the curb. If necessary, chock the wheels by putting a stone, brick, or other object behind the tire. Then, get everything you will need out of the trunk. Get the lug wrench, the jack, and the spare tire. Use the lug wrench to loosen the lug nuts on the flat tire. After the lug nuts are loosened slightly, place the jack in the location described in the owner's manual and raise the wheel off the ground. You may have to use the lug wrench as part of the jack handle on some makes of cars. After the wheel is raised, completely remove the nuts and then the wheel and tire assembly. Place the spare on the hub and tighten the lug nuts with the lug wrench as tightly as possible. (This will not be very tight because the tire will spin.) Lower the car. Tighten the lug nuts again with the lug wrench, taking care to tighten every other one until you have tightened each one. Pack the jack, the flat, and the lug wrench back in the car. Get the flat fixed as soon as possible

Comparison Development (Including Contrast)

To contrast two items is to emphasize their differences. To compare two items is to delineate their similarities and their differences. Thus, when asked to write a comparison, it is always best to ask for clarification. Does the instructor want you to concentrate on similarities or to discuss both similarities and differences? Comparison generally means concentrating on both similarities and differences unless you are instructed otherwise.

You already know the three patterns of comparison intuitively; but, here it is in black and white. Generally, comparison paragraphs fall into one of these three categories. The categories depend on how the information is grouped. One type of grouping is by similarity and difference: all of the similarities are grouped together, and all the differences are grouped together. Which one comes first is up to the writer. Another type of grouping is by subject: one subject is discussed first, and the second subject is then discussed and tied together with the first subject. The last kind of grouping is point by point. Each point is discussed in relation to each subject before the next point is approached.

No matter which kind of grouping pattern is selected, a strong topic sentence is essential.

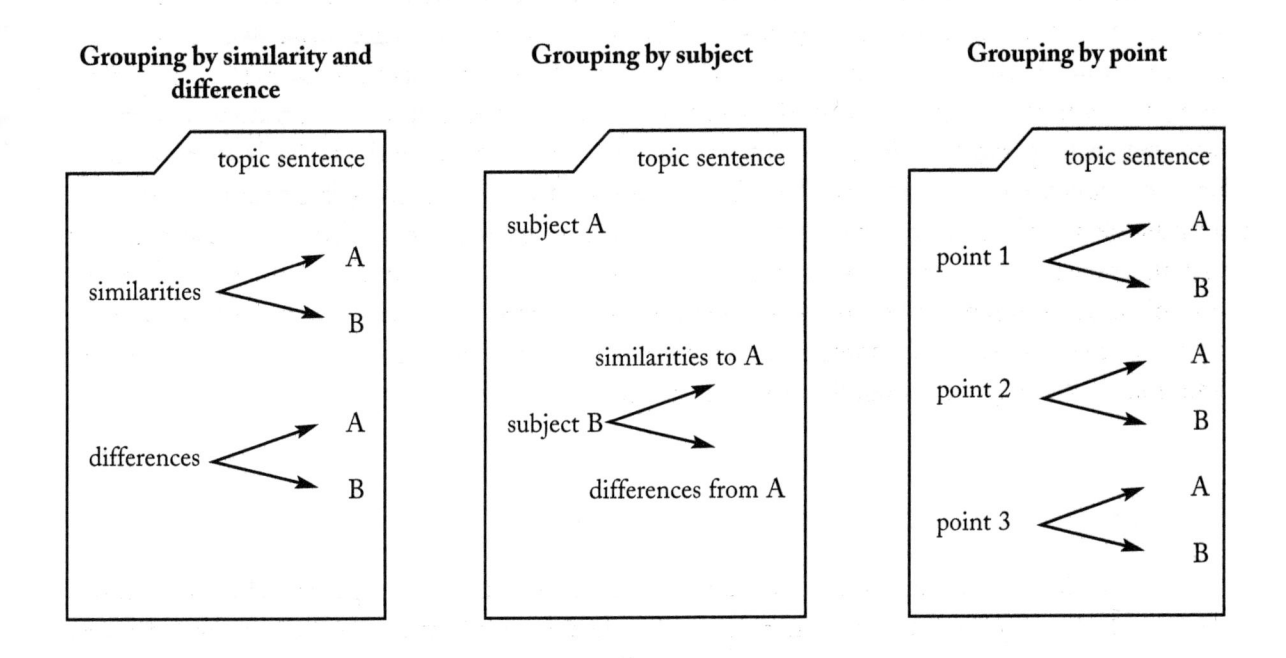

Grouping by similarity and difference

topic sentence

similarities → A
            → B

differences → A
            → B

Grouping by subject

topic sentence

subject A

subject B → similarities to A
         → differences from A

Grouping by point

topic sentence

point 1 → A
        → B

point 2 → A
        → B

point 3 → A
        → B

Example (Comparison Paragraph Grouped By Point)

> Even though they look alike, my two brothers are not alike. One is twenty-two; one is twenty-three, and both have brown eyes and salt-and-pepper hair, receding rapidly. Neither one could be called tall and elegant: they are more short and stocky. Everyone who sees them knows they are closely related. But they do not act closely related. My brother Bob is so calm and so even-tempered that the arrival of a maniac or a tiger in the backyard would bring a yawn and a quiet statement that he would take care of the situation. My brother Ted acts as though he sticks his finger in a battery charger every morning before breakfast. If the toast is a shade too brown, the paper is five minutes late, or even if the world news from Zaire is not good, he begins to rant and stomp. Bob is generous; he has never known a stranger. He gives time, effort, and dollars to every worthy and unworthy cause. Ted is not like Bob. He never gives time and effort except in situations that will get him some social gain, and he only gives money when "everyone else" will know. Similar looks do not make similar actions.

Comparison development in an essay generally means concentrating on both similarities and differences unless you are specifically instructed otherwise. Comparison essays usually fall into one of three patterns. One pattern is grouping by similarity and difference. If you are writing a short standard college essay using this pattern, you might have two major body sections, one on similarities and one on differences. Each of the sections might be more than one paragraph long, depending on the length of the essay. Another way to organize a comparison essay is to group by subject, so that you have two major body sections. Each section might be more than one paragraph long. The first section focuses on the first subject that you address and the next section on the other subject. Make sure to discuss the similarities and differences of both subjects. The third type of comparison organization is grouping by point. When you use this kind of organization, you would probably group the information into three major body sections: the first section addresses a point in relation to both subjects, the second section addresses another point in relation to both subjects, etc.

Analogy

One kind of comparison is the analogy. An analogy makes comparisons between things that are not usually considered similar. Analogy is usually used when the writer wants to reveal something with which most people are not familiar. The writer chooses something that people are familiar with to compare to his or her subject so that the subject becomes more real and believable to the reader. Familiarity with one part of the paragraph helps make the reader familiar with the other part as well.

Example (Analogy Paragraph)

> In the mornings, our house is like an army field training camp. In an army camp before the sun is up, reveille sounds to wake up all of the sleeping, still-tired soldiers. If a soldier does not arise immediately and assemble the correct clothing and field gear, the sergeant comes to his or her aid, to the chagrin of the soldier. The same thing is true at our house. Before the sun is up, reveille sounds. My father turns on the radio and the television at high volume. If a child or teen has trouble rising from the bed, my father will help, first by pulling the bed clothes from the bed and then by pulling on the toes of the errant child or teen. Toes are only delicately attached to the rest of the foot, so fear of mutilation brings the miscreant promptly upright. Appropriate clothes are next on the agenda. If the temperature is 35 degrees Fahrenheit outside, my father does not want to see shorts. Nor does he want to see T-shirts. He wants to see fully clothed bodies, with sweaters and scarves. Next is field gear. School bags must be ready by the door, full of the correct items. When at the car, no child, and especially no teen, dares to admit that some item, such as homework or lunch, needs to be retrieved. It would be safer to admit there were no clothes under the coat. It might even be safer to be at those army field exercises.

Division And Classification Development

Division divides things. Classification groups things. Division and classification divides things into groups. Usually, a division and classification paragraph begins with a topic sentence identifying the subject to be discussed. The paragraph then continues by showing how the parts of that subject are related to each other.

To plan the division and classification paragraph, begin by dividing and grouping. Pick a subject. Write down all of the "pieces" of the subject (divide) and then group all of the similar pieces together (classify).

Example (Developing a Division and Classification Paragraph):

- Suppose that the subject is media. List some forms of media with which you are familiar. Then decide what some of those media have in common and make those into a group. Continue until you have found groups for all of the media. Then experiment with other types of groupings. In your paragraph, choose only one type of grouping to discuss and use as examples only those media that are most representative.

- Write down the types of media.

radio	newspaper	newsletter
television	weekly	books
commercial	daily	audio
public	monthly	Braille
private	mainstream	hardback
film	tabloid	paperback
video	magazine	correspondence
audio tape	weekly	
compact disc	monthly	
audio	bi-monthly	
video	sporadically	
audio/video	journal	

- We could go on and on and on.

- Now find common groups for the types of media. They could be divided into visual, audible, and both. Another possible set is means of transmission and/or distribution. Another is frequency of appearance. Another is ownership. Yet another is audience. We could divide by a number of other criteria.

- Last, select the type of division and classification that you want to discuss and write the paragraph.

- **Division and Classification Paragraph**

    Although media come in a variety of forms, they can be divided into two major categories. Those two categories are responsible and irresponsible, as shown by the language of the writers. The responsible category includes what are generally called mainstream publications, those that are read by a large number of different kinds of people. Mainstream publications include *Time*, *Newsweek*, and *New Republic*. Even though each of those publications has a different political slant, each generally takes responsibility for reporting accurately. Each one's penchant for responsible journalism is revealed in the language of the publication. Each one tends to use measured terms and avoid loaded words, i.e., words that elicit immediate emotional responses, like "femi-Nazi" and "jerk." On the other hand, the irresponsible category includes tabloid-style periodicals and television and radio shows, like *The National Enquirer* and some talk shows. These periodicals and shows are watched, read, or heard by specific audiences, occasionally audiences that are isolated from mainstream society. They tend to skirt the edge of journalistic ethics, rushing to get a story, if not the facts of the story. Their tendencies are revealed in the language they sometimes use, resorting to stereotyping and name-calling; they sometimes use words like "lesbo-femininst" and "cretin." This is not the kind of word usage that appeals to reasonable people who are looking for facts, not for "slams."

Analysis or Cause And Effect Development

Analysis begins with a fact and goes backward from that fact—to find out why it happened—or forward—to find out what will happen next. In other words, analysis investigates cause and effect.

Causes and effects are not simple, and they are not isolated. Most causes go beyond the scope of history, and most effects go beyond our lifetimes. The cause of an earthquake in Mexico City began eons ago with the first shift of a tectonic plate. The effect of someone's losing a newspaper in 1790 may be the development of a free, unlimited power source. But it would be a little hard to write a paragraph of this scope. So you must isolate. You must make causes and effects look more simple and discrete than they actually are.

Example (Cause And Effect Paragraph)

> I did not do well in calculus for a number of reasons. First, as a freshman in college, I did not have the background for calculus. I had trigonometry in high school and made an "A," but I did not learn it well. So I entered class inadequately prepared. Second, I had a graduate student for an instructor. He knew math, but he could not get it across to those of us who were struggling. Of course, my not doing well was not his fault because, third, I did not do the homework. It frustrated me to struggle with the problems so I just did not struggle. Fourth, I began to cut class. I had the class at 7:00 in the morning on the fifth floor of a building all the way across a cold, dark, windy campus from my dormitory which was warm and lighted. Fifth, I was having much too good a time doing other things to worry about a detail like five hours of engineering calculus. I passed, but barely: I still do not know how.

Argumentation or Persuasion Development

Argument centers around controversy. In argumentation (also known as persuasion), you attempt to persuade the reader to your view. You offer evidence that your view is the reasonable one to hold. Collecting this evidence may involve doing research, as well as collecting case histories and analogies, so that you can support your point of view.

To write using argumentation development, first choose a controversial subject and take a position on it. Then, before beginning to write, ask yourself if you (1) want to convince the reader or only to raise his or her awareness of the issue, (2) want to promote action or to change attitudes and behavior, and (3) know enough about the subject to write knowledgeably or need to do research. Then decide (1) what your strongest point is, (2) what kind of appeal to make (emotional or intellectual, covert or direct), and (3) what tone to take. For example, you may decide that, for your purposes, irony is better than a direct approach.

Example (Argumentation or Persuasion Paragraph)

> Children with AIDS should be allowed to attend public schools. All children, handicapped, ailing or ordinary, are entitled, by law and by social custom, to an education. Furthermore, these innocent victims need the support and care of the community, as represented by the school. But, what about risk of infection to the other children in the school? All medical and scientific evidence points to the fact that AIDS is not transmitted through casual contact. No verified cases of transmission to primary care givers exist, even in those situations in which the care giver must deal with body fluids. Only when those body fluids come in contact with an open sore or cut is contagion possible. And even that risk can be alleviated through the use of rubber gloves. Since the risk of infection to caretakers is slight and to classmates is none, the fear of contagion is not a valid reason to keep children with AIDS from the public schools. To refuse them this entitlement would be to imply that these children are not worthy of being part of society. Children with AIDS are not pariahs: they are victims. They deserve our consideration. Yes, children with AIDS should go to public school.

You may, of course, have more than one kind of development in an essay; even if you do, you probably have only one kind of development in each paragraph of the essay.

REVISION

Refer to the peer consultation sheets in the back of the *Guide to College Writing* for specific information on how to make suggestions on revisions for other people's papers.

Essay Organization

In general, make sure the organization of the essay is clear: the thesis statement is clearly stated as the last sentence in the introductory section, each topic sentence supports the thesis statement, each sentence in each paragraph supports the topic sentence of the paragraph, the paragraphs are arranged in logical sequence, etc.

Introductory Section

Check to see that the introduction catches the reader's attention, leads logically to the thesis statement, and shows the tone and style you use in the essay.

Thesis Statement

Be sure the thesis is clear and specific and that it reveals the structure of the essay.

Body Paragraphs

Make sure that each paragraph is fully and completely developed and adheres to the principles of coherence and unity. Remove any information that does not support, develop, or illustrate the thesis.

Conclusion

Finally, check to see that the conclusion does not introduce new material that has not been covered in the essay but that it does develop logically from the thesis statement and body.

Editing

The last step in revision is checking for spelling, sentence structure, grammar and usage, and punctuation. If you have difficulty with any of these aspects, ask a friend, tutor, or someone else with good skills in writing mechanics to help you.

MANUSCRIPT PREPARATION

After you have revised and edited the paper, you need to prepare it for submission. No matter how well you learn to write, papers that are neatly prepared to hand in are always more impressive than sloppy ones: they show that you take pride in your work. Follow these simple guidelines for proper manuscript preparation. Submit only the best.

For handwritten papers,
1. Use regular notebook paper, 8 1/2 by 11 inches.
2. Never submit papers written on spiral notebook paper.
3. Write only on the front of the paper.
4. Use black or blue ink.
5. Skip lines at your instructor's request.
6. Leave the marked margins on both sides of the paper.
7. Leave a double line margin at the bottom.
8. The title should not be in quotation marks unless it was originally used by someone else. Center the title. Skip a line after the title and before you begin the text. The title is not part of the text; if you wish to make the title words part of your paper, use them in the text.
9. Indent the first line of each paragraph an inch.
10. Write legibly in upper- and lower- case letters.
11. Proofread and correct.
12. Staple papers together with one staple in the upper left-hand corner or fold all papers together, as the instructor requires. Do not dogear any papers.
13. Write your *full* name on each page in the upper right corner. Include the page number. Include class time and date on the first page. If papers are folded, write your *full* name, class time, and date on the outside.

For typed papers,
1. Use regular typing paper, 8 1/2 by 11 inches. Do not use erasable bond or onionskin.
2. Doublespace unless otherwise instructed.
3. Type on only one side of the paper.
4. Use letter-quality print, legible and dark. Use only typefaces such as Arial, Times New Roman, Helvetica, Courier, etc. Use type sizes of approximately 8 letters per inch.
5. For MLA format papers, use 1-inch margins on all sides of the paper, unless you are to bind the paper. In that case, leave a margin of 1 1/4 inches on the left.
6. Indent paragraphs by 1/2 inch or five spaces, whichever is greater.
7. The title should not be in quotation marks unless it was originally used by someone else. Center the title. Skip a line after the title and before you begin the text. The title is not part of the text; if you wish to make the title words part of your paper, use them in the text.
8. Staple papers together with one staple in the upper left-hand corner or fold all papers together, as the instructor requires. Do not dogear any papers.

9. Write your *last* name and the page number on each page in the upper right-hand corner. Include *full name*, class time, and date on the first page on the left side. If papers are folded, write your *full* name, class time, and date on the outside.
10. Use Arabic numbers (with no periods or parentheses) in the upper right-hand corner of the pages.
11. Do not justify the margins on both sides of the paper. Left justify only.
12. Proofread and correct all mistakes. If necessary, use black ink or even dark pencil.

Example (MLA Format: Typed Paper, First Page)

```
                                                              ↕ 1/2"
                                                            Student 1

↔ John Student
1"  Prof. Who
    ENGL1113
    September 22, 2009
                            Title Goes Here:
                                Center It
    1/2"
    → Always proofread and correct the paper. If it is necessary, you may correct any last-
      minute mistake with black ink or even dark pencil. Never leave a mistake.        ↔ 1"
                        ↕ 1"
```

Example (Typed Page, Not The First Page)

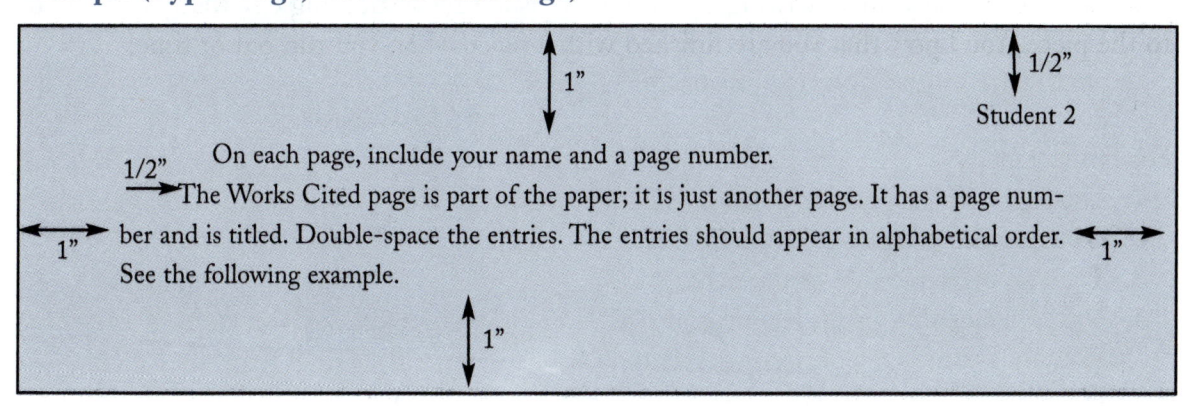

```
                         ↕ 1"                                ↕ 1/2"
                                                            Student 2

         On each page, include your name and a page number.
    1/2"
    → The Works Cited page is part of the paper; it is just another page. It has a page num-
↔   ber and is titled. Double-space the entries. The entries should appear in alphabetical order. ↔
1"  See the following example.                                                                    1"
                        ↕ 1"
```

Example (Research Paper, Works Cited Page)

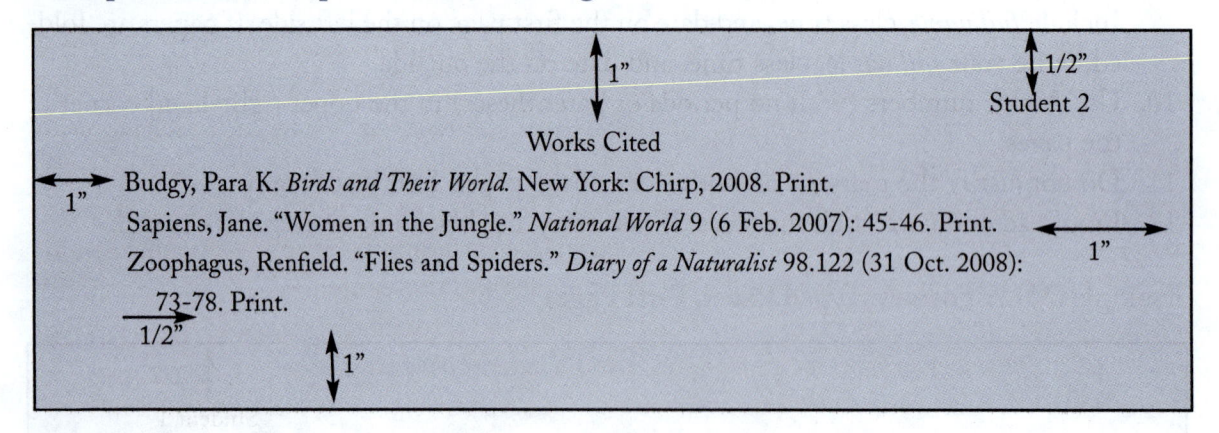

```
                            ↕1"                              ↕1/2"
                                                           Student 2
                         Works Cited
←→ Budgy, Para K. Birds and Their World. New York: Chirp, 2008. Print.
1"  Sapiens, Jane. "Women in the Jungle." National World 9 (6 Feb. 2007): 45-46. Print.   ←→
    Zoophagus, Renfield. "Flies and Spiders." Diary of a Naturalist 98.122 (31 Oct. 2008):  1"
        73-78. Print.
        1/2"
                    ↑1"
```

WRITING: THE RECURSIVE PROCESS

Writing is a recursive process! Recursive means that you can return to a previous step or process at any time. This book has presented the writing process as though it takes place in discrete steps: first you plan; then you organize; then you write a first draft; then you revise, etc. As you probably already know, that is not actually the way writing works. You are always planning, organizing, and developing simultaneously. You are in a constant process of revision. At any point, you can go back to a previous point and revise and repeat the step.

So the process is not straightforward, but more circular or spiral, a constant recurrence of steps.

How do you know when you are finished writing if the process is not a straight one? You do not ever really finish writing, because there is always something else that you could do to the piece. You know that you are finished with a piece when you run out of time!

READING FOR CONTENT AND READING FOR WRITING

One of the things that you need to be aware of is how to read texts. "Text" in this instance does not mean textbook, but any piece of writing. To begin with, think about how writing is usually structured. Earlier sections discussed the idea that essays, or other pieces of academic or informational writing, generally have a statement of the main point that the author wants to make, called the thesis statement. The thesis statement is generally supported by the remainder of the essay, which is contained in paragraphs. Each of the paragraphs generally has a topic sentence supported by the rest of the sentences in the paragraph. Basically, with the inclusion of an introductory section and a concluding section, this describes the structure of the majority of informational and academic writing.

With this in mind, we can take a piece of text and determine how that piece corresponds to the model we have described. You can make the same determination when you are reading a textbook, studying for a test, or reading for information. Obviously, the main idea of the information is of vital importance. And the major support for that information is also of importance. So, being able to pick out these points helps you understand what the author is trying to convey. In addition, being able to pick out these points helps you learn the material.

Look at this piece of writing, a short essay that could be written in fifty minutes.

Example (Short Essay, 50-Minute Essay)

Note: Student essay examples are above-average papers, but not necessarily "A" papers.

Ainperson 1

Cert Ainperson

Prof. Elle

ENGL 1113

May 10, 2005

Models

If we look around, we can see models for planes, trains, and automobiles. Models introduce us to the miniature worlds of transportation, people, and imagination.

The most obvious miniature world is probably the world of tiny transportation. Even in a supermarket, children can find and lust for metal space shuttles and plastic dump trucks. They can drive and ride these through the air and over the mud or carpet and imagine that they are astronauts or garbage collectors, truckers or race car drivers, pizza deliverers or mechanics. In the majority of cases, the transport looks much like the original, but only the mind powers these miniature machines.

We can find another small world peopled by dolls and doll houses. In this world, furniture looks like furniture, even if the upholstery is hard and plastic. In this world, people can look like

> people and babies like Cabbage Patch dolls. Women can look like Barbie and men can style their hair like Ken.
>
> These worlds are representations of the "real" world but there are other imaginary, miniature worlds. There are miniature universes that resemble and reflect reality and imagination almost equally. Out there are worlds of trolls with emerald navels; of ponies with manes and tails longer than their bodies; of plastic potatoes with eyes, noses, and hats; of green slime and pink Slinkies.
>
> Realistic or imaginary, these models become the world when they are played with. These miniatures, these models, allow children, and all the rest of us, to ride our dreams and shape our futures in the present, plastic and malleable.

Now that you have read the previous piece of writing, look at it and call it names! If we had to describe what kind of writing it was, we could call it a very short, descriptive essay. (See, we have already started to label it!) We could determine that, yes, it does fit the model by having a thesis statement: "Models introduce us to the miniature worlds of transportation, people, and imagination." That thesis is introduced by a comment about models in general and is supported by three points. Those points appear in the topic sentences of the paragraphs in the body of the piece. The first topic sentence discusses "tiny transportation"; the second, "people"; and the third, "imaginary worlds." Each of the topic sentences is supported by the remainder of the sentences in the paragraph. The piece concludes with a general statement, giving us a judgment on where the author stands on models.

Now that we have decided on what basic information is conveyed in the text, we can decide whether the author uses that structure in an appropriate way. First, is the thesis statement descriptive of the information contained in the text? In this case, we could probably make the judgment that the thesis is *fairly* focused. It does imply that the text will be about miniature worlds, which it is, but the thesis also implies that the text will focus on plastic, glue, and superglue, but neither kind of glue is mentioned in the essay.

Now we can decide whether the points revealed in the topic sentences support the main point made in the thesis. In this case, the topic sentences tell us that at least three miniature world models exist: transportation, people, and imagination. Does this support the contention in the thesis statement? Yes. Very well? Probably not very well, but the essay is so short that something has to be left out. Does that mean the thesis should be more focused? Yes, it probably does.

> *Be a careful reader.*

Next, is each paragraph complete? Does each paragraph contain enough information to support or illustrate the topic sentence? After rereading the piece, we can say, yes, probably, each paragraph has sufficient examples to support the topic sentence. Of course, the paragraphs could all be longer and more complete, but that is a decision that the author has to make—what to put in and what to leave out.

Does the conclusion sufficiently end the piece? This conclusion not only ends the piece but leaves the mind of the reader thinking further on the same subject. If this is the intention of the author—and it seems to be—the conclusion is successful.

In doing this analysis, or "engaging the text," we could proceed several ways. We might think through the structure, as we have done here. We might outline the main points and evaluate their effectiveness. (See the section on outlines.) We might annotate the text itself. This is a popular method. Annotating is sometimes known as highlighting and underlining, but it goes further than that! However, it works best if you read the piece first and then go *back* and underline and/or highlight. If we annotated the text, we would go back, after reading the text, and underline/highlight the main points. We would also make notes in the margins of the text as ideas occurred to us. We would make notes about whether we agreed or disagreed with what was said, with what connection we could make to other pieces we have read or other information we knew, with what we felt or thought when we read the passage.

Annotation of the text goes beyond a simple discovery of the structure of the text or the main points of the piece. It is actually an engagement of you and the text. You are actively involved with reading. Reading is not a passive activity. You have to filter what you read through your mind, assessing the relevance of what you read to you and to your situation, deciding how the new information agrees or disagrees with what you already know or think you know, discovering how the new information fits into your own knowledge of the world and yourself. If you do not do this, you are not reading and being engaged with the text. You are a couch potato who might as well be asleep! The information will not become *yours* without *your* participation. All of these possible ways to engage text work well, if a little differently. You need to find what works best for you.

Now, aside from learning the information by studying and for tests (and, of course, for your own personal satisfaction!), why would you want to follow any of these procedures? For one thing, you may be required to write pieces for classes or for your jobs that require this kind of analytic thinking. Summaries, reports, evaluations, précis, abstracts, reading cards, journal entries—all of these are names for writing that incorporates engaging text.

> *Think about what you read.*

One of the reasons to "engage text" is to evaluate it. Evaluation may tell whether you liked or disliked the article and why, whether you thought it was good or not and why, whether you found the information interesting or not and why. It may tell what you thought about the work's topic, what you thought about the work's writing, how you assessed the effectiveness or the importance of the topic or the presentation, or how you could relate the work to others you have read—all of which must be supported by reasons why you made the evaluation you made—and many other possibilities.

The evaluation is the part of the report in which your opinion is vital. You are evaluating the work. In the evaluation, you can express how you feel about the article, the subject, the writing, and the relative value of each of these.

Or you can go beyond a personal reaction to a more analytic response. You can consider the author, the publisher, and the date of publication. This would enable you and your reader to determine whether the selection was written by a reputable author, published by a reputable publisher, and is dated or timely. What difference might these things make? Well, what if you had read an article that asserted that eating raw pork prevented trichinosis (which, as you know, may be carried in raw pork)? And what if you found that the author was the owner of the largest pig farm in the world and had just been admitted to a psychiatric hospital? You might use this knowledge to decide whether the article contained accurate information!

If you are going to make a more formal report, you might consider the length, organization, and style of the work. In that case, you would have to decide whether the work were too short for the amount of information, if it gave enough information, if it were well organized, if it had a valid and well-supported thesis, and so on. You might want to comment on whether the work made sense. You might want to consider any or all of these factors when you decide on what you want to comment in the reaction or evaluation part of the report.

As you read, you can tell whether or not you like a work. In addition, you can make another determination. You can decide if it is good or bad. However, you have to realize that those are two different determinations. In other words, liking something does not necessarily mean it is good, and not liking something does not necessarily mean it is not good. Deciding whether you like it is different from deciding whether the work has merit.

For example, many people like to read series fiction—such as the Destroyer novels or Harlequin Romances. Reading these is a lot like eating at McDonald's. You know exactly what you are getting. And so, if that is what you want, you like it. But that does not mean you cannot decide that some other works might be "better" in the sense of more artistic or more important, such as Rachel Carson's *Silent Spring* or Oliver Sacks's *The Man Who Mistook His Wife for a Hat* or *Awakenings*.

> *Evaluate and assess what you read.*

Making a decision about the quality of a work does not mean that there are aspects of it that you should not like. It does mean that you should look at why you make the decisions about what you like and know that the decision about liking something does not mean the same as deciding about worth or importance.

An evaluation can also be a decision on whether the information or judgment is correct or incorrect, whether the information or judgment is applicable to your situation or that of another, or whether the information or judgment is right or wrong—in a moral, social, or political sense. Actually, you are making a judgment on a judgment!

It can be difficult or easy to make the evaluation. Sometimes it is obvious that what you have read is incorrect or irrelevant. For example, an article on beekeeping that suggests that you keep bees in the bathtub is hardly credible. In some circumstances, you may not be able to distinguish between the possibilities so easily. However, there are some steps that you can use to make this decision easier.

First, as a base, decide what the author actually says by finding the main idea and the major supporting ideas of the work. This is the basis of all evaluation and is also the basis for a summary.

Then decide what the author means by determining whether the statements are fact or opinion, whether the author might be biased in any way, and whether you can relate the information to knowledge that you already have.

For example, in an article about food use, an author might say that eating ice cream leads to drowning. The article contains figures that show a relationship between the number of people drowned in a month and the number of gallons of ice cream consumed in that month. As one figure goes up, the other does too. As one goes down, the other does too.

Well, the argument looks as though it might make sense. But does it really? Are the statements fact or opinion? On the surface, the statements of the author seem to be fact. The numbers of people drowned and the numbers of gallons consumed are fact.

Is the author biased in any way? We find that the author has credentials and that the data in the article were gathered by two reputable organizations. The author does not own swimming areas or dairy farms. So the author is probably not biased in any sense that we can determine.

Then, can we relate the information to information we already have? Well, we know that ice cream consumption rises in the summer. This is borne out by the figures in this and in other articles. It makes sense that more people eat ice cream in warmer weather. We know that the number of people drowning rises in the summer because the number of people swimming increases in the summer. Such is delineated by figures in this and other articles. It makes sense that if more people swim, more people drown because the number of possibilities for drowning increases.

Does that mean that one causes the other? We also know that many things that are not related to each other rise and fall cyclically: hemlines and the stock market, the number of sparrows in fields and the number of aircraft. But they do not cause each other. They are not related as supply and demand are related. So you also can decide that the author has mistakenly determined that two things rising and falling cyclically have a cause and effect relationship. We can evaluate the article and conclude that the author is in error.

> *The more you bring to a work,*
> *the more you receive from the work.*

SPECIALIZED FORMS OF WRITING

Summarizing

A summary may be referred to as a précis or an abstract. (In technical writing, a distinction is made between these terms. If you are doing technical writing, you need to know the distinction. In that case, refer to a good technical writing text or manual or to the style sheet of the company initiating the report.)

The writer of a summary reduces material in an original work to its main points and key supporting details. A summary may consist of a word, a phrase, several sentences, or one or more paragraphs. Usually a summary is one or two paragraphs. This paragraph or paragraphs includes a statement of the main idea of the article (the thesis statement) and refers to the major points that support the main idea.

A report (which may also be called a review) usually contains two sections: a summary of the material and a statement of the report writer's reaction to the material. If you are the report writer, the reaction is your own evaluation of the article—whether you liked or disliked it and why, whether you thought it was good or not and why, and/or whether you found the information interesting and useful or not and why. (In technical writing, there are different types of reports. If you are doing technical writing, you need to know the different kinds. Refer to a good technical writing text or manual or the style sheet of the company for which you prepare the report.)

To write a summary well, and relatively painlessly, follow the steps listed:

1. Read the selection carefully, rereading as much as necessary.
2. In your own words, write a summary of the selection.
   A. At the top of the page, give the bibliographic information for the selection. Use the MLA format unless otherwise instructed. (See the section on documentation.)
   B. The first line of the summary section should repeat the name of the selection and the author.
   C. The summary should convey your understanding of the main idea (thesis) of the selection and the major points used in developing this idea *or* the major events in the short story or novel.
   D. Usually confine the summary of an article to one paragraph. (See the section on paragraph development.) This may seem brief, but a summary has one purpose—to summarize.
   E. A summary should not exceed one-fourth of the length of the selection being summarized. Be skeptical of any summary that seems to require more than a page and a half.
   F. Phrases or clauses quoted from the selection should be enclosed in quotation marks.
   G. Do *not* include your opinion of the selection or your own knowledge of the subject in the summary paragraph. (This information belongs in the reaction paragraph of a *report*—not in a summary.

Example (Summary of an Article or Essay)

Trillin, Calvin. "It's Just Too Late." *The Bedford Reader*. 2nd ed. Ed. X. J. Kennedy and Dorothy M. Kennedy. New York: St. Martin's, 1985. 4556. Print.

Trillin's "It's Just Too Late" is an account of a sixteen-year-old girl's death. FaNee Cooper is the "perfect child" who, at thirteen, is discovered no longer perfect. She turns to alcohol and drugs and the people who use these substances. One night her father, wanting to take her from the company of one of her friends, chases her in a car. The car FaNee is riding in is wrecked. FaNee dies; the boy driving is convicted of involuntary manslaughter.

Example (Summary of an Article or Essay)

Etzioni, Amitai. "Parenting as an Industry." *The McGraw-Hill Reader*. 7th ed. Ed. Gilbert H. Muller. Boston: McGraw-Hill, 1997. 106-12. Print.

In Amitai Etzioni's essay "Parenting as an Industry," Etzioni analyzes the woeful condition of parenting. He says the condition is a result of increased numbers of parents leaving "the nest" to seek careers outside the home. Etzioni believes the lack of quality and quantity time parents have to offer their children is resulting in insufficient bonding and education. In turn, these children will have difficulty growing into well-adjusted adults. In addition, Etzioni discusses the growing numbers of children being placed in child care centers and the failure of these centers to give children the quality care they require because of understaffing and poorly paid, unqualified personnel. Because of these conditions, the turn-over rate at child care centers is very high, making bonding between child and caregiver difficult. Etzioni expresses concern about whether parents should trust strangers to raise their children and form their personalities. Furthermore, Etzioni suggests that parents become more responsible in selecting child care and remain involved after placement. Etzioni recommends increased government supervision of centers and home facilities and financial assistance for parents struggling to afford quality care for their children. In conclusion, Etzioni asks the reader the following question: What is most important in our country—making more money in pursuit of the "American Dream" or striving to be effective nurturing parents to our children?

A specific kind of summary is the rhetorical précis. The emphasis in the rhetorical précis is on the rhetorical aspect of the work, written or spoken, that you are considering. Rhetorical study is the study of language use and communication. Thus, a rhetorical précis is designed to show the main points of the work, such as the name of the writer, the name and genre (or type) of the work, the manner of information delivery, the main and supporting points, and the relation between the writer and audience. The rhetorical précis consists of four sentences:

1. Sentence 1: The first sentence names the author, the genre (essay, novel, speech, etc.), the title (with the date of the work in parentheses) followed by a verb ("claims," "posits," "argues," etc.), followed by "that" and a phrase or clause in which you state the thesis of the work.
2. Sentence 2: The second sentence explains the manner in which the author supports the thesis. You do not do this by restating details but by explaining the rhetorical method that the author used to develop the support, such as narration, comparison, classification, etc.
3. Sentence 3: The third sentence states the purpose of the work. This may reflect the thesis but must include why the author has created the work. The third sentence contains a phrase or clause beginning with "in order to," such as "The writer delineates his vision of the future in order to. . . ."
4. Sentence 4: The fourth sentence states the intended audience for the work and how the author positions himself or herself in relation to that audience. (See the following example.)

Example (Rhetorical Précis)

Gray 1

Laura Gray

Guide to College Writing

July 1, 2005

Minsky, Marvin. "Will Robots Inherit the Earth?" The Writer's Presence: A Pool of Readings. Ed. Donald McQuade and Robert Atwan. Boston: Bedford/St. Martin, 2000. 460-470. Print.

In his essay "Will Robots Inherit the Earth?" (1994), Marvin Minsky posits that the inevitable synthesis of human and machine offers an optimistic future for the human race, which will be "delivered from the limitations of biology" (461). Minsky supports his futuristic vision through scientific facts and statistics of Darwinian theory, biochemistry, genetics, and nanotechnology. His purpose is to convince his readers of the feasibility and desirability of machine/human augmentation in order to indict those who fail to embrace the inevitable merging of human and machine. Minsky establishes a problematic relationship with his audience through his dismissive tone that labels those who take issue with his particular world-view as "dangerous" (469).

For a *short story summary*, see the summary of "Young Goodman Brown" in the section on writing in response to literature.

REPORTS AND REVIEWS

To write a *report* or *review*, follow the previous steps for writing a summary. Follow Step 1; then follow Step 2 A–F. Then, instead of using the previous Step 2 G, include G from the following:

G. *Do* include your opinion of the selection and your own knowledge of the subject in the reaction or evaluation paragraph.

When writing the reaction paragraph(s) of the report or review, you may consider the author, the publisher, and the date of publication: this enables you and your reader to determine whether the selection were written by a reputable author, published by a reputable company, and is dated or timely. (See the section on reading for writing and reading for content.) You might consider the length, organization, and style of the selection.

The reaction paragraph or paragraphs can be, and probably should be, analytical. (See the section on reports and reviews: making evaluations.) Relate the information to your own thoughts and feelings and to your own knowledge of the subject. Decide whether or not the information is useful, you liked or disliked the subject and/or the author's style of writing, you thought the selection was good or not. Do not stop with a simple statement such as "I liked it." Tell why you liked or disliked it!

Example (Report on an Article or Essay)

> Trillin, Calvin. "It's Just Too Late." *The Bedford Reader*. 2nd ed. Ed. X .J. Kennedy and Dorothy M. Kennedy. New York: St. Martin's, 1985. 4556. Print.
>
> Trillin's "It's Just Too Late" is an account of a sixteen-year-old girl's death. FaNee Cooper is the "perfect child" who, at thirteen, is discovered no longer perfect. She turns to alcohol and drugs and the people who use these substances. One night her father, wanting to take her from the company of one of her friends, chases her in a car. The car FaNee is riding in is wrecked. FaNee dies; the boy driving is convicted of involuntary manslaughter.
>
> This essay was very distressing. I enjoyed reading it even though it made me feel uneasy. It shows how any child from any family in any community can go "bad." FaNee seems to be ordinary until she turns to drugs, but the essay shows that she is surrounded by hypocrisy and high expectations. Her parents turn against her because her mother discovers cigarettes in her drawer. The community and school reveal hypocritical standards: the "Ins" talk about not drinking, but there is no evidence that they actually do not. Against these expectations, false standards, and the knowledge she never can be "perfect," FaNee escapes to places and people of imperfections. Her escape leads ultimately to her death because she made wrong choices. Others, however, might feel guilt. Ironically, her father says he would chase her again, knowing his actions would cause her death. What kind of father is this?

Example (Rhetorical Précis with Reader Response or Rhetorical Report)

Gray 1

Laura Gray
Guide to College Writing
July 15, 2005

Minsky, Marvin. "Will Robots Inherit the Earth?" *The Writer's Presence: A Pool of Readings*. Ed. Donald McQuade and Robert Atwan. Boston: Bedford/St. Martin, 2000. 460–470. Print.

In his essay "Will Robots Inherit the Earth?" (1994), Marvin Minsky posits that the inevitable synthesis of human and machine offers an optimistic future for the human race, which will be "delivered from the limitations of biology" (461). Minsky supports his futuristic vision through scientific facts and statistics of Darwinian theory, biochemistry, genetics, and nanotechnology. His purpose is to convince his readers of the feasibility and desirability of machine/human augmentation in order to indict those who fail to embrace the inevitable merging of human and machine. Minsky establishes a problematic relationship with his audience through his dismissive tone that labels those who take issue with his particular world-view as "dangerous" (469).

I found this essay both intriguing and problematic. Minsky sets an early tone of optimism for the future as he discusses science and technology as tools for improving human existence. He establishes ethos with his audience by presenting complex scientific information in easily readable prose. His rhetorical style is engaging and informative. Minsky's tone changes, however, as he addresses the possible criticisms of his particular world vision, and as he dismisses the deep spiritual and philosophical questions with a swift "I have no patience with such arguments" (467). Overall, I believe Minsky's argument fails because he refuses to adequately address the major concerns that his readers will likely have—what it means to our sense of humanity if we alter something considered fundamental to our makeup, the brain, through technological tinkering. Just because we can do something does not necessarily mean that we should.

Making Evaluations

Sometimes you will be required to make evaluations of articles or books that are written to be persuasive or informative and that contain judgments of one kind or another. An evaluation is a decision on whether the selection is correct or incorrect, etc. (See the section on reading for writing and reading for content.)

To make rational evaluations of selections containing judgments, you might follow this process:

1. Summarize the main idea and supporting points.
2. Does the selection offer new information or a fresh approach or a new interpretation? What questions does the selection answer or fail to answer?
3. Determine whether statements are facts, opinion, or both. Be sure to identify any authorial bias; i.e., an article on cars, praising Fords, that was written by the Ford Motor Company president may well be biased. Does the author's opinion mar or enhance the selection? Does he or she plead for a special view? Is his or her plea based on fact or on prejudice?
4. Analyze the selection in terms of what you know. Have you experienced or researched the topic? Does your experience agree with the author's? (It is not sufficient simply to agree or disagree. You must have some basis for agreement or disagreement.) Is the work credible?
5. Decide whether you will accept the work as accurate, reject it, or defer judgment on it until you have collected more information.

Reviews, Critiques, and Evaluations

You may also be required to review artistic works. This kind of review is also called an evaluation or critique. In essence, you are making your own judgment of the worth of the work; you are critiquing the work.

Some reviews include bibliographic data and a summary. (See the section on summaries and reports.) Some reviews, especially those for newspapers and for some classes, do not include either bibliographic data or a summary. Be sure to check with the person making the assignment to see what the requirements are. Then follow directions!

ESSAY TESTS

Taking an essay test is an experience you will undoubtedly have in college if you have not already had it. Taking an essay test may be frightening, as taking any kind of test can be, but it should not cause you to panic if you are familiar with the material to be covered.

Just follow these simple guidelines to a successful experience.

1. *Follow instructions.* Bring the designated supplies to the test—pen, paper, "blue book," and anything else specified. Write your name in the designated position. Read the instructions first so you know what instructions to follow. Remember that there are *two kinds of essay tests*: one in which you write a full, short essay of four or five paragraphs in answer to a question (see timed essays for examples) and one in which you write a paragraph or two in answer to a question. Note the instructions to see which kind of answer you should make.
2. *Read through the test.* Partly this is to make sure you know what the instructions are (see Step 1), and partly this is to reassure yourself that not everything sounds strange or new!

3. *Select the questions you will answer.* Often, the test lists a number of questions from which you select. In that case, decide which questions you think you can answer best. Be sure you answer what the question is asking and not what you wish the question were asking.
4. *Jot down ideas.* Either in the margin of the test paper, on a scrap of paper, or in the back of the "blue book," write down your thoughts as they occur to you. As you select the questions you plan to answer and as you think of points you might be able to use in your answer, write a little note to yourself. If you do not, you may forget that wonderful thought and not be able to recapture it when you write the answer. It is too late to recall it as you walk out the door. Make sure this does not happen to you—write it down as you think of something.
5. *Time yourself.* As you select the questions, decide how much time you can safely spend on any one answer. Allow ten minutes at both ends of the class for Steps 1, 2, 3, 4, 6, and 11. That leaves you half an hour for answering questions if you are taking a fifty-minute exam. If you are answering five questions, you can only spend six minutes on each answer. (This calculation assumes that all the questions are of equal weight and importance.) When you come to the end of the time you have allotted for the question, quit. You have programmed into your plan a cushion at the end in which to fill in additional information if necessary. Remember that it is better to omit a couple of sentences in a few answers than to omit a complete answer, which is likely to happen if you do not plan your time.
6. *Look for direction words in the question.* Answer the question that is asked.

Analyze	means to *examine* closely, separating basic parts, steps or features, to look for cause and/or effect, to tell why or how.
Attack or *defend*	means to take a position, for or against.
Compare	means to explain similarities, parallels and differences. Sometimes people mistakenly assume that to compare means only to describe the similarities (because *contrast* means to stress the differences). When you are in doubt about the instructor's desires, *ask*. It is too late to find out what the instructor wants after the test is returned with the answer marked wrong.
Contrast	means to stress the differences.
Define	means to explain what something means or what it is. Begin with a basic definition and then use examples to clarify what you mean.
Discuss	means to explain, to analyze, to elaborate, even to debate. This is a general and fairly vague term, so decide carefully which direction you are going to go and then stay with your plan.
Elaborate	means to explain further, to develop a detailed explanation. Be careful to use both primary and secondary support. Make major points (primary support); include examples and details (secondary support).
Evaluate	means to judge or to *analyze* critically, discussing the pros and cons. Write a pros and cons argument or a critical analysis. If writing a pros and cons argument, be clear about which side you prefer, even if you feel you need to spend time on both sides.

Examine	means to *analyze*.
Explain	means to clarify, interpret, explicate, or summarize. The term explain covers all expository writing strategies. This is a general term, so decide carefully which direction you are going to go and then stay with your plan. Do not write an argument (*attack* or *defend*).
Illustrate	means to clarify. Begin with the basic generalization called for and then elaborate with a long example or with several short examples.
List	means to write down a series of points. Use the 1, 2, 3 or the first, second, third approach.
Outline	means to discuss briefly, give a skeletal discussion, skip details.

7. *Plan your answer.* Plan your time, and plan your answer. Read the question and decide what points to cover before starting to write. You may want to jot down ideas or even do a simple outline. Do not just begin writing and trust to luck and your fairy godmother to make sure you hit all of the important points before you run out of time or memory. If you just begin to write and write and write, you may find that you have been writing the wrong things.

8. *Write neatly so that the grader can read your answer.* No matter what you have heard or read, the grader must be able to read your paper. Otherwise, the grader is likely to assume that you do not know the information at all and are trying to cover up by being messy. In addition, the grader will be subconsciously prejudiced in favor of your paper by its neat, pleasing appearance. Fair? No, but make it work for you, not against you.

9. *Write a good answer.* Write in complete sentences. The more that a grader can easily read your answer, the more it is likely that the grader will be happy to read your answer. Be coherent and logical. Answer the question that is asked, not the one you wish had been asked. Believe it or not, graders can recognize blah blah blah.

10. *Write part of the question in the answer.* The grader should be able to tell what question you are answering by reading your answer. The grader should not have to refer to the question number, which you *must* include. For instance, as you are answering a question that says, "What were the three major causes of Black Friday?", you should start your answer by saying, "The three major causes of Black Friday were. . . ." This makes the grader happy. Probably more important, it solves the major problem for most people—starting out. You already have written part of what you are going to say. You are started on the answer, so the worst is over.

11. *Determine the length of the answer by how long you have to answer it.* No other guideline can be applicable to the length of an essay question. Some questions could be answered in a short paragraph; some could take a book. But you do not have time to write a book. Judge how long the answer should be by how long you have to answer it. If you have two questions to answer, the answers should be 20 minutes long. If you have four questions to answer, the answers should be 10 minutes long.

12. *Reread and revise, but do not rewrite.* After you have answered all of the questions and run out of answering time, you still have the ten minutes that you have allotted to go over your paper. Take this time to check your answers for various things, such as spelling and

punctuation errors. Even if an instructor says that spelling and punctuation "do not count," you can be sure that they influence the grader's reaction to your answer, even if only subconsciously. Check also for accuracy, coherence, logic, and readability. This is also the time to go back and complete those questions that you may not have completely finished. Do not take the time to rewrite the paper. You do not have time. If you have been neat and have planned, you will not need to rewrite.

13. *Turn in the paper!*

Example (Essay Question Answer)

- The test you have been handed says to answer both of the following questions:
    1. Discuss the irony in "Appointment in Samarra." Include in your discussion some comments on how the female figure of death functions as part of that irony.

    2. Discuss the two major images in "The Tell-Tale Heart." Include in your discussion how the images function as symbols.

- Your answer looks something like this:
  1. "Appointment in Samarra" is an ironic short story. First, the servant thinks that Death has threatened him, so he runs away from Baghdad to Samarra. But Death has only made a gesture of surprise because she has an appointment with the servant in Samarra. When the servant flees, he is running to his fate instead of away from it. This is an ironic aspect. Another ironic aspect is that Maugham has made Death female. In most stories, Death is seen as male. Usually, the female is considered the life-bringer, the fruitful one. Usually, the male is seen as the force of destruction and death. Maugham has chosen to portray Death as female in an ironic reversal of the usual role for death. Because Death is female and because the servant is running to death at her hands, the story is ironic on two levels.
  2. The two major images in "The Tell-Tale Heart" are the "evil eye" and the beating heart. The madman sees the eye of the old man as evil because it is filmy and clouded. He says he loves the old man but that the eye is evil and must be destroyed. The eye becomes the symbol for the madness of the killer, and it becomes the symbol for the attitude of the killer as well. Because the killer says he loves the old man but is willing to kill him to kill the eye, the eye becomes the symbol for the madman's ability to divorce his fear of the eye from his "love" for the old man. He makes the old man into a bundle of parts, and he wants to wipe out one of those parts. He makes the old man into an object by only looking at one aspect of him.

     The beating heart is a symbol for madness and for conscience. The heart is symbolic of the madman's conscience, which will not let him rest until he confesses to the crime. The image of the heart beating more and more loudly under the floor becomes the symbol of the conscience crying out more and more loudly for the truth. The heart is also symbolic of the killer's madness because he imagines it beating long after the old man is dead.

Example (Essay Question Answer)

- The test you have been handed asks,
    1. How has a film affected your life and/or your philosophy of life?
- Your answer looks something like this:

Renetta Harrison

Comp. II/Cinema

Sept. 4, 1997

1. The film *Schindler's List* affected my life by making me more aware of discrimination, more knowledgeable on the history of the period of the film, and very angry. I am now much more against all forms of discrimination because of the film's depiction of the cruel treatment of the Jewish people during the Holocaust. I am appalled that anyone would treat others badly, not to mention kill them, based on religious preference. I am also more knowledgeable on the history of Hitler and the Holocaust because of the film. I can now actually hold an intelligent conversation with my "history buff" husband. That fact pleases us both. I feel it is very important for me to know about the events in history in order to help prevent recurrence. This movie also stirred my angry feelings toward those who continue to believe in a supreme race. This anger has made me stand more strongly for what I believe: racism is wrong. I feel *Schindler's List* brought me to a deeper understanding of what it will involve, including taking a stand and facing dangers, to defeat racism. Therefore, I believe *Schindler's List* definitely affected my life.

Example (Essay Question Answers)

- The test question says,
  1. Define one of the themes in *Much Ado about Nothing*.
- One answer says,

  Mike Mitchell
  1. The theme of a film is the central or controlling idea. Although the film *Much Ado about Nothing* has several themes, the predominate one is that reputation is desperately important. For example, Claudio is successful at displaying social grace; however, his strict adherence to social propriety enslaves him. Claudio abandons Hero at the wedding because he believes she is unfaithful. Leonardo is embarrassed as well because he thinks he matched Claudio with someone unchaste. Leonardo slaps his daughter, Hero, and she desires death when she is publicly humiliated. These events show the code of social values in the society.

- Another answer says,

  Debbie Stubblefield
  1. A theme of *Much Ado about Nothing* is that no matter what a person does to change things, the truth will always come out. Hero is vindicated in the end because the truth comes out that she was not the unchaste woman in the window. Also, the truth prevails because Don John, the villain, is punished in the end; evil and lies lose. And, the truth that Beatrice and Benedict love each other is also revealed in the end.

Example (Short Essay in Response to a Prompt)

> - The instructions follow:
>   You have 50 minutes to write this essay. Respond to one position in this statement: Students should/should not have to write research papers.
>
> Foreman 1
>
> Kevin Foreman
> Composition II
> 50-Minute Essay
> Sept. 10, 1998
>
> Writing Research Papers
>
> Many people do not like writing or, for that matter, spending endless hours in a library doing research, especially if that research is on a topic that is as dry as a cardboard box. But I believe writing a research paper should be a required activity in college for several reasons.
>
> First of all, the valuable experience gained in using the library, such as experience with the computer system, the business index, the card catalog, or the Internet, gives individuals tools helpful in other parts of their daily lives. Many people are not exposed to computer systems such as a library can provide. If a person needed information he or she were not getting from a local car dealer, a library business index could provide valuable information for that person. An Internet connection might provide more information that will aid the customer.
>
> Job-related situations may call for skills learned by doing a research paper. If a veterinarian needed up-to-date information on the treatment of exotic disease in a dog, he or she could use research skills to get information from books, periodicals, or the Internet. If a local newspaper reporter needed information on a celebrity visit to the community in order to write a feature, he or she could use the library skills to get quick and easy access to the needed information.
>
> General exposure to the library is good for people. The necessity to write a research paper would give people great exposure to the library and its resources. They would then have the skills they needed to find information or just to check out a book for recreational reading.
>
> Students should have to write research papers.

ELECTRONIC COMMUNICATION

E-mail is a communication device that is prevalent in the affluent 21st century. However, the most effective e-mail uses standard, professional "netiquette." Of course, any communication to a friend or relative can be written in the form and style preferred by the two of you. But any communication to a professor or for business purposes should follow the standard guidelines.

1. E-mail should be concise and clear. It should not be full of "pretties," such as colored backgrounds, pictures, and fancy fonts. Some servers cannot handle backgrounds and odd fonts, and, thus, your fancy communication might not reach the recipient.
2. In addition to avoiding unusual fonts, you should also avoid "smilies" or "emoticons," such as the smile :). These symbols might be misinterpreted and do not look very professional or academic.
3. *Subject lines must be clear.* The recipient should know from the subject line exactly what the topic of the message is. *Do not use a subject line such as "Hello" or "Hi."* Such generic subject lines on e-mails are known to most recipients as clues that the e-mail may contain a virus.
4. The salutation may be formal, such as "Dear Professor Smith" or "Dear Dr. Beans," but you may begin the e-mail message without a salutation.
5. Be sure to *put your full name at the end of each message.* Your e-mail address and/or screen name are not usually sufficient identification for the recipient of your message. At any rate, it's only polite to identify yourself in the message.
6. Avoid using quotations (unless very short) or graphics at the end of the message.
7. The *main part of the message must be complete* enough so the recipient knows exactly what you are asking and/or answering and does not have to guess anything or try to reconstruct the previous communications.
8. The message should *use standard conventional grammar*, punctuation, capitalization, and spelling.
9. *Do not use all caps*, which is the electronic equivalent of shouting.
10. Remember that *e-mail is not private communication*: businesses, system administrators, etc. can and may access it.
11. Think about your message before you send it. E-mail is so fast and efficient that you may have the impulse to initiate a message or respond to one in the fire of emotion. This could be a mistake. Compose the e-mail; let it sit while you cool; consider it calmly; maybe you will want to recompose the message. It might be wise.

> *Follow simple rules for e-mail etiquette.*

THE RESEARCH PAPER

Writing a research paper is not as difficult as you may fear. If you follow some simple steps and allow yourself plenty of time, you should be successful in turning out a product of which you can be proud.

RESEARCH PAPER STEPS

Following are the steps in writing a research paper. The remainder of this section of the *Guide* is a full explanation of each step.
1. Choose a limited topic. Remember the audience.

2. Collect a preliminary bibliography.
3. Make notes.
4. Plan the paper.
5. Write out a first draft, including necessary internal documentation and a Works Cited page.
6. Revise the draft. Type a second draft with internal documentation and a Works Cited page.
7. Correct, type, and assemble your final paper. Proofread!

> *Simple steps make successful research writing.*

Step One: Limited Topic

Choose a topic and limit it so that your subject is not too broad or complex for the length of paper you are writing. Your instructor will probably give you a general subject—such as Civil War generals. But, in a single semester, you cannot write about all of the Civil War generals or even all about one Civil War general. So you must limit the subject to something you can handle within the time and space requirements—such as General Pemberton's defense of Vicksburg.

Step Two: Preliminary Bibliography

After you select the topic, find out what resources are available. Research the topic by looking in the card catalog and in various indexes and bibliographies. (See the section on library discovery.) Keep track of the available resources by making "bib cards"—index cards on which you keep bibliographic information for each source you find. Or use another method that works for you and keeps track of the information about sources.

Sources should be well-known magazines and/or newspapers, books and/or special references. Do *not* use general encyclopedias. General encyclopedias are useful to read for background information but should not be used as sources.

You may decide to search the Internet for sources, using search engines, which are programs that work with an Internet browser to locate information on the World Wide Web. Search engines include http://www.altavist.digital.com/, http://google.com, http://www.excite.com/, http://www.lycos.com/, <http://www.metacrawler.com/, http://www.yahoo.com/, and http://www.netscape.com/escapes/search, among others. You might need to use more than one engine to search a subject.

Whether you find books, articles, or Internet sources, the bibliography cards (or alternate method) contain the bibliographic information you need to complete a Works Cited page. The Works Cited page contains an alphabetical list of the sources to which you have actually referred in your paper.

You may be more familiar with the term *bibliography* than with the term *Works Cited*. The bibliography is an alphabetical list of works to which you refer in your paper; it may also contain works that you researched and that are relevant to the subject, but to which you did not actually refer in the text of your paper. A Works Cited page, not a bibliography page, is designated by the MLA (Modern Language Association) documentation style. An MLA

Works Cited page includes *only* works to which you refer in the paper. (See section on manuscript preparation.) The APA (American Psychological Association) style requires a References page rather than a Works Cited page.

Bibliography information for the "bib cards" should be written in the format in which it appears on the Works Cited page. (See section on documentation.) For your own convenience, you may include other information that does not appear on the Works Cited page.

Example (Bibliography Card)

You have found a magazine article by Gina Kolata called "Cannibalism: Fact or Fiction?" appearing in volume 17, number 12 of the *Smithsonian* magazine dated March 1987.

> Kolata, Gina. "Cannibalism: Fact or Fiction?" <u>Smithsonian</u> 17.12 (Mar. 1987): 150-71.

DOCUMENTATION

When gathering source information, be sure to collect the information that is applicable.

<u>For Books</u>
1. Author(s)
2. Chapter or part of book
3. Title of the book
4. Editor, translator, or compiler
5. Edition
6. Number of volumes
7. Name of the series
8. Place, publisher, and date
9. Volume number of the book
10. Page numbers (when citing part of a book, such as citing a chapter on Plato in a book about the Greeks)

<u>For Articles</u>
1. Author(s)
2. Title of the article
3. Name of the periodical
4. Series number or name
5. Volume number
6. Issue number
7. Date of publication
8. Page numbers

Some of this information is not relevant; however, if you have it all, you do not have to go back and look up anything again. You need to examine some of the examples found in the section on documentation. These examples are not complete: there are other situations that you may find when doing research. For a complete explanation of how to write entries, see the MLA or APA handbooks.

Remember that MLA style is not the only "style" that you can use to write a paper. You might use MLA style, which requires footnotes; you might be using APA; or you might be using another style entirely. The principles are the same; the differences are in format. When you are assigned a paper, you need to find out what format the instructor requires. If the instructor does not specify or says, "I don't care," pick a style and be consistent.

DIFFERENCES IN DOCUMENTATION FORMS FOR MLA AND APA STYLES

Title of Source Listing
- MLA — Works Cited
- APA — References

Entry Format
- MLA — indents the second and subsequent lines one-half inch
- APA — indents the second and subsequent lines 5–7 spaces or one-half inch

Author's Name
- MLA — includes first name and any middle initials
- APA — uses only initials for first name and includes middle initials

Order of Author's Names (More than One Author)
- MLA — reverses the order (last name, first name) only for the first listed name; uses regular order (first name, last name) for all subsequent names
- APA — reverses the order (last name, first name) for all names

The Word *and* for Listing More than One Author
- MLA — uses the word *and*
- APA — uses the ampersand (&)

Year of Publication
- MLA — gives the year toward the end of the citation
- APA — gives the year in parentheses, followed by a period immediately after author name

Capitalization in Titles
- MLA — capitalizes in accordance with capitalization rules
- APA — capitalizes only the first word, a word after a colon, and proper nouns

Quotation Marks for Names of Shorter Works (Articles, Short Stories, etc.)
- MLA — uses quotation marks around the names of shorter works

Publisher
- MLA — uses short forms if they are clear: Prentice for Prentice Hall, for example
- APA — uses the complete name but drops words such as Inc., Co., and Publishers

Publication Month Abbreviations
- MLA — abbreviates all months except for May, June, and July by using the first three letters, followed by a period
- APA — does NOT abbreviate months

Inclusive Page Numbers

Inclusive page numbers give the starting page number and the ending page number of a cited work, such as one article in a journal or one chapter in a book. Using inclusive page numbers signals that the cited work is on those pages and all pages in between. If that is not the case, use the following style for discontinuous pages.

MLA	uses the full number through 99, then uses only the last two digits unless confusion would result: 101–09 is clear, but full numbers are needed for 897–910.
APA	uses complete numbers

Discontinuous Numbers

MLA	uses the starting page number, followed by a plus sign (+): 44+
APA	lists all pages, with discontinuous numbers set off by commas: 43–44, 47–49, 54–66, 76

- *Note:* In the following pages, you will find examples of both MLA and APA documentation. Be sure that you are using the correct format for the assignment that you are given. Also remember that you may have to look at more than one example in order to find the necessary information. For example, you might have to look at both "article in a magazine, signed" and "newspaper" to find how to do the entry you are working on.

SAMPLE MLA DOCUMENTATION EXAMPLES

BOOK with one author.
Dickens, Charles. *Great Expectations.* New York: Rinehart, 1948. Print.

BOOK with two authors.
Biddle, Arthur W., and Kenneth M. Holland. *Writer's Guide: Political Science.* Lexington: Heath, 1987. Print.

BOOK with three authors.
Frye, Northrup, Sheridan Baker, and George Perkins. *The Harper Handbook to Literature.* New York: Harper, 1985. Print.

BOOK with more than three authors.
BOOK with an edition after the first.
BOOK with several volumes.
BOOK with several volumes, one of the volumes.
Blair, Walter, et al. *The Literature of the United States.* 3rd ed. Vol. 2. Glenview: Scott, Foresman, 1969. 3 vols. Print.

BOOKS by the same author.
BOOKS with date of publication unknown.
Dickens, Charles. *The Old Curiosity Shop.* Garden City: International Collectors, n.d. Print.
    —-. *Oliver Twist.* Garden City: International Collectors, n.d. Print.

BOOK translated by another writer.
BOOK edited by another writer.
BOOK reprinted.
Gogol, Nicolai. *Dead Souls*. 1842. Trans. George Reavey. Ed. George Gibian. New York: Norton, 1971. Print.

BOOK edited by another writer (citing material written by the editor).
Gibian, George, ed. *Dead Souls*. By Nicolai Gogol. 1842. Trans. George Reavey. New York: Norton, 1971. Print.

REFERENCE BOOK/ENCYCLOPEDIA/DICTIONARY *(Give entry author, if known.)*
"Raze." Def. 7a. *Famous American Dictionary*. 14th ed. 1980. Print.

ANTHOLOGY/REFERENCE BOOK with an editor.
Kennedy, X. J., and Dorothy M. Kennedy, ed. *The Bedford Reader*. 2nd ed. New York: St. Martin's, 1985. Print.

ARTICLE (or SHORT STORY) reprinted in an anthology.
ARTICLE appearing on more than one page, paginated in the hundreds.
Vidal, Gore. "Drugs." *The Bedford Reader*. 2nd ed. Ed. X. J. Kennedy and Dorothy M. Kennedy. New York: St. Martin's, 1985. 38284. Print.

TWO OR MORE ARTICLES reprinted in an anthology.
Baldwin, Gail. "The Hard Sell." Goshgarian 159–64. Print.
Goshgarian, Gary, ed. *The Contemporary Reader*. 5th ed. New York: HarperCollins, 1996. Print.
Persky, Bill. "Conan and Me." Goshgarian 259–61. Print.

ARTICLE from a collection of reprinted articles.
Smythe, George. "Not in My Backyard—Nor Anyone Else's." *Public* 6.6 (2005): 67–78. Print. Rpt. in *Social Science Series*. Ed. Semi Evans. Privacy. Vol. 3. Article 14. Boca Raton, FL: Social Issues Resources Series, 2002. 7–13. Print.

ARTICLE in a magazine/journal, signed.
ARTICLE with part of the title in quotation marks.
ARTICLE in a magazine/journal with volume and issue number.
ARTICLE appearing on only one page.

- *NOTE:* In citing dates, abbreviate the names of months except for May, June, and July.

Wolkomir, Richard. "For the 'Tied Up' Businessman." *Smithsonian* 17.12 (Mar. 1987): 192.

ARTICLE in a magazine/journal with no volume number.
ARTICLE appearing on more than one page, inclusive pages.
ARTICLE from a magazine/journal published bi-monthly.

Fautin, Daphne Gail. "The Anemone Is Not Its Enemy." *National Wildlife* Oct.-Nov. 1987: 22-25. Print.

ARTICLE unsigned.
ARTICLE appearing on more than one page, discontinuous pages.

"Saving Time." *NewsMag* 18 Apr. 1997: 70–76+. Print.

ARTICLE, signed, in a daily NEWSPAPER.

McUsic, Teresa. "Stillwater Designer Followed Her Nose." *Tulsa World* 8 Mar. 1987, late ed.: G1. Print.

EDITORIAL and LETTER in a daily NEWSPAPER.

"Campus Unrest." Editorial. *University Times* 14 May 1996: B6. Print.

Davis, Marion. Letter. *University Times* 15 May 1996: B8. Print.

BIBLE.

Today's English Version Good News Bible. New York: American Bible Society, 1976. Print.

FILM.

Witness for the Prosecution. Dir. Billy Wilder. Perf. Tyrone Power, Marlene Dietrich, and Charles Laughton. MGM/United Artists, 1957. DVD.

TELEVISION PROGRAM.

The Grizzly. National Geographic Special. PBS. KXON, Tulsa. 9 Mar. 1987. Television.

RECORDING.

Holiday, Billie. "God Bless the Child." Rec. 9 May 1941. *Billie Holiday: The Golden Years.* Columbia, 1962. CD.

INTERVIEW.
Martin, Dr. Richard. Personal interview. 5 Mar. 1993.
Docmanter, Eric. Interview by James Taylor. "In the Name of Unity." *Spotright*. UBS.
    KMIX, Cowinka. 31 Oct. 1996. Television.

PAMPHLET with author credited.
• *NOTE:* If no author is given, begin the entry with the title of the pamphlet.
Drury, Matt. *Ant Farms*. Altus: Sheffield Press, 1987. Print.

PAMPHLET or GOVERNMENT PUBLICATION.
United States. Dept. of Transportation. National Highway Traffic Safety Admin. *Driver*
    Licensing Laws Annotated 1980. Washington: GPO, 1980. Print.

UNITED STATES CODE/FAMILIAR HISTORICAL DOCUMENTS.
These items are not listed on the works cited page; they are, however, cited parenthetically in the text.

PERFORMANCE.
• *NOTE:* If, in your paper, you refer to one performer, author, etc., begin the citation with that name, as in the following:
Aldridge, Joyce Spivey, dir. *Dracula*. By Hamilton Dean and John Balderston. Based on
    Bram Stoker's *Dracula*. Rogers State College, Claremore. 23 Oct. 1987. Performance.

• *NOTE:* If referring to the performance as a whole, the entry reads as follows:
Dracula. By Hamilton Dean and John Balderston. Based on Bram Stoker's *Dracula*. Dir.
    Joyce Spivey Aldridge. Rogers State College, Claremore. 23 Oct. 1987. Performance.

LECTURE.
Lurz, Diana. "The Goths and the Vandals." Humanities Image Forum. Rogers State
    University, Claremore. Baird Hall 202, 16 June 1998. Lecture.

LETTER/E-MAIL.
• *NOTE:* If the letter is directly accessible, use the following format. If it is reprinted in another work, use the longer format as follows.
Driver, Jeana. "1996 Senior Class." Message to E. R. Cagill. 27 May 1996. E-mail.

CD-ROM, DISK, or MAGNETIC TAPE.
Recomp, Erica. "Computers and Film Focuses." *Little University News* 15 Aug. 1996: E6. CD-ROM. *University Newspapers On-disc*. New York: UPI-UP, Sep. 1996.

ON-LINE SOURCES.
• *NOTE:* The format for online sources follows this model:

Author's last name, First name Middle initial. "Title of Short Piece or Document." Print Publication Data, using guidelines for print. Site Title. Name of Editor. Version Number. Name of Sponsoring Institution or Organization. Publication date or date of last revision. Medium. Date of access.

ON-LINE NEWSPAPER/PERIODICAL.
Recomp, Erica. "Computers and Film Focuses." *Little University News* 15 Aug. 1996: E6. Milling University. Web.1 Sept. 2002 .

James, Wilfred. "*Emark*, the Published Text." *English Eclectic* 13.13 (8 July 1996). Milling University. Web. 17 Aug. 1996.

WEB SITE with credited author.
Driver, Jeana. *Meteorology Pictures*. Oklahoma School of Science and Mathematics. 2001. Web. 1 May 2005.

WEB SITE with no credited author.
The Romanov Conspiracy. 1 Jan. 2002. Web. 16 Mar. 2004.

LIBRARY SUBSCRIPTION SERVICE.
Merrick, John. "GTO's and Other Hot Rods." *Hot Rod Magazine* Spring 2004: 61. *Academic Search Premier*. Web. 4 May 2004.

SAMPLE APA DOCUMENTATION EXAMPLES

BOOK with one author.
Dickens, C. (1948). *Great expectations*. New York: Rinehart.

BOOK with two authors.
Biddle, A. W., & Holland, K. M. (1987). *Writer's guide: Political science*. Lexington: Heath.

BOOK with three authors.
Frye, N., Baker, S., & Perkins, G. (1985). *The Harper handbook to literature*. New York: Harper.

BOOK with more than *seven* authors.
BOOK with an edition after the first.
BOOK with several volumes.
BOOK with several volumes, one of the volumes.
Blain, J., Blair, K., Davis, L., Walter, M., Smyne, H., Former, G., et al. (1996). *The life of Rexan* (3rd ed.). (Vol. 2). Bloomington, IN: Exra University.

BOOKS by the same author.
Dickens, C. (1952a). *The old curiosity shop*. Garden Center: Collectors.
Dickens, C. (1952b). *Oliver Twist*. Garden Center: Collectors.

BOOK translated by another writer.
BOOK edited by another writer.
BOOK reprinted.
Gogol, N. (1971). *Dead souls*. (G. Reavey, Trans.). G. Gibian (Ed.). New York: Norton. (Original work published 1842)

REFERENCE BOOK/ENCYCLOPEDIA/DICTIONARY.
The new dialect encyclopedia (2nd ed.). (2004). Marietta, OH: Maze.

ANTHOLOGY/REFERENCE BOOK with an editor.
Kennedy, X. J., & Kennedy, D. M. (Eds.). (1985). *The Bedford reader* (2nd ed.). New York: St. Martin's.

ARTICLE (or SHORT STORY) reprinted in an anthology.
ARTICLE appearing on more than one page, paginated in the hundreds.
Vidal, G. (1985). Drugs. In X. J. Kennedy & D. M. Kennedy (Eds.), *The Bedford reader* (2nd ed., pp. 382-384). New York: St. Martin's.

ARTICLE from a collection of reprinted articles.
Snark, M. (2002). More nasty stuff around than ever: Theory and practice. In H. H. Mandel (Series Ed.) & Q. E. Dee (Vol. Ed.), *Resources for a dying planet: Vol. 3. Dumping* (3rd ed., pp. 33-36). Nearl, FL: Wimple.

ARTICLE in a magazine/journal, signed.
ARTICLE with part of the title in quotation marks.
ARTICLE in a magazine/journal with volume and issue number.
ARTICLE appearing on only one page.
Wolkomir, R. (1987, March). For the 'tied up' businessman. *Smithsonian 17*(12), 192.

ARTICLE in a magazine/journal with no volume number.
ARTICLE appearing on more than one page, inclusive pages.
ARTICLE from a magazine/journal published bi-monthly.
Fautin, D. G. (1987, October-November). The anemone is not its enemy. *National wildlife*, 2225.

ARTICLE, unsigned, in a newspaper.
ARTICLE appearing on more than one page, discontinuous pages.
Saving time. (1997, April 18). *Newsmag*, pp. 70-76, 89, 91, 94.

ARTICLE, signed, in a daily NEWSPAPER.
McUsic, T. (1987, March 8). Stillwater designer followed her nose. *Tulsa world*, p. G1.

FILM.
Wilder, B. (Director). (1957). *Witness for the prosecution* [Motion picture]. United States: United Artists.

TELEVISION PROGRAM.
Cristobal, P. (Writer), & Forcer, F. (Director). (2002, May 11). Moving [Television series episode] In C. Sansobal (Producer), *Time of Despair*. Los Angeles: Backyard.

PAMPHLET with corporate author credited.
Center for Abundant Life. (2004). *Living on yoga* (6th ed.) [Brochure]. Altus. OK: Sheffield Press.

GOVERNMENT PUBLICATION.
- *NOTE:* When the authoring agency prints the publication, use the word "Author" in place of the publisher's name.

United States Department of Transportation. (1980). *Driver licensing laws annotated 1980* (NHTSA Publication No. 55-5). Washington, DC: author.

ON-LINE SOURCES.
- *NOTE:* The format for online sources follows this mode. Note that, if the source is originally a print source, you do not use the retrieval date or URL, but the words "Electronic version" in brackets.

Author's last name, First initial. Middle initial. (Publication date). Title of document [Electronic version]. *Title of complete work.* Retrieved November 30, 2004, from URL.

ON-LINE NEWSPAPER/PERIODICAL BASED ON PRINT SOURCE.
Recomp, E. (1996, August 15). Computers and film focuses [Electronic version]. *Little university news 17,* 17-25.

ON-LINE ONLY PERIODICAL.
Garth, B., & Remington, W.R. (2004, March 6). Referring to references. *Journal of on-line data, 6,* 18-32. Retrieved May 30, 2004, from http://source.data.stuff.htm.

WEB SITES.
Meteorology pictures. (n.d.) Retrieved June 17, 2004, from http://www.ucco.edu/stud/met/99.

LIBRARY SUBSCRIPTION SERVICE.
Merrick, J. (2004, Spring). GTO's and other hot rods. *Hot rod magazine,* 61. Retrieved May 4, 2004, from Academic Search Premier database.

Step Three: Notes

After finding out what is available in the way of resources, investigate those resources for applicability and usefulness. Look at each of the resources and cull them. Some are not especially useful; discard these. Others are relevant; take notes on information to use in your paper.

ASSESSING SOURCES

Always assess the value of the sources you find. If you follow the principles in "Reading for Content and Reading for Writing," you can decide whether the text of sources you read is plausible. Assessing Internet sources is more difficult.

Generally, you can expect that the sources available in data bases from the University library, such as FirstSearch and in InfoTrac, are credible. However, you may not be able to expect that other sources you find on the Internet are credible. Some people tend to think that whatever is in print or on television is true. Because you know that "everything" cannot be true, you need to evaluate the sites you find.

Print periodicals and books have generally been through an editorial process in which at least one other, and sometimes an entire board of people, has agreed that the information to be printed is trustworthy. Even these sources may be slanted, depending on the editorial stance of the editor(s) and publishers. You have to determine how credible all sources are. For example, if the publication is printed by a company that owns a chemical processing plant and the article you see asserts that chemicals in the environment have never been proved to show harm, you might question the impartiality of the article.

Internet sources do not necessarily go through an editorial process. Anyone can be published on the Internet, which means you need to spend even more effort determining the value of information on Web pages. You need to be aware of the Web address. If the address is a <.com> address, you know the site is commercial, posted by a commercial interest. If the address is an <.org> address, the site was posted by an organization. If the address is an <.edu> address, the site was posted under the aegis of an educational institution, either by the administration and/or faculty or by a student or students at that institution.

When evaluating a site, look for the following items:
- *Author:* with credentials and contact information: if you cannot attribute the information to a source, the information is not useful.
- *Date(s):* the site was posted and/or updated: without a date, you cannot consider the site a resource.
- *Clear citations:* an online source must be held to the same standards as a print source. If the site does not give references on which the writer based his or her conclusions, the site is not holding to the standards of scholarship.

Evaluate sources carefully.

- *Language:* poor grammar and spelling are clues that the site is not posted by a careful, reputable scholar. In addition, you can sometimes distinguish "slanted" sites by language, which may call names or appeal to prejudices or convey stereotypes.
- *Site associations:* a site belonging to a company, offering products for sale, or associated with a movement (political, social, or religious) may have an agenda. At the very least, look carefully at the information for validity and confirm it with other, non-affiliated sites.
- *Appearance:* if the site is so visually distracting that the information is difficult to perceive, this may not be an accident.
- *Verifiability:* a site that takes a stance that is not taken by other reputable scholars may be questionable.

These points are only guides for you to use. Experience will lead you to your own conclusions. Ultimately, it is your decision what sources to use in your work, because you are responsible for what appears in your paper.

PLAGIARISM

Be sure that you avoid plagiarism. Plagiarism is unacknowledged use of someone else's words or ideas. To avoid plagiarism, follow these rules:

- *Never* copy *word for word* without quotation marks and without mentioning the author's name.
- *Never* copy *key words or phrases* without quotation marks and without mentioning the author's name.
- *Never* paraphrase, summarize, or otherwise borrow an *idea* that belongs to a specific author without mentioning that author's name.
- To be safe, *always* introduce the quotation or paraphrase by using the source's name.
- *Always* document each and every quotation, paraphrase, or idea originating from a source other than yourself.
- *Always* put quotation marks around *all* quoted material.
- *Always* include a Works Cited or Bibliography entry for each source used in your paper.

You do not need to document items that are common knowledge.

Examples (Plagiarism and Avoidance Measures)

Rogers 1

Chip Rogers
Guide to College Writing
June 15, 2005

Plagiarism Issues

What Is Plagiarism?
Generally, plagiarism is presenting as your own the work of someone else without properly acknowledging the source or sources; plagiarism is submitting material from a source without attributing the source. When ideas or information are common knowledge (and there is very little of this), you do not need to acknowledge sources.

Why Do We Need to Know about Using Sources?
Integrating the words and ideas of others into your own work is an important feature of academic expression.

How Can We Avoid Plagiarism?
But plagiarism occurs whenever we incorporate the intellectual property of others into our own work without proper acknowledgment of whose words, ideas, or other original material we are bringing into our work, either with quotation marks and direct mention of the source or through other means of clear and precise acknowledgment.

Plagiarism can of course be a purely intentional attempt at deceit, but whether or not there is conscious intent to deceive, plagiarism occurs any time you do not give proper acknowledgment of others' contributions to your work. Ignorance of the responsibility of acknowledging sources is not a legitimate defense against a charge of plagiarism, any more than not knowing the speed limit on a given road makes a person stopped for speeding less at fault. Because the consequences of being charged with plagiarism are serious, you must pay attention to the following definition of plagiarism to ensure your more precise understanding of what constitutes plagiarism, intentional or unintentional.

1. **It is plagiarism to copy another's words directly and present them as your own without quotation marks and direct indication of whose words you are copying. All significant phrases, clauses, and passages copied from another source require quotation marks and proper acknowledgment, down to the page number(s) of printed texts.***

Source material from the "Notice" to Mark Twain's *Adventures of Huckleberry Finn*: "Persons attempting to find a motive in this narrative will be prosecuted; persons attempting to find a moral in it will be banished; persons attempting to find a plot in it will be shot."

Plagiarized: Surely it is an exaggeration to say that *persons attempting to find a moral in Huckleberry Finn will be banished* and *persons attempting to find a plot in it will be shot.*

Proper acknowledgment of source: Perhaps the author is exaggerating when he says that "persons attempting to find a moral" in his novel "will be banished" and "persons attempting to find a plot in it will be shot" (Twain 3).

Note that even brief clauses and phrases copied from source material require quotation marks. Also note that acknowledging the source without putting the quoted words in quotation marks is still plagiarism: put *all* quoted words in quotation marks.

2. **It is plagiarism to paraphrase another writer's work by altering some words but communicating the same essential point(s) made by the original author without proper acknowledgment. Although quotation marks are not needed with paraphrasing, you must still acknowledge the original source directly.**

Source material from *Adolph Hitler* by John Tolland: "Ignored by the West, the Soviet Union once more looked to Germany. Early in 1939 it accepted a Hitler overture to discuss a new trade treaty by inviting one of Ribbentrop's aides to Moscow; and a few days later Stalin gave credence to a sensational story in the London *News Chronicle* that he was signing a non-aggression pact with the Nazis" (721).

Plagiarized: When Western nations continued to shun the Soviet Union, the Russians drew closer to Germany, meeting with a senior Nazi official in Moscow to arrange a trade agreement in early 1939. Shortly after, Stalin admitted his intent to sign a pact of non-aggression with Germany.

Proper acknowledgment of source: In *Adolph Hitler*, John Tolland notes that when Western nations continued to shun the Soviet Union, the Russians drew closer to Germany, meeting with a senior Nazi official in Moscow to arrange a trade agreement in early 1939. Shortly after, Stalin admitted his intent to sign a pact of non-aggression with Germany (721).

3. **Plagiarism includes presenting someone else's ideas or factual discoveries as your own. If you follow another person's general outline or approach to a topic, presenting another's original thinking or specific conclusions as your own, you must cite the**

source, even if your work is in your own words entirely. When you present another's statistics, definitions, or statements of fact in your own work, you must also cite the source.

Example 1: Say that you read Paul Goodman's "A Proposal to Abolish Grading," in which he claims that an emphasis on grades results in students' caring more about grades than learning subject matter, causing them to have a bad attitude when their grades are low and sometimes even leading them to cheating. In order to make these same essential points in your own work without plagiarizing—even if your development of these ideas differs markedly from Goodman's in examples and order of presentation—you must still acknowledge Goodman as the basis for your approach to the topic.

Plagiarized: Abolishing grades at the college level would allow students to focus on subject matter instead of grades, it would prevent students from getting a bad attitude towards a class when they receive low grades, and it would virtually eliminate the temptation to cheat or plagiarize.

Proper acknowledgment of source: As Paul Goodman argues in "A Proposal to Abolish Grading," doing away with grades would allow students to focus on subject matter instead of grades, it would prevent students from getting a bad attitude towards a class when they receive low grades, and it would virtually eliminate the temptation to cheat or plagiarize.

Example 2: If you found a source indicating that Americans consume more beer on Friday than on any other day of the week, to make this claim in your work you must cite the source to avoid plagiarism. If the source indicated that American beer-drinking on Fridays accounts for 21% of the whole week's total consumption, mentioning this statistic, or even approximating it, requires acknowledgment of the source.

Plagiarized: Americans consume more beer on Fridays than on any other day of the week.
Proper acknowledgment of source: Americans consume more beer on Fridays than on any other day of the week (Cox 31).

Plagiarized: Beer consumption on Fridays accounts for more than 20% of total U.S. consumption throughout the week.
Proper acknowledgment of source: Beer consumption on Fridays accounts for more than 20% of total U.S. consumption throughout the week (Cox 31).

4. **Plagiarism includes allowing someone else to prepare work that you present as your own.**

Allowing a friend, parent, tutor, or anyone else to compose any portion of work you present as your own is plagiarism. Note that plagiarism includes copying, downloading, or purchasing an essay or any other material in part or in whole via the Internet. Note also that plagiarism includes using online "translator programs" in foreign language classes.

5. **Plagiarism applies in other media besides traditional written texts, including, but not limited to, oral presentations, graphs, charts, diagrams, artwork, video and audio compositions, and other electronic media, such as Web pages, PowerPoint presentations, and postings to online discussions.**

Conclusion:
- If you are uncertain about any portion or aspect of this definition of plagiarism, ask your instructor to clarify or explain immediately. If at any point later in the semester, you have questions about potential plagiarism issues, talk to your instructor about them before submitting the work in question.
- Students who plagiarize often feel pressured into submitting plagiarized work because they have either struggled with the assignment or waited until the last minute to get the work under way. You will always be better served discussing your situation with your instructor, however grim it seems, rather than submitting any work that is not entirely your

*The examples of proper acknowledgment of sources above follow the MLA (Modern Language Association) conventions for in-text parenthetical citation used in English classes and many other courses in the humanities. The parenthetical references point the reader to a list of "Works Cited" at the end of an essay. Other courses and disciplines may follow different conventions, such as footnotes, endnotes, or a variety of other methods of documentation (APA, Chicago Style, etc.).

Now that you know about plagiarism, you can feel free to add quotations to your notes. You may take notes on note cards or use another method of keeping notes. No matter what system you choose, use the same principles: search out material and put the relevant material into a form that can be used in the paper.

There are four points to remember in making note cards:
1. When writing a paper requiring many notes, each note should have a heading that identifies the specific subject that the note covers. Keep the notes arranged by topic.
2. These items should also appear in the heading:
    (1) the author's name (at least the last name);
    (2) the title of the book or article (if you have multiple sources from an author); and
    (3) the page number of the information.
If you do not know who wrote the information and where it comes from, the information is of no use to you when you write your paper.

3. In using direct quotations, find the sentences or phrases to best convey the idea you want to use and quote the author word for word. Delete irrelevant information by using the ellipsis (see the section on the ellipsis).
4. Distinguish your notes from the author's words by using quotation marks around any quoted material.

Remember: There are three things that must be on each note—author, page, and a way to distinguish noted from quoted.

Example (Note Card)

Cravotta 20   Java on Internet

Java works as a virtual machine

"Java has security and authentication features, so users don't have to worry about letting strange programs into their computer from the Internet without testing them for viruses or other harmful processes. 'A thing called a verifier examines your program, and it does a certain amount of testing to see whether it plays by the rules,' says Gosling."

ANNOTATED BIBLIOGRAPHY

Sometimes you may need to include an annotated bibliography with your paper. An annotated bibliography is nothing more than a combination of notes and works cited entries. When you have determined exactly which sources to use in your paper, create the equivalent of a works cited list and add to it a summary of what each work is about.

Example

> Johnson, Dirk. "Where the Beer Flows Easy, Calls to Sober Up." The New York Times 16 Nov. 2008: A16. LexisNexis Academic. Web. 10 May 2009.
> Johnson says even children can drink at a bar in Wisconsin, with parental permission. Wisconsin has lenient drunk driving laws and high accident rates for drunk drivers.
>
> OU Public Affairs. "Alcohol Poisoning Can Have Fatal Consequences, Warns Oklahoma Poison Control Center." University of Oklahoma Health Science Center. University of Oklahoma 1 May 2009. Web. 10 May 2009.
> OU Public Affairs announces that drinking too much and binge drinking (too much too fast) can lead to death through alcohol poisoning. Symptoms range from confusion to unconsciousness.
>
> "Weekend Edition Sunday, Health and Science: Intervening with Teen Drinking." Narr. by Liane Hansen. NPR. National Public Radio. 22 Mar. 2009. Web. 10 May 2009.
> "Weekend Edition" reports that, increasingly, preteens and teens arrive in emergency rooms with symptom of binge drinking, which should be a wakeup call to U.S. society.

STEP FOUR: PLAN AND OUTLINE

Now that you know what information is available and what you can use in your paper, plan your paper. Consider audience, purpose, logic, structure, and support. With all these things in mind, prepare a general outline to follow when writing your paper. (See the section on the organization page and outline.) Structure your paper so that each point can be well developed and presented. The outline need not be too detailed. It is for you to use so that you stick to your subject and do not stray into unnecessary or ill-supported areas.

STEP FIVE: FIRST DRAFT

Collect and organize all of your information. Compose a first draft of your paper, either by writing neatly and legibly or by typing. It is probably best to skip lines so that you have space to revise. Be sure to include all of the necessary internal documentation. (See the section on documentation.)

Using Quotations in the Paper

If you take care not to be guilty of plagiarism, you need not fear using quotations to support or to give examples about what you have said in your paper. Quotations are easy to handle if you use the following simple guidelines.
- If you are quoting, you must quote *exactly*. That is what quoting means. The exact words of the author are reproduced in your paper (in quotation marks, of course).
- Quotations are incorporated into the text of the paper. *You must introduce the quotation in some way with your own words.* The quotation does not stand alone.

Example (Using Quotations)

- The periodical that contains the information you need is *Carnegie Mellon Magazine*. In it you find the following passage, written by Cravotta, about Java programming language:
Java has security and authentication features, so users don't have to worry about letting strange programs into their computer from the Internet without testing them for viruses or other harmful processes. "A thing called a verifier examines your program, and it does a certain amount of testing to see whether it plays by the rules," says Gosling.

- You decide to use part of this passage in your paper. You write the following in your own words and include a quotation:

Java, a programming language, "has security and authentication features, so users don't have to worry about letting strange programs into their computer from the Internet without testing them for viruses or other harmful processes. 'A thing called a verifier examines your program, and it does a certain amount of testing to see whether it plays by the rules,' says Gosling" (Cravotta 20).

- *Note:* As you can see, the quotation is made part of what the paper is about. It does not function on its own without the support of your words to explain its relationship to what you have written elsewhere.

USING QUOTES IN THE PAPER: INTERNAL DOCUMENTATION

MLA Citation

You should know now that you must give credit every time you use words, phrases, sentences, or ideas from someone else. (See the section on plagiarism.) When using the MLA format, do one of the following things each time you borrow words, information, or ideas from someone else.

1. Cite in parentheses the information the reader needs in order to find the complete entry in the list of works cited.
    or
2. Cite part of this information in the text and part in parentheses at the end of the passage. (It is possible to cite all of the information in the text, but it can be exceedingly awkward.)

Example (MLA Citations)

MLA Internal Documentation for Printed Material
- Suppose you are quoting from a book, *A Handbook to Literature* (third edition), written by C. Hugh Holman and published in 1972 in New York by Bobbs-Merrill Company, Inc. Information about Holman's book appears on the Works Cited page in your paper like this:

    Works Cited
    Holman, C. Hugh. *A Handbook to Literature*. 3rd ed. New York: Bobbs-Merrill, 1972. Print.

- If this is the only work by Holman listed on the Works Cited page, the only information you need to include when citing it in your text is the author's last name and the page number on which the quotation appears:

1. *Author and page number cited in parentheses:*
    One authority on literature has observed that a "characteristic quality of this Amerind language is its building of many ideas into one term" (Holman 18).
2. *Author cited in text and page reference noted in parentheses:*
    Holman has observed that a "characteristic quality of this Amerind language is its building of many ideas into one term" (18).

- What if more than one work by this author is listed on the Works Cited page? Then you need to cite a full or an abbreviated title as well as the author's name and the page number in the text so that the reader knows to which work you were referring. With the addition of this information, the Works Cited page and the parenthetical reference look like this:

Works Cited

Holman, C. Hugh. *Dictionary of Literacy*. New York: Kellman, 1987.

—. *A Handbook to Literature*. 3rd ed. New York: Bobbs-Merrill, 1972.

- Then the text of your paper says,

One authority on literature has observed that a "characteristic quality of this Amerind language is its building of many ideas into one term" (Holman, *A Handbook* 18).

- or

Holman has observed that a "characteristic quality of this Amerind language is its building of many ideas into one term" (*A Handbook* 18).

MLA Internal Documentation for Web Sites

- What if you use an Internet source that has no credited author? Use the title of the Web page, the information closest to the left-hand margin. You also have no page number, because Web pages seldom list page numbers. The Works Cited page and the parenthetical reference look like this:

Works Cited

The Romanov Conspiracy. 1 Jan. 2002. Web. 16 Mar. 2004.

- Then the text of your paper says,

Theories about the Romanov family continue today (*Romanov*).

Further examples of internal/parenthetical documentation of Web pages follow:

Robin Pryor Murphy
Guide to College Writing
June 15, 2005

- In MLA, when using a Website that does not have a credited author, place the name of the Website in the phrase introducing the quoted, paraphrased, summarized, or mentioned material *or* in the parentheses at the end of the sourced material.

The title of the site is *dogallergies.com*. The title of the page is "Top Ten Foods to Avoid."

1. Web page cited in text:

On the "Top Ten Foods to Avoid" page of *dogallergies.com*, John Smith, a ten-year veterinarian, "suggests food with no corn products for dogs prone to allergies."

> **2. Web page cited in parentheses:**
> John Smith, a ten-year veterinarian, "suggests food with no corn products for dogs prone to allergies" ("Top Ten").
>
> - When you summarize or paraphrase information from a Website, you *must* refer to the Website in the connecting phrase or parentheses. Failure to acknowledge the source of the material is considered plagiarism.
>
>   In addition, according to the "Susceptible Breeds" page on *dogallergies.com,* Smith suggests watching a breed like the Dalmatian for excessive itching and a pink undertone to the skin.
>
> - A Works Cited page for these two sources would look like this:
>
>   Works Cited
>   "Susceptible Breeds." *dogallergies.com.* 12 March 2005. Web. 30 May 2005.
>   "Top Ten Foods to Avoid." *dogallergies.com.* 12 March 2005. Web. 30 May 2005.
>
> - **NOTE:** When you are citing material that was originally print and that is accessed from a database, remember that the internal or parenthetical citations are identical to the citations you would use if you had accessed the work from a print source.
>
>   Also remember that, in summarizing and paraphrasing, you must make clear at what point the summary or paraphrase begins. Usually, you begin the paraphrase or summary with a phrase such as the prior statement by John Smith.

CITING LITERARY TEXTS

A knowledge of the methods in this section enables you to document most types of sources, but there are also some special literary cases of which you should be aware.

When citing a literary work, either in the text (internal documentation) or on the Works Cited page, follow the conventions for each genre. (See the *MLA Handbook* for details.)
- For poems, use line numbers rather than page numbers.
- For plays, give act and scene rather than pages. Use Roman or Arabic numbers.

Specialized Forms of Writing • Writing in Response to Literature

Example (Citing Literary Works, MLA Format)

Paradise Lost begins with a call to the poet's Muse to "assert eternal providence, / And justify the ways of God to men" (Milton 1.25-26). Iago makes an ironic statement when he says, "He that filches from me my good name / Robs me of that which enriches not him / And makes me poor indeed" (Shakespeare, *Othello* 3.2.159-61).

- **NOTE:** The 1 following the author's name is the number of the book from which the quote comes, not an abbreviation for line. When quoting lines of poetry, insert a slash (/) at the end of each line.

A paradox can be as simple as "the last shall be first, and the first last" (*King James Bible*, Matt. 10.16).

- **NOTE:** When you quote a religious work, give version (which should be underlined), book, chapter, and verse.

After writing your paper, use the bibliography information to compile a Works Cited page. (See the sections on documentation and manuscript preparation.) The entries on the Works Cited page should be doublespaced, as should the space between entries.

SPECIAL PUNCTUATION FOR QUOTATIONS
Brackets and Ellipses

When you are quoting from a source, you sometimes need to use special punctuation to make the sentences read clearly or to clarify a point. One of these special punctuation marks is brackets. Brackets are punctuation that enclose information that is inserted within a quotation.

Example (Use of Brackets in a Quotation)

- Although it is not strictly necessary, you might have inserted the word *downloaded* in the passage to make the sentence easier to understand:

Java "has security and authentication features, so users don't have to worry about letting strange programs into their computer from the Internet without testing them for viruses or other harmful processes. 'A thing called a verifier examines your [downloaded] program, and it does a certain amount of testing to see whether it plays by the rules,' says Gosling" (Cravotta 20).

Brackets help when you run into a problem in exact quoting. The absolute rule is to quote *exactly* as it appears in the text. What if there is an error of some kind in the text? Can you fix it? No, you must quote exactly. Will the instructor assume it is your error or mistake and count off for this? Yes, probably. Is this a Catch-22? No. The way to solve this problem is through a special use of brackets and of one Latin word, *sic*, which means "as it stands." Using *sic* means that you have quoted the text exactly "as it stands," because there is nothing else you can do, and you recognize the error or problem. Using *sic* lets the reader know that you found the error; you are no longer responsible.

Example (Use of Brackets and sic)

- Suppose the text reads, "Columbus descovered America in 1492." You must quote this exactly but to avoid being charged with a spelling error, you do it this way:

  According to G. Wrong, "Columbus descovered [sic] America in 1492" (72).

- Voilà!

Another special kind of punctuation is the ellipsis mark—punctuation that allows writers to eliminate inessential words or sentences. The ellipsis is a clue to the reader that the quote has been altered. For example, you might not need to quote transitional words, parenthetical expressions, repeated words, or sentences that amplify a previous statement. The ellipsis does not mean you can change the intent of the author in your writing. It does mean that you can smooth out your text or omit repetitious words that are unnecessary to what you are saying.

When you delete part of a quoted passage, use an ellipsis. The ellipsis is three spaced periods if you omit only part of a sentence. If you omit one sentence or more, use four periods (three for the ellipsis and one for terminal punctuation). (See the section on the ellipsis in punctuation.)

If an author uses an ellipsis in his or her text, you must differentiate between the author's ellipsis and the one you are using to show a deletion by putting brackets around the ellipsis you add. Leave no space between the bracket and the initial and final period but do space before the second and third period. If the author does not use ellipses, do not add brackets around the ellipsis you add.

Example (Use of Ellipsis)

PART I

- Perhaps in your paper you might want to quote only part of the section in *Carnegie Mellon Magazine*. You might have the following as a passage in your text:

  Java, a programming language, "has security . . . so users don't have to worry about letting strange programs into their computer from the Internet. . . . 'A thing called a verifier examines your program, and it does a certain amount of testing . . .'" (Cravotta 20).

- The writer of the research paper has left out part of the quotation and shown that omission with the ellipsis. The part left out inside the sentence is shown with three spaced periods. The part left out at the end of the first sentence is shown with four spaced periods. Notice also that, because parenthetical documentation is included at the end of the second sentence, the omitted words are designated by three spaced periods, and the parenthetical citation is followed immediately by the end period.
- The section the writer has quoted, which appears in quotation marks, also includes a sentence that Cravotta quoted. That sentence appears in single quotation marks.

PART II

- Perhaps you want to use part of the prior section about ellipses in your paper. You might say,

  The ellipsis can be used to show omitted material. For example, "The writer of the research paper has left out part of the quotation and shown that omission with the ellipsis. . . . The part left out at the end of the sentence is shown. . . . Notice also that, because parenthetical documentation is included at the end of the second sentence, the omitted words are designated by three spaced, bracketed periods . . ." (Dial-Driver 100).

- If you omit an entire sentence, use three bracketed periods spaced before and after the bracket.
- If you omit one end of one sentence and the entirety of another, use the bracketed spaced periods and space them for the requisite end of the sentence. You can see that the end of one sentence and the entirety of another are omitted in the prior example.

As you can see from the examples, brackets and ellipses offer a convenient way to add or delete information within a quotation. Remember that they should be used sparingly so that the flow of reading is not excessively interrupted. Instead of over-using these special forms, you can usually quote selectively and integrate short quotations into your own sentences.

Summary and Paraphrasing

In addition to using quotations, you will also want to summarize some information and to paraphrase other information. (See the section on summaries.) Remember that you must still document the source of that information. (See the section on plagiarism.)

To summarize, you must shorten and rewrite. To paraphrase, rewrite in your own words, but do not substantially shorten.

Example (Summary and Paraphrase)

- A *summary* from the *Carnegie Mellon Magazine* about Java language might say,
  Crovotta says Java is a programming language that has features that check for viruses (20).

- A *paraphrase* in your paper of that same passage might say,
  Cravotta says Java is a programming language with safety features so users will not have to worry about downloading programs from the Internet because Java will inspect them for viruses or other invasive computer problems. According to Java's creator, James Gosling, a feature of Java looks at the program and checks it for appropriate use of rules (Cravotta 20).

LONGER QUOTATIONS

Long quotations are defined as quotations of more than four typed lines in your paper. Long quotations are incorporated into your text; you use your words to connect them to what you are saying, but they are also set apart from that text in the way they appear on the page. MLA style specifies indenting long quotations one inch and double-spacing. Because longer quotations are set apart from the text, they are not surrounded by quotation marks. Be sure that any long quotation is actually necessary. Use long quotations sparingly.

Example (Using a Long Quotation in the Paper)

- Your paper includes information from the previous paragraph and looks like this:

  Quotations of more than four typed lines are considered long quotations and are handled differently from quotations less than four typed lines long. As Dial-Driver maintains,
  > they are . . . set apart from that text in the way they appear on the page. MLA style specifies indenting long quotations one inch and double-spacing. Because longer quotations are set apart from the text, they are not surrounded by quotation marks. Be sure that any long quotation is actually necessary. (101)

  A writer uses long quotations to support points and to elaborate on ideas but not to fill space or to save effort.

- Note that the final punctuation in this case comes after the quotation itself, not after the parenthetical citation.

APA Citation

Of course, in APA style, as in all formats for documentation, you must give credit every time you use words, phrases, sentences, or ideas from someone else. (See the section on plagiarism.) When using the APA format, use one of the following types of citation each time you employ words, information, or ideas from someone else.

When you quote material, always include the page number, with *p.* for one page or *pp.* for more than one page. If you do not mention the name of the author or the year in the sentence, include that information with the page number in the parenthetical reference immediately after the end of the quotation, even in mid-sentence. If your sentence includes the author's name, give the year of publication and the page directly after the author's name, even if the quotation appears earlier or later in the sentence. If your sentence includes the author's name and the date of publication, only the page number(s) appear in the parenthetical citation. In writing quotations in the paper, note that the inserted ellipsis is not surrounded by brackets in APA format.

For paraphrased or summarized material, APA style allows the writer to decide whether or not to give a page number, depending on whether or not the reader is likely to want to know the specific location of the information. As a student writer, you may be required to furnish the page number so the grader or reader can verify your source. Always check the requirements of the assignment with the person assigning it.

Example (APA Citations)

- *Direct quotation:*
  The language "has security and authentication features so users don't have to worry about letting strange programs into their computer from the Internet" (Cravotta, 1997, p. 20).

  or

  Cravotta (1997) says, "Java has security and authentication features so users don't have to worry about letting strange programs into their computer from the Internet" (p. 20).

- *Summary:*
  According to Cravotta (1997), Java is a programming language that has features that check for viruses (20).

- *Paraphrase:*
  Cravotta says Java is a programming language with features for safety for users who will not have to be concerned about downloading programs from the Internet because Java will inspect them for viruses or other invasive computer problems. According to Java's creator, James Gosling, a feature of Java looks at the program and checks it for appropriate use of rules (Cravotta, 1997, p. 20).

Step Six: Revision

Revise and rewrite the first draft. You might have other people read over the draft to check for mechanics and logic. (See the section on checking the paper.) Type a second draft, double-spaced.

Type a draft? Yes, the reason to type the draft is to enable you to check accurately and easily the punctuation, spelling, internal documentation, and Works Cited entries. Of course, if you use a computer, you save yourself some typing!

Step Seven: Final Draft

Correct, type, and assemble your final paper. Be sure to proofread for errors. If you detect an error after you are ready to turn the paper in, correct it. Use black pen or even pencil, if necessary. *Never* leave an error. When assembling the paper to turn in, either staple the upper left corner with one staple or enclose the paper in a folder, according to your instructor's request.

HINTS FOR SUCCESS:
1. Of course, content, style, and appearance are important; but form is also very important, especially on the Works Cited page. Be sure that you follow the format described.
2. The paper should be typed.
3. The paper must meet superior criteria (including original style, quality content, good mechanics, and accurate format) to earn the maximum number of points.
4. One elementary mistake is one mistake too many. *Accuracy and proofreading are your responsibility.* The typist is not responsible for any mistakes—*you are.*

Research papers reveal what you know about research, what you know about a topic, and what you know about writing. Make your research paper show what you know!

CHECKING THE PAPER FOR YOURSELF OR FOR SOMEONE ELSE

Because the best papers are usually written in multiple drafts, the problem arises of how to review the paper before the next draft is written. Checking a paper for yourself is usually harder than checking one for someone else. This may seem odd, but you have written all of the words in your own paper and they already seem familiar and right to you. Checking a paper for someone else can be easier because you are looking at it with fresh eyes. Checking either kind of paper can also be frustrating because you are not quite sure what to look for. The following simple check list can help you check someone else's paper; it can also help you check your own.

Check for Contents

1. Is there a thesis statement (or guiding idea) that you can easily find?
   Is there support for the thesis statement?
   Is there an introduction leading up to the thesis statement?
2. Does each body paragraph have a topic sentence?
   Is the thesis statement supported by the topic sentences?
   Does every sentence in the paragraph relate to the topic sentence?
   Do the quotations and other evidence from sources pertain to the topics in the paragraphs?
   Do the quotations and other evidence read as part of the text?
   Are the quotations tied into the text by the paper writer's own words?
3. Does the paper make sense?
   Is it convincing? Is it logical?
4. Does it end satisfactorily with some concluding remarks?
5. Is it enjoyable to read?

Check for Mechanics

1. Are the sentences well structured?
2. Is the spelling correct?
       Punctuation?
       Agreement between subject and verb?
       Pronoun and antecedent?
       Capitalization?
       Underlining?
       Quotation marks?
       Etc.?
3. Is the internal documentation correct?
   Is every statement drawn from a source documented?
   Is every quotation in quotation marks with parenthetical documentation following?

Is every quotation adequately tied into the text?
Is every quotation adequately introduced by the paper writer's own words?
Are the mechanics of the documentation correct?
> Parentheses?
> Placement of quotation marks?
> Placement of end marks, etc.?

4. Is the Works Cited page correct?
Are all of the works on the Works Cited page actually cited in the text?
Are the mechanics of the documentation correct? (See the section on documentation.)

5. Do the pages look as though the format (margins, etc.) corresponds to manuscript preparation form? (See the section on manuscript preparation.)

REVIEWING RESEARCH PAPERS

Writing a research paper is difficult; it may be tedious; it can be extremely rewarding and revealing. Reviewing a research paper also can be extremely rewarding and revealing. The reader may discover a number of things about the writer, among them whether or not the writer can use coherent, logical prose about specific subject matter. The paper can show whether the writer has a good grasp of one aspect of the course. Another discovery may be whether the writer can, in fact, use the reference books required to function in the discipline. The reader may determine whether the writer can follow directions and function consistently within a specified format. Most important, the research paper reveals whether the writer has a grasp of the essentials of the course itself and of the college experience, namely how to accumulate knowledge.

The reviewer needs to assess certain criteria for a research paper in any class:

1. Does the paper have a structure that is easily followed? In other words, does the writer tell the reader what the paper is going to tell about? Does the writer show a clear purpose for writing? Does the writer discuss the major subjects and divide them logically? Are the points sufficiently supported? Does the writer end with some kind of concluding remarks?

2. Is the paper coherent and logical? Can the reader follow the arguments without trouble? Does the paper make sense? Is it convincing? Is it interesting?

3. Are the sources used well? Do the quotations support what the writer has said, or do they stand alone and have no clear relationship to what is being discussed? Are the sources reputable? Does the writer choose proper sources for the subject, or are the major sources on the order of *National Enquirer* or even the *Desktop Encyclopedia*? Is the material quoted only enough to make the arguments convincing, or has the writer quoted (or copied) large blocks of material (with or without giving credit)?

4. Are the mechanics of the prose (punctuation, spelling, sentence structure, etc.) good enough that the reader is not distracted by problems in these areas?

5. Are the mechanics of the paper, including documentation, acceptable? Does the writer consistently follow the guidelines of the required style of documentation? Does the writer give credit to the writers from whom he or she uses words, phrases, passages, or ideas?

All factors are generally tied together, and a paper that is strong in content is probably also strong in mechanics.

WRITING IN RESPONSE TO LITERATURE

Before beginning a writing assignment of any kind, the most important step is to understand fully the expectations of the instructor. Listen carefully to what is assigned. In the case of literary or artistic assignments, there are three words that you might hear: analysis, interpretation, and criticism. You must be able to distinguish between these words.

- Analysis of literature involves "taking the work apart" to see how it is made, to see how it "works," to discover what the parts are and what they do.
- Interpretation involves deciding what the work says.
- Criticism involves deciding how well the work says what it means to say and how well it is crafted. Criticism is not looking for the "bad stuff" in a piece of literature. Criticism in a literary or artistic sense means examination. Literary criticism is examining a work, section by section, aspect by aspect, very carefully, seeing how the work is put together and determining how well it is put together and how well it fulfills the function for which it is written. (See the section on evaluation.)

> *Literary work begins with careful reading.*

To analyze, interpret, or criticize, follow these general steps:
1. Read the story or poem or drama.
2. As you read, keep in mind the questions of *who, what, when, where, how,* and *why*.
3. Remember the definitions of analysis, interpretation, and criticism. Decide what the parts of the work are and how they function together. Decide what the author means and how you know what he means. Decide how or why the author does what he does. Decide how well the author does what he means to do.

It is necessary to cite evidence to prove your points. As you begin to search for a point from which to begin, consider a number of aspects. You may focus on the theme (or ethical insight), plot, character(s), point of view, setting, or language (sometimes called style). For example, you may choose to explain figurative language that involves examples of metaphors, similes, alliteration, allusions, etc. Whatever you choose to focus on should be significant and should be interesting to you. Your focus becomes the thesis of your paper.

4. Once you have identified a focus, read the work again, taking note of evidence you can cite in your essay.
5. Shape that evidence around your thesis and write a first draft.
6. Read your essay and revise it. Be sure that you have developed the thesis in the supporting paragraphs and used illustrations and evidence from the work.
7. Really good papers sometimes go through several revisions, so do not hesitate to revise until the paper pleases you and represents your very best efforts.

Literary analysis, interpretation, and criticism are not simple summaries or the retelling of a story. For examples of a summary, a report, and a four-section evaluation of the short story "Young Goodman Brown" see the following. (See also the section on summaries and reports for a summary and a report on a nonfiction literary work.)

Example (Summary of "Young Goodman Brown")

Hawthorne, Nathaniel. "Young Goodman Brown." *Imaginative Literature: Fiction, Drama, Poetry.* 4th ed. Ed. Alton C. Morris, Biron Walker, and Philip Bradshaw. New York: HBJ, 1983. 324. Print.

"Young Goodman Brown" by Nathaniel Hawthorne is the story of a young man recently married who leaves his wife to go on a journey into the forest. According to Young Faith, Young Goodman Brown's wife, this "night of all nights" is not a good time to be left alone; and Young Faith is near tears when she whispers softly and a bit sadly, "Dearest heart, prithee put off your journey until sunrise and sleep in your own bed tonight . . ." (Hawthorne 13). But Brown insists on making the journey. Brown's journey is filled with surprises, from seeing the staff bearing the likeness of a great black snake to finding Goody Cloyse, who had taught Brown his catechism, to discovering Faith's presence in the wood and to spying the devil lurking behind the tree. The fiend-worshippers make one cry, "Welcome!" (Hawthorne 23), before Young Goodman Brown resists them with his shout, "Look up to Heaven, and resist the Wicked One" (Hawthorne 23). The narrator asks whether or not Brown has fallen asleep in the forest and only dreamed a wild dream of a witch-meeting. The question is not answered. Young Goodman Brown leads a dreary existence for the remainder of his life, and, "when he had lived long and been borne to his grave . . . they carved no hopeful verse on his tombstone, for his dying hour was gloom" (Hawthorne 24).

Example (Report on "Young Goodman Brown," Including Bibliographic Data Section and Summary Section)

Hawthorne, Nathaniel. "Young Goodman Brown." *Imaginative Literature: Fiction, Drama, Poetry.* 4th ed. Ed. Alton C. Morris, Biron Walker, and Philip Bradshaw. New York: HBJ, 1983. 3-24. Print.

"Young Goodman Brown" by Nathaniel Hawthorne is the story of a young man recently married who leaves his wife to go on a journey into the forest. According to Young Faith, Young Goodman Brown's wife, this "night of all nights" is not a good time to be left alone; and Young Faith is near tears when she whispers softly and a bit sadly, "Dearest heart, prithee put off your journey until sunrise and sleep in your own bed tonight . . ." (Hawthorne 13). But Brown insists on making the journey. Brown's journey is filled with surprises, from seeing the staff bearing the likeness of a great black snake to finding Goody Cloyse, who had taught Brown his catechism, to discovering Faith's presence in the wood and to spying the devil lurking behind the tree. The fiend-worshippers make one cry, "Welcome!" (23), before Young Goodman Brown resists them with his shout, "Look up to Heaven, and resist the Wicked One" (Hawthorne 23). The narrator asks whether or not Brown has fallen asleep in the forest and only dreamed a wild dream of a witch-meeting. The question is not answered. Young Goodman Brown leads a dreary existence for the remainder of his life, and, "when he had lived long and been borne to his grave . . . they carved no hopeful verse on his tombstone, for his dying hour was gloom" (Hawthorne 24).

I enjoyed "Young Goodman Brown" very much. It seems to be an allegory of sorts, and I appreciate reading stories that are multi-level. One level is the interesting story itself, with the relationship between Brown and Faith and the relationships between Brown and the villagers. Another level is the psychological one, with the development of Brown as a person who lives with a self-fulfilling prophecy. Another level is the religious allegory, with Brown allowing doubt to overcome faith. It could be, of course, that what Brown sees is not his own doubts but reality, and that is the ambiguity in the story, an ambiguity that the author leaves deliberately since there can be no certainty in relationships, in psychology, or in religion. I think it is the ambiguity that appeals to me the most, leaving me to wonder exactly what Brown saw. As an optimist, I prefer to think that Brown sees only what he fears and that he is deceiving himself about his wife and his neighbors, that he brings his despair on himself. I prefer that scenario to the opposite one, that in fact everyone is evil and corrupt and Brown finally realizes the reality of the world. That thought is so depressing that I reject it!

Example (Four-Section Report on "Young Goodman Brown," Including a Bibliographic Data Section, a Summary Section, a Reaction Section, and an Evaluation Section)

Hawthorne, Nathaniel. "Young Goodman Brown." *Imaginative Literature: Fiction, Drama Poetry.* 4th ed. Ed. Alton C. Morris, Biron Walker, and Philip Bradshaw. New York: HBJ, 1983. 3-24. Print.

"Young Goodman Brown" by Nathaniel Hawthorne is the story of a young man recently married who leaves his wife to go on a journey into the forest. According to Young Faith, Young Goodman Brown's wife, this "night of all nights" is not a good time to be left alone; and Young Faith is near tears when she whispers softly and a bit sadly, "Dearest heart, prithee put off your journey until sunrise and sleep in your own bed tonight . . ." (Hawthorne 13). But Brown insists on making the journey. Brown's journey is filled with surprises, from seeing the staff bearing the likeness of a great black snake to finding Goody Cloyse, who had taught Brown his catechism, to discovering Faith's presence in the wood and to spying the devil lurking behind the tree. The fiend-worshippers make one cry, "Welcome!" (Hawthorne 23), before Young Goodman Brown resists them with his shout, "Look up to Heaven, and resist the Wicked One" (Hawthorne 23). The narrator asks whether or not Brown has fallen asleep in the forest and only dreamed a wild dream of a witch meeting. The question is not answered. Young Goodman Brown leads a dreary existence for the remainder of his life, and, "when he had lived long and been borne to his grave . . . they carved no hopeful verse on his tombstone, for his dying hour was gloom" (Hawthorne 24).

I enjoyed "Young Goodman Brown" very much. The story itself is interesting and the relationships between the characters are fascinating. Poor Faith tries to keep her husband from leaving her on a dangerous night. Her fears are borne out in Brown's subsequent attitude toward her and his suspicions of her and of all of his acquaintances. In addition to interesting characters, the author has supplied the reader with vivid imagery. The staff which is a living snake is a picture that will stay in my mind! The section that describes the "meeting" is also vivid, with Brown's fears about his neighbors come to life. Ultimately, I think it is the story's ambiguity that appeals to me the most, leaving me to wonder exactly what Brown saw. As an optimist, I prefer to think that Brown sees only what he fears and that he is deceiving himself about his wife and his neighbors, that he brings his despair on himself. I prefer that scenario to the opposite one, that in fact everyone is evil and corrupt and Brown finally realizes the reality of the world. That thought is so depressing that I reject it!

When I investigate "Young Goodman Brown" from a stance of evaluating significance of the plot, I find that the story functions on a number of levels. One level is the literal story itself, with the relationship between Brown and Faith and the relationships between Brown and the villagers. Faith tries to prevent Brown from taking his journey into despair but fails. That journey brings him to the belief that his world is peopled only with the corrupt and the fraudulent, leaving him to feel he faces evil alone and unprotected. Another level in the story is the psy-

> chological one, with the development of Brown as a person who lives with a self-fulfilling prophecy. When Brown determinedly sets out on a journey he need not make, he then decides that his neighbors and his wife are all evil. This causes him to further determine that his life is nothing but gloom. Each of those progressive steps into bleakness is made deliberately by Brown: he decides his reaction to each event, even choosing to accept the "meeting" as a reality and not as a dream. Another level is the religious allegory, with Brown allowing doubt to overcome faith. He refuses to keep his faith in the goodness of the world, instead preferring the gloom of despair. It could be, of course, that what Brown sees is not his own doubts but reality, and that is the ambiguity in the story, an ambiguity that the author leaves deliberately since there can be no certainty in relationships, in psychology, or in religion.

Literary criticism goes much further than a summary. It incorporates only enough summary to make the thesis and support understandable to the reader.

Three elements actually comprise literary criticism: analysis, interpretation, and criticism.

ANALYSIS

Analysis is attention to elements of a literary or artistic work. For example, if you are analyzing "Young Goodman Brown," you can look at the structure, such as plot elements of inciting incident, conflict(s), climax, resolution, dénouement, the characterization, the images, the symbols, the theme(s), the literary language, etc.

In class, during a discussion or lecture about literature, you may find yourself saying, "I did not see that at all." Do not get discouraged. It takes practice to discover literature fully. You never learn all there is to know about it. You never come to the end of discovery. A person who has studied and taught literature for years is often surprised by a new insight that a student offers. This same student (maybe you) may have said, in other circumstances, "I do not see where you got that."

The study of literature is the study of themes—ideas that are reflected in the literature, structure—how the work is put together, and of genre—the types of literature. *Genre* means type: a literary genre is a type of literary work. Generally, the literary genres are considered to be short story, poem, play (or drama), film, and also include the nonfiction genre, the essay.

> *You bring insight to each literary work.*

To study any subject, you must be familiar with the specialized vocabulary that people use to discuss that subject. In the glossary is a list of very common literary terms. All of the terms are applicable to each genre of literature.

We can start our discussion of literary terms with *fiction*. Fiction can be based on fact, but it is not fact. If an author starts with an event and adds elements to the event that did not actually occur, the author is fictionalizing the event, no longer sticking to "just the facts, ma'am." If an author makes something up, he or she is creating pure fiction. If an author just tells what happens, as a newspaper reporter should report a news story, this is not fiction because the author is not "making up" anything.

One of the places fiction and nonfiction seem to get mixed up is in the "docu-drama," which is a romanticized or fictionalized television program based on an actual event. The writer takes an event and, to suit the desires of the media audience or to suit the needs of the network or production company, makes the event "larger than life" and more saleable. The "docu-drama" is supposed to be a combination of documentary and of dramatization of the subject to be documented, but the docu-drama is usually more drama (and much less fact) than documentary. Little, if anything, may be left of the "truth" when the normal docu-drama airs.

Now look at what happens in the work of fiction. What are the events in the short story? These are the things you undoubtedly notice first when reading or viewing anything. What happens, of course, is *plot*. And one of the things you should be aware of is whether the piece contains any *flashbacks*.

You can notice flashback most easily in a television "soap opera," now known as a daytime drama. If you watch a "soap," you may notice that characters and couples have their own theme music; that is, when the character or couple is on screen, the music accompaniment is distinctive, and distinctive to them.

When a plot line calls for a flashback, a character, usually a woman, accompanied by her character music, is on screen and says something such as "I remember when . . ." and her voice fades off. The music changes and becomes slightly eerie or out of sync with her character. The edges of the picture blur, and there is a fade to black. When the scene clears and the music comes back up, another scene is on the screen, one that has already played days or weeks ago. The scene plays over, as it was originally filmed, with the original music and other sound. When the portion the director wants to replay finishes, the music again changes, the screen becomes fuzzy and fades to black. The original scene returns with the character saying something such as "Yes, that was how it was. I remember." That was a flashback.

Another aspect of plot is the *climax*, the highest point in the plot. The climax is the point of greatest intensity in the events of the story. It is the culmination of all of the conflict.

The climax often occurs with an *epiphany*, in which a character suddenly realizes something about himself or herself, the situation, or others. The movie about the good guy and the bad guy may end with the good guy being forced to kill the bad guy at the climax. If the good guy realizes that he is now a bad guy because he too is now a killer, this is the epiphany.

The *dénouement* occurs after the climax. M*A*S*H is one of the television shows with a dénouement. All of the action in M*A*S*H occurs before the last set of internal commercials (the ones before the half-hour show break commercials). The climax is reached. The story is over. But the program continues. Between the last set of internal commercials and the credits, the program returns to the screen: Hawkeye and B. J. have a martini, or somebody apologizes to Margaret, or they all go to the club, or someone tells a joke. These things are not necessary to the storyline, although they are connected. What they do is leave the viewer with a good feeling, or at least a feeling of completion. This is the dénouement.

The *conflict* in the story is what gives the story its action and spice. Conflict does not have to be Rambo shooting up the local terrorist camp. It may be very subtle. It may not even be external. The protagonist, or main character, may oppose, may be in conflict with, the antagonist, or second main character. These people may be just characters, or they may represent something outside themselves, larger ideas. In the Superman comics, television programs, and movies, Superman represents "truth, justice, and the American way!" Usually the opposition, whether it is Lex Luthor or someone else, represents evil in one form or another, maybe "lies, injustice, and un-American activities!"

> *Literary terms apply to fiction, films, television, etc.*

Conflicts usually fall into one of five categories. One category, *person against person*, is a conflict in which two characters are in opposition. All of the Rambo movies, the Rocky movies, the Superman movies, and lots of other movies have this conflict. It is very easy to pick out. If someone hits someone else or blows him or guns down that person, the conflict is person against person.

Another category, *person against society*, is a conflict in which someone is in conflict with the society in which he or she lives, either with its mores and values or with its laws or with the representatives of those laws or mores—the people around him or her. This conflict can be seen in the film *Straight Time*, starring Dustin Hoffman as an ex-convict. The Hoffman character is on parole and comes into conflict with various segments of society and with each segment's expectations. His parole officer (a representative of the government and the law) expects him to stay away from all of his old friends and companions; his old friends and companions (representatives of the fringe criminal society) expect him to take up his old life at the point at which he left it; society as a whole expects him to get a job, support himself, and become a responsible citizen despite the fact that he has no skills. So the Hoffman character comes into conflict with societal elements in various ways.

Person against God (alternately known as *person against fate*) is the conflict seen in the Oedipus plays by Sophocles, perhaps most easily in the first play of the cycle, *Oedipus the King*. In *Oedipus the King* (also known as *Oedipus Rex*), Oedipus's father is warned by Teiresias, the blind prophet, that his son will grow up to kill the father and marry the mother. To escape that fate, Oedipus' father has Oedipus exposed on the hillside. The king of a neighboring kingdom rescues the boy and brings him up as the king's own son. The boy does not know that he is adopted; and, when he hears a prophecy that he will kill his father and marry his mother, Oedipus runs away from the kind king. On his travels, Oedipus sees an old man at a crossroads who will not get out of the way. Oedipus, who is extremely arrogant, kills the old man and continues to a nearby kingdom, finding a beautiful queen who is widowed, marrying her, and becoming king. Plagues fall on the kingdom. Teiresias says that the plagues are caused by the fact that an evil man who has married his mother and killed his father lives in the kingdom; Oedipus vows to rid the kingdom of him. Oedipus discovers that the man is himself. Neither he nor his father is able to escape the fates prophesied for him.

Another conflict is a *person against nature*, seen in "To Build a Fire," the story by Jack London. In this short story, the main character, despite warnings from the "old-timers" in the "frozen North," takes his dog team, which he treats with cruelty, and begins a search for gold. Various adventures befall him, causing him to lose all of his supplies except for a few matches and all of his dogs except for one. He determines to light a fire and warm himself, feeling confident that he can endure the cold and survive. He drops matches, or snow falls on the fire, etc., until he is left with one match. His hands are too cold to feel the match, and he knows that he will not succeed in lighting a fire with the match unless he can first warm his hands. He calls the dog to him, planning to kill the dog and warm his hands inside the body. The dog runs away. The story ends. In "To Build a Fire," a man has come in conflict with nature and lost.

The conflict of *person against self* is one of the conflicts in "Eveline," a short story in which a young woman must decide whether to stay with her abusive, but known, family or to accept a proposal of marriage and to enter a probably better, but unknown, situation. This conflict is largely internal, taking place inside a character. This kind of conflict is seldom seen to any large extent in a "bang, bang, shoot-'em-up" story.

A short story, novel or film, etc., may have more than one conflict. Usually, a short story contains one major conflict; and a novel, because it is so much longer, may contain several.

Aside from plot and aspects deriving from plot, literature has other aspects. The *setting* of the work is its time and place location. Sometimes the author leaves this deliberately vague. Sometimes the setting is very specific: Faulkner's "A Rose for Emily" is set in the South in the early 1900s or late 1800s.

An *image* in literature involves the reader in the imagining of a sensory experience, of sight, sound, taste, touch, or smell. One visual image in "The Tell-Tale Heart" by Edgar Allen Poe is the eye of the old man. The reader can "see" the eye in his or her imagination.

A *symbol* may also be an image, but it is more than an image. A symbol is something in the work that stands for something outside the work or that stands for something that is more than itself. A flag is a symbol. It *is* a piece of cloth, but it is a symbol of a country. A symbol may mean different things to different audiences. The flag of our country means more to us than does the flag of another country. A symbol also may change through time, meaning one thing to a child and another to an adult: Santa Claus is a good example of a symbol that changes with the age of the observer.

A symbol may also be an *allusion*, but not all allusions are symbols. An allusion is simply a reference to something outside the work, perhaps a political event or a person from another literary work. For example, a short story about a camping trip might allude to Huck Finn and his trip down the river with Jim. This is an allusion to the character in Mark Twain's *Huckleberry Finn*.

An *anomaly* may be an allusion or a symbol, or it may be neither. An anomaly is something that does not seem to fit into the work,

> *Santa Claus is a symbol.*

either in terms of plot or of setting or of theme, etc. A very simple example of something anomalous is a movie with Indians attacking the wagon train and wearing sneakers. This is not a significant anomaly; it is simply terrible movie-making. Most of the time, anomalies are significant in a literary work and must be considered carefully. For example, in "Appointment in Samarra," a reader might consider the female figure of death to be anomalous because death is usually portrayed as a male figure. What point is Maugham trying to make when he presents death as female?

The *style* of the work is how the author has written or presented the work. Sometimes style also involves *tone*. The tone of the work can be serious, comic, ironic, etc. The style contributes to the tone and to the overall effect of the work. Style is the way the work is presented. The author may use short sentences or long sentences; short journalistic-style paragraphs (Hemingway) or long, involved paragraphs (Faulkner); much description (Welty) or hardly any description at all (Asimov), etc.—all of these are aspects of style.

Another aspect of style is the decision of the writer on the *point of view* with which to write. The writer develops a *narrator*, a person telling the story. This person (called a *persona*) does not necessarily represent the writer and his or her feelings and views. The narrator tells the story from his (or her) point of view. The narrator may be the main character and tell the story in first person, saying, "I was at the store to buy some milk. I saw a robber who pulled a gun on the storekeeper and then ran away. I was really scared." The narrator is the key figure. This point of view is known as first person central. You can see this point of view in "The Tell-Tale Heart."

The narrator could say, telling the same series of events, "I saw my friend John rob the store. He pulled a gun on the storekeeper and then ran away." John becomes more important than the narrator. This is *first person secondary point of view*.

Or the narrator with the *first person observer point of view* could say, "I saw a person in a store pull a gun and rob the storekeeper and then run away." The narrator, except for his or her presence as the narrator, stays out of the account.

In addition to first person points of view, there are several third person points of view. The writer still develops a narrator who tells the story but the narrator is not as personal as the narrator of a first person account.

In a *third person objective* account, the narrator tells the story as if the story were seen by a movie camera. The narrator gives just the facts and does not offer any opinion, nor does the narrator give the reader any idea of the thoughts or feelings of the characters involved. The reader does not know what any of the characters are like except through what they do and say.

> *The narrator's point of view establishes how you see the story.*

In a *third person limited* account, the narrator gives thoughts and feelings for a few of the characters, but not for all. The reader gets to know something about a few of the characters by seeing how these characters feel without their expressing their feelings to other characters. The reader also finds out what these characters think by "hearing" what they think and not by watching only the actions and dialogue of the characters. "A Worn Path" is written in third person limited. The reader sees thoughts and feelings of only the main character, Phoenix, and not of any of the other characters.

In a *third person omniscient* narration, the narrator gives the thoughts and feeling for a majority of the characters, if not for all of them. Third person omniscient is the point of view in "The Open Boat;" the reader sees into the minds, sees the thoughts and feelings, of all of the characters in the boat.

One of the most important aspects of a literary work is *theme*, what the work means or what it is trying to teach. This does not mean that the work preaches a moral, but that the work has one (or more) main idea(s) to present or to reveal. Finding the theme is part of interpretation; interpretation is based on the reader's decision on what the theme is. A theme is always stated in sentence form. You would not say, "The theme is love." You would say, "The theme is that love conquers all." One of the themes in "Appointment in Samarra" can be stated in this way: "a person cannot run away from fate."

INTERPRETATION

Interpretation is deciding what the work—the film or short story or poem or play—is "all about," determining meaning. It is the weaving of all of the elements into a coherent whole so that each part functions to illuminate all of the other parts. Interpretation can function on more than one "level." The lowest level, and the simplest interpretation, is literal. In literal interpretation, all that the reader has to decide is what happened; *literal interpretation* is the equivalent of a plot summary.

Biographical interpretation is interpretation in light of the events of the author's life. It is looking at the work and trying to find what of the author is reflected in the work, aside from his or her imagination and craft. It is looking at the plays of Tennessee Williams and finding that at least one of the female characters in most of his plays is "flawed" in some way, usually psychologically, and making a connection between that fact and the fact that Williams had a dearly-loved sister who had mental problems.

Literature can be interpreted in terms of how it fits into a historical pattern or how it reveals a historical period (*historical interpretation*). Most of the novels of Charles Dickens can be interpreted historically because he reveals the culture and class problems and struggles of the times about which he writes. Literature can be interpreted in terms of how it fits into sociological or psychological theory or how it illuminates one of these theories (sociological and psychological interpretation). For example, the play *Oedipus Rex* can be interpreted in terms of the Oedipus complex, named by Sigmund Freud. Of course, because Freud named the complex for the play, this is rather circular.

Religious interpretation is interpretation of literature in terms of religious symbols and images. Langston Hughes's short story "On the Road" can be seen in terms of religious interpretation. The story

> *Interpretation determines meanings.*

abounds with religious symbols and images. The main character stands between two pillars and pulls a building down, reminiscent of Samson in the Bible. He is released from jail by a suddenly and mysteriously opened door, reminiscent of Peter. Of course, the fact that the main character converses with Christ is probably the key to religious interpretation of this story.

Each piece of literature can probably be interpreted in more than one way. For example, if you were interpreting "Young Goodman Brown," you might decide that the short story is about how a weak man's search for faith in a threatening world can lead him to despair, a religious interpretation and/or a psychological one. Or you might decide that the story reflects Hawthorne's society and its emphasis on faith, a *sociological interpretation*.

Just because someone else has not mentioned what you see does not mean that you cannot interpret the work in that way. However, this does not mean that you can read just anything you want to into a work. You must have internal evidence. Internal evidence is lines and actions occurring in the work itself that serve as evidence to back up your interpretation. In other words, you cannot say that "The Tell-Tale Heart" is about Abraham Lincoln's dog's doctor because you can find no internal evidence to back up this far-fetched idea.

CRITICISM

Criticism is determining the worth of a work, deciding whether the work has artistic, social, or personal value. Remember that criticism is not negative: it is a balanced look, a precise look at the relative importance of the work. If you were criticizing "Young Goodman Brown," you might say it has social merit because it reflects one of the cultural tones of early America, or you might decide that it is of no worth to you personally because you are not interested in people's relationships with each other and with God, or you might assert that the work is important artistically because it is well crafted and engaging.

> *Criticism determines value.*

Example (Literary Analysis of "Young Goodman Brown")

Amanda 1

George Amanda

Prof. Zeta

ENGL 1213

April 11, 19–

Contrasting Symbols in "Young Goodman Brown"

"Young Goodman Brown," by Nathaniel Hawthorne, is the story of a man's encounter with evil. That encounter affects the rest of his life. Throughout the story of Young Goodman Brown's journey into the woods and his subsequent life are symbols that represent the contrasting forces present in his world. Investigating the symbolism of Faith and her pink ribbons, the man with the serpent staff, and the tombstone with no hopeful verse illustrates some of the conflict in the story and the life of Young Goodman Brown.

Young Goodman Brown's wife, Young Faith, with her flying pink ribbons, represents the good in Brown's life. Pink is a color of innocence and freshness, and it is innocence and freshness that Young Goodman Brown leaves behind in the person of his wife of three months. She has begged him not to leave her, on this night "of all nights" (Hawthorne 14). He turns from her and insists on making the journey into the forest. His turning away from her pleading represents his subsequent turning away from faith in the innocence, freshness, and goodness of humanity.

In addition, her name is an obvious symbol. Her name is Young Faith, and in fact the name represents that faith which is young and fragile. The faith that Young Goodman Brown turns away from at the beginning of the story is not only his own wife, it is his own faith. His own faith is so weak that he cannot hold to it. When tested, he resists by calling out, "Faith! Faith! . . . Look up to Heaven, and resist the Wicked One!" (Hawthorne 23); but his faith is so fragile that he cannot believe that Young Faith also resists. After Brown suspects he meets Faith in the forest at the witch meeting, Young Goodman Brown allows this to color his future relationship with his wife, causing him on various occasions to look "sternly and sadly into her face . . . without a greeting" and to shrink from her on "awaking suddenly at midnight" (Hawthorne 24).

After leaving Faith at home, Young Goodman Brown meets the stranger who has a staff, "which bore the likeness of a great black snake, so curiously wrought, that it might almost be seen to twist and wriggle itself like a living serpent. This, of course, must have been an ocular deception, assisted by the uncertain light" (Hawthorne 15). This stranger with the deceptive staff represents the evil that Young Goodman Brown meets. More important, this stranger represents the uncertainty and deception that will plague Brown the rest of his life. The stranger takes Brown into the forest to meet all the people near whom he resides and whom he has trusted and loved. Brown is not strong enough to realize that not only his vision and the staff can be deceptive. Perhaps the whole episode is an illusion. Whether it is deception or not is immaterial because the stranger has succeeded in ruining Brown's life. The deception and "ocular deception" is the basis for Brown's ensuing actions.

The grave of Brown is headed by a tombstone, on which there is "no hopeful verse" for "his dying hour was gloom" (Hawthorne 24). This tombstone represents the conflict in Brown's life. After meeting the stranger and living through either the witch-meeting or the dream of the witch-meeting, Brown returns to his home. But he does not return joyfully. All of his relationships are soured by the memory of the night in the forest. His young faith is not strong enough to live as if the meeting had been a dream. He lives instead with doubt. Did it happen? It does not matter because doubt destroys him. The tombstone comes at the end of his life, but it very well could have been set at the moment he returned to the village and shrinks from its people "as if to avoid an anathema" (Hawthorne 24).

> Brown has experienced an episode in which he allows himself to lose innocence and faith. He discovers that the world can be deceptive. But it is his choice, his actual reaction to that conflict between faith and doubt, in which doubt wins, that leads him to his gloomy death and gloomier life.
>
> Works Cited
>
> Hawthorne, Nathaniel. "Young Goodman Brown." *Imaginative Literature: Fiction, Drama, Poetry.* 4th ed. Ed. Alton C. Morris, Biron Walker, and Philip Bradshaw. New York: HBJ, 1983. 13-24. Print.

FILM ANALYSIS

In your classes, you may have to deal with short stories, novel, plays, or poems. In addition, you may have to learn about films. Films affect your life if you go to the movies, rent videos, or watch television. Short stories, novels, and plays have been translated into film. Screenplays have become novels. Literature moves back and forth across the line to the visual art that is film. Films may begin with a story idea from literature, with a script, with a concept, and/or with a vision. Films are usually made in something like the following manner.

If a film begins with a concept, a *scriptwriter* writes a film script. The script is the skeleton that becomes the production. The words are interpreted by actors, director, editor, etc.

Although the *actors* are not the first people involved in making the film, the actors interpret the writer's concept and allow the translation of that concept to film. The skeleton that is the script begins to take form when the actors bring it to a kind of life. Just as no two people have exactly the same vision of a character in a short story, no two actors interpret a part in exactly the same manner. The background and concept of the character, the actions and reactions of the character, the motivations of the character, the character itself is interpreted differently by each actor playing the role.

Remember all of the remakes of the old movies? Or the remakes for television of old movies? Did any remake ever duplicate the original? Were any characters for the remake just like characters in the original? Undoubtedly not. An actor brings a personal view to a role and is not even able to (or wants to) duplicate what was done before.

Probably the first person who actually deals with the making of the film is the *producer*. The producer looks for financing and supervises the production, especially in terms of budget. In some cases, the producer also supervises the film in terms of concept, ensuring that the concept of the film remains true to the original concept.

The *director* is also a supervisor. The director supervises the actual making of the film. In most cases, the director is the person who has in mind the film as an entirety and directs the actors and camera personnel so that the concept in the director's mind becomes translated to the final product.

Some directors (and even some producers) become well known for the personal stamp they put on films. You can pick out who made the film from seeing what kind of film it is. Some of the directors who are easily distinguishable from other directors are Brian dePalma, Steven Spielberg, Alfred Hitchcock, Robert Altman, and Francis Ford Coppola, among others.

Either the *director* or a *camera director*, or the director and the camera director together, decide on the camera shots and angles. How you see a scene depends on how the camera sees a scene.

The camera becomes the eye of the viewer. You are manipulated by the action of the camera. You wander up the stairs in the *Psycho* house with the detective and are startled at the appearance of the knife in the hand of the murderer. Because you are frightened and fixed on the knife (and because the knife is what the camera lets you see), you do not see the face of the murderer.

What the camera sees at the beginning of *E.T.* is portions of people. You see feet in heavy boots, large hands holding swinging flashlights, key rings on belts, other large hands holding guns of various kinds. You do not see the whole person. The whole sequence of shots creates a mood, as do all of the sequences of shots. In this case, the mood is ominous. We see the people in the sequence as objects, objects with frightening items. We know something not too good is going to happen.

The person in charge of *continuity* insures that each scene flows smoothly and continuously, one to another. In most cases, films are not made in sequence. That means that each scene is not shot as it appears in the script or as it appears in the final product. Instead, the scenes are filmed in the most efficient manner.

Perhaps all of the outdoor scenes in the rain are all filmed, then all of the indoor scenes of the mansion, then all of the outdoor scenes at the pool, and then all of the indoor scenes in the restaurant. This is despite the fact that, in order of time (and in the final order of the finished film), the scenes would run in this sequence: first an indoor scene in the mansion, then an outdoor scene at the pool, then an indoor scene in the mansion, then an indoor scene at the restaurant, then an outdoor scene in the rain, and then an indoor scene in the mansion, etc.

You can see that someone needs to keep track of how the actors have their hair combed and what clothes they are wearing in the restaurant, etc. Otherwise a male actor may appear in the restaurant in a gray suit and move outside to catch a cab in a green blazer and jeans. Keeping all of this straight is up to continuity.

Lighting is important, not just for visibility. Lighting creates a mood and enhances the emotional quality of a scene. The lighting in the 1940s version of *Cat People* lets the viewer see bars of light across the main female character in several scenes, foreshadowing and symbolizing her imprisonment in her plight and the leopard's imprisonment at the zoo.

Low light may create a feeling of impending doom or of fright. At the beginning of *E.T.* (and indeed through the bulk of the film), the lighting is subdued, leading the viewer to suspect that a relatively unpleasant event is coming.

Sound is also a critical part of a film. The soundtrack of a movie may be a work of art in its own right. The music enhances and reinforces the action and emotion portrayed on the screen and contributes to the effect of the film.

The *editor* of a film takes the final rolls of film and the soundtrack and combines all of the parts into a whole. Under the direction of the director, the editor decides how long a shot actually lasts, what remains in the final product, and what is deleted.

Some techniques that an editor uses are *fade-in, fade-out, close-up, cut,* and *montage*. Fade-in and fade-out are rather obvious terms. In these technique, the film either fades out to black or fades in to the picture from black. Close-up is rather obvious as well. In close-up work, the camera frames a subject so that you can see it closely.

Cutting and montage are more complicated, but not much more. Montage is the rapid juxtaposition of shots. One shot is quickly followed by another, which is quickly followed by another, etc. Montage is a form of cutting. Cutting is switching from one scene to another. Cutting between several scenes is montage. Cutting between two scenes is just cutting.

Cutting also affects what you see in the film and how you react to it. Cutting can either allow the viewer to carry an emotion over from one scene to another, if the scene is cut early enough, or allow the viewer to enjoy a scene fully before reacting emotionally to the next scene.

> *Films can be analyzed, interpreted, and criticized.*

In *E.T.*, Spielberg allows many scenes to continue and does not cut at the point that many directors would. In the scene in which E.T. "dies," the camera continues to roll until every member of the audience is drained of emotional reaction to the "death."

This is a different cutting technique than that used by the editor in *An Officer and a Gentleman*. In the scene in which the main character helps his classmate over the wall, the joy of the audience at seeing this arrogant, self-centered, and self-contained man reach out to someone struggling (and to someone who has been struggling in several scenes in the film) is hardly experienced before the scene is cut and the next scene begins. The next scene is not a joyous one, and the joy of the viewer is juxtaposed with his or her subsequent sadness. The cutting allows the viewer the almost simultaneous experience of the up-and-down of real life. And the spillover from the first scene makes the second more palatable and acceptable, as well as sadder.

Other members of the film crew are important, including other sound and lighting experts, various camera personnel, production and director's assistants, go-fors of all kinds, etc.

The viewer is manipulated by film. Your emotions are involved, and your response is motivated by what you see and how you see it. You should be aware of the techniques of film so that you are aware of how you are affected. Knowing about techniques and effects does not subvert your enjoyment of a film. This knowledge allows you to enjoy and appreciate the film from a new perspective.

Example (Film Analysis, Literary Analysis of a Film)
NOTE: Student essay examples are above-average papers, but not necessarily "A" papers.

Denita Hancock

Prof. Dial-Driver

ENGL 2613

February 23, 2000

Toy Conflicts in *Toy Story 2*

What do toys do when their owner is gone? Do they really just sit there lifeless? Most children wonder this at some time during his or her young life. *Toy Story 2* is an outstanding movie that makes toys come to life. An investigation into *Toy Story 2* reveals conflicts that toys may have: rejection of owner, identity crises, and the possibility of leaving their present life to move on to a new life where they are more appreciated.

One of a toy's worst fears is that of being rejected or no longer wanted by its owner. Woody has been Andy's most beloved toy for several years and is looking forward to his most exciting summer yet with Andy at camp when tragedy strikes: "When Woody's arm accidentally is torn, Andy decides not to take him to camp, and Woody worries that his days might be numbered" (Caro 2). Todd McCarthy puts it this way, "Andy's mom adds the final sting with the comment, 'Toys don't last forever'" (83). These are the dreaded words every toy hates to hear. Woody feels very rejected by being left behind. Woody is again reminded of Andy's rejection later on in the movie. Stinky Pete, a member of a toy collection that Woody would complete, asks, "Do you really think that Andy is going to take you to college or on his honeymoon?" (Caro 3). Woody realizes that Andy will outgrow him someday, but does it have to be now? Andy isn't the only one dealing with owner rejection in the movie. Jessie, another member of the rare toy collection tells Woody "about her former owner, Emily, who tossed her under the bed and forgot her" (Ebert 2). Buzz sums it up best when he says, "You never forget kids, but they forget you" (Ebert 2).

Identity crisis is another conflict represented in *Toy Story 2*. Joe Morgenstern describes Buzz Lightyear as "a lantern-jawed space ranger, struggling with the realities of his existence—he's not really the intrepid galactic explorer he'd like to be but a plastic plaything manufactured in Taiwan" (W1). Not only is he a mere toy, but he also finds out (while trying to rescue Andy) that there are hundreds of him: "Buzz discovers that he is only one of many Buzzes and must come to terms with existential questions about being mass-produced, one of the crowd" (Maslin E1). Even more devastating is the fact that he is the old model. There is now a "new and improved version of his likeness" (Caro 3). If this isn't enough to make a toy feel bad, Buzz is overcome by one of the new toys and stuck in his box impairing him from helping with the rescue of Woody. Eventually Buzz escapes from the box to return to Andy's rescue mission, showing no signs of inferiority. Buzz handles his identity crises quite well and continues with his mission as a friend.

The biggest conflict is *Toy Story 2* is the choice Woody must make in deciding whether to be rescued by his old friends to return to Andy or stay with his new friends and complete the collector's set, which will be sent to Japan and placed in a museum forever. This decision is very difficult as Todd McCarthy says in his review, "[Woody] is torn between the 'blood' family of his old TV cohorts and his closest friends from Andy's house" (83). Woody is excited to know that he was once famous. He finds out that he starred in a TV show with his horse, Bullseye, a cowgirl named Jessie, and a Prosecutor named Stinky Pete. Jessie and Pete want Woody to stay with them to complete the collection so they can be sent to Japan. If Woody leaves to go back to Andy's house, "they'll be put back in storage" (Nichols E24). Jessie tries to persuade Woody by "tugging at Woody's heart . . . by pointing out that unlike Woody, who has enjoyed many years with a loving owner, she has endured a long purgatory in storage, bereft of any life worth living" (Nichols E24). Woody is in a terrible mess. Should he stay or go? "Besides, in the museum he'll be admired by many children for years, instead of living under the threat of being outgrown by Andy" (Vice 2). Lisa Schwarzbaum describes it by saying, "Woody weighs the safety of lying low with his new, untouchable teammates against the perils (and pleasures) of being loved and played with (but likely eventually discarded) by an imperfect little boy" (72). Just when Woody has made his decision to go to the museum, his group of old friends show up to rescue him. Buzz tries to persuade Woody to come home with several touching lines, such as, "It is better to be loved for the length of a childhood than admired forever behind glass in a museum" (Ebert 2); "You're not a collector's item, you're a toy" (*Toy)*; and "Life's only worth living if you've been loved by a kid" (*Toy*). Woody refuses to go with his "old pals" and sends them on their way. It's only when he hears the song "You've Got a Friend in Me" that his heart is touched and he comes to his senses, knowing that he cannot forsake Andy. Woody comes up with the great idea of inviting Bullseye, Jessie, and Stinky Pete to come along with him to Andy's house. Everyone is thrilled except Stinky Pete who has never been out of his box to be loved by anyone. He tries to make trouble for the rescue team and eventually ends up in a backpack with a Barbie. Bullseye and Jessie are welcomed new toys at Andy's house as expected. Andy closes with the thoughts, "It will be fun while it lasts, and besides, I will still have Buzz Lightyear to infinity and beyond!" (*Toy*).

Toy Story 2 may be about what toys do when no one is around, but it also can relate to real life situations in today's world. Many children deal with the same kind of conflicts that the toys do: owner (or parent) rejection, identity crisis (self-worth), and choices to stay with the old or join in with the new. It would be great if real life stories could end as happily as this story and everyone could have their own Buzz to be with "to infinity and beyond!"

> **Works Cited**
>
> Caro, Mark. "Toy Story 2." *Metromix: A Chicago Entertainment and Restaurant Guide*. 17 Feb. 2000: 1-4. Metromix. Web. 22 Feb. 2000.
>
> Ebert, Roger. "Toy Story 2." *Chicago Sun Times* 17 Feb. 2000: 1-3. Ebert. Chicago Sun Times. Web. 22 Feb. 2000.
>
> Maslin, Janet. "Animated Sequel Finds New Level of Imagination." *New York Times* 24 Nov. 1999, late ed.: E1. Print.
>
> McCarthy, Todd. "Toy Story 2." *Variety* 377.2 (22 Nov. 1999): 83. Print.
>
> Morgenstern, Joe. "What? A Good Sequel? A Brilliant 'Toy Story 2' Proves It Can Happen." *Wall Street Journal* 26 Nov. 1999: W1. Print.
>
> Nichols, Peter M. "The Terrors of Toyland: Collectors." *New York Times* 26 Nov. 1999, late ed.: E24. Print.
>
> Schwarzbaum, Lisa. "Second That Emotion: A Rare Sequel That Lives Up to Its Predecessor, the Blissful Toy Story 2 Makes You Feel as Giddy as When You First Thrilled to the Adventures of Woody and Buzz." *Entertainment Weekly* 515 (3 Dec. 1999): 72. Print.
>
> *Toy Story 2*. Pixar/Disney, 1999. DVD.
>
> Vice, Jeff. "'Toy Story 2' Among the Disney Studios' Best Film Ever." *DesertNews* 24 Nov. 1999: 1-2. 17 *DesertNews*. Web. Feb. 2000.

POETRY ANALYSIS

Many people say they hate poetry. Some people panic when asked to read or analyze a poem. Others say they do not understand it, so they don't like it. If you look at the subject in one way, much as you would look at music, you might realize that you do not have to understand poetry to enjoy it, just as you do not have to understand what a contralto voice sings or what harmonic relationships are in order to appreciate a song or a tune. It is enough that the sound and the feeling are appealing and satisfying.

But it does add to the appreciation and understanding of the meaning of the poem to analyze, interpret, and criticize the poem (called by some people "picking it to death"). Poetry analysis is not difficult. It is something you have to learn how to do. With practice, it comes more easily, until you can do it without thinking about it or breaking the process down into steps. Until you reach that point, you might consciously follow the steps of the following process.

> *Poetry can be analyzed and understood. Answer the questions to begin the process.*

1. What is your immediate emotional reaction to the poem?
   Does it make you feel depressed? Does it make you feel happy or uplifted? Does it make you feel sad? (No, *bored* is not a valid answer to this question.)

2. What is the title?
   What is the significance of the title? The title of a poem is frequently related to the theme or, at least, gives a starting point that the first line of the poem takes for granted.
   Does the title specify a locale for the poem?
   Does the title specify a person? Is the poem addressed to this person? Is the poem about this person?
   Does the title specify an incident or action about which the poem is written?
   Does the title specify a dominant purpose for the poem?
   Does the title allude to some incident or event in literature, life, the Bible, or a myth that the poem assumes as its starting point?

3. What is the form of the poem?
   Is there regular rhyme pattern? What is it?
   Is there regular rhythm pattern? What is it?
   Does the poem have a recognizable verse form? What is it? Is the form significant to the purpose or theme of the poem?
   Is each line a single thought unit, or does the thought continue to the next line or lines?
   Is each stanza a separate thought unit, or do some of the thoughts continue to the next stanza or stanzas? Why do you think this is so?
   Is the poem arranged on the page in any manner that does not look usual to you? Why do you think this is so? Are the words arranged or used in unusual ways? Are the stanzas used or arranged in unusual ways? Why?

4. Determine the context of the poem.
   Who is the speaker of the poem? Convention assumes that almost all poems have a speaker. Some speakers simply function as an organizing point of view. Other speakers are clearly someone other than the poet. This kind of speaker is called a persona and may be as multifaceted as a character in a play or short story.
   Is the speaker male or female, young or old? Does the speaker have a name? What are the speaker's characteristics? Does he or she have a well-defined identity or is the speaker only a focus or narrator?
   How does the speaker feel about the events, incidents, people, or objects described in the poem? Does the speaker express any feelings in the poem? Do the attitude and emotion of the speaker coincide with the way a "reasonable person" might be expected to feel?
   Who is spoken to? Is the person whom the speaker addresses different from the reader? What kind of person is the one addressed? What significance might this have?
   Where is the speaker? Why is the speaker at that place?

5. Summarize the events of the poem.
   What happens? Tell the events or emotions of the poem in your own words. Do this line by line. This is called explication; it helps you understand what is actually happening in the poem.

6. Discover the mechanics of the poem.
   What kind of imagery does the speaker use in the description? Do these images have anything in common? Do they cluster around a dominant impression?
   What kinds of words does the poem contain? What is the diction of the poem? Are slang words used? Is the language formal or informal; is it standard or a dialect? What do the word choices reveal about the situation and the speaker?
   Are there allusions to events or works outside the poem? Do the allusions serve to broaden the significance of the poem, to universalize the experience, or to give you added insight?
   Are there anomalies in the lines? Do the anomalies serve to give you a new view of what is said or meant?
   What words or ideas are repeated? Anything repeated is worth investigation, because it must be of some significance. A poem is a kind of shorthand; if the poet feels something is worth repeating, it must be important.
   What are the symbols in the poem? What is their significance? What do they mean? How do they function?

7. What is the theme of the poem?
   What is the poet trying to say to the reader? It is customary to consider all of the things that you have discovered about the poem—all of the characteristics, the effects, the minor meanings—and develop an expression of the theme of the poem.
   Once the theme is discovered and stated, the purpose of the analysis is to demonstrate that the theme is appropriate and that the statement of theme can be supported by references from the poem itself. Any statement of theme must have this support. A poem may have many themes. You may discover a theme that a classmate overlooks and vice versa. But a poem (or a short story or a novel or a play or a movie) does not mean whatever you want it to. You cannot say that a poem about the discovery of the alphabet is about Abraham Lincoln's doctor. The statement of the theme must be defensible with internal evidence from the poem, and all of the parts of the poem must fit into this statement.

8. Evaluate your reaction to the poem.
   Your response to the poem is a factor that must be taken into account. Did you like or dislike the poem? On what do you base this reaction? Did the reaction change as you came to understand the poem better?

Example (Analysis of Poetry)
NOTE: Student essay examples are above-average papers, but not necessarily "A" papers.

Gay 1

Rick Gay

Prof. Sesso

ENGL 1213

April 15, XXXX

Carnal Poetry

Poetry could be described as "painting with words." It is man's attempt to give linguistic form to thoughts and emotions. While a short story or novel may use pages to build a scene, poetry strives to create vivid imagery with only a minimum of language, achieved by any number of ingenious methods. The styles of poetry are as myriad as the number of poets themselves. For example, some poets are reasonably straightforward about their subject. But, others teasingly offer only brief glimpses of profundity while demurely concealing their velvet message. Still others use symbolism and metaphor to obscure the message with an equivocal haze. Although any subject can be treated in a variety of poetic styles, every technique endeavors to push the reader toward a climactic epiphany.

Sharon Olds's "Sex without Love," for instance, is an example of literal poetry that purports to be about the same subject as the symbolic "she being Brand" of e. e. cummings. These verses both extol the joys of sex, but each uses widely varied means to achieve their ends. Although cummings's work is ostensibly about a new car, it actually details a youthful sexual romp, perhaps taking place in the back seat of a car (cummings 1-38). Olds's poem, on the other hand, is more open and obvious about its subject, even incorporating it into the title so that its meaning is unmistakable (Olds 1-24). While these two poems are about the same subject, their poetic techniques are of a decidedly contrasting nature.

The style and tone of these two works contrast. Cummings uses a light and almost comedic tone to accent his already bizarre style of poetry. This forces the reader to look beyond the words themselves in their given form and dig for a more abstruse meaning. Moreover, cummings's use of extended metaphor creates an ambiguous framework, showing how one scene or setting can elicit a message entirely apart from its interpretation. When the car is viewed as being symbolic of a women, all the poem's descriptive language consequently takes on sexual connotations. Like "she being Brand," many poems draw their power from the vagary of double meanings. Conversely, some poems find strength in a decidedly singular approach.

Olds's "Sex without Love" presents itself with a serious tone and a literal style, utilizing metaphor to impart its message. The words display their meaning with an open directness that is designed to allure the reader. The poem begins by asking how a person can have sex without love, "How do they do it, the ones who make love / without love?" (Olds 1-2), seemingly presenting a moralistic admonishment on promiscuity. However, this message becomes diluted as the reader reaches the mid-section of the poem in which the physicality of sex seems to be celebrated but asks how lovers can "come to the / still waters" (Olds 9-10). The movement continues as the narrator's metaphor compares sex to exercise, a solitary pursuit: the lover knows "they are alone / with the road surface" (Olds 18-19), and the partner is "just factors" (Olds 21), like cold and wind. Then, by the end, the "single body alone in the universe" (Olds 23) is brandished by the lover as the center of importance, but still ironically "alone."

Both Olds's and cummings's verses use a traditional technique, the metaphor, to reach the climax of the poem. However, cummings's extended metaphor delves into some curious avenues with its unusual use of a car as metaphor for a woman and a ride in the car as a metaphor for sexual activity. Cummings's first lines, "She being Brand / -new;and you / know consequently a / little stiff" (1-4), begin the extended metaphor. He continues the metaphor as the driver continues the trip, turning the "corner of Divinity / avenue" (21), and finishing as the trip ends with the car "tremB / -ling / to a:dead. / stand- / ;Still)" (34-38). In the end, both methods, simple and extended metaphors, achieve their desired goal, but the degree of satisfaction depends on individual tastes.

Although the traditional style of poetry may be the most socially accessible, it does not sate the appetite of all who indulge. Some hunger for darker and more bizarre poetic practices. While mainstream society continues to prefer a more missionary approach, double meanings and unusual wording hold an undeniable allure for a certain segment. This extreme style is not for the faint at heart. Poetry virgins would be well advised to begin their experimentation with a subject that is easy to grasp and has limited moral characteristics. Once this conquest is made, the reader can move on to a more intimate affair with an enjoyable subject. But the intense satisfaction that poetry offers can only be fully experienced when the reader becomes completely immersed in the subject. As one moves beyond the surface, into deeper areas, the readings should slowly build and build toward cummings. One should always save the best for last.

Works Cited

Cummings, e. e. "she being Brand." *The Compact Bedford Introduction to Literature.* 4th ed. Ed. Michael Meyer. Boston: Bedford, 1997. 484-85. Print.

Olds, Sharon. "Sex Without Love." *The Compact Bedford Introduction to Literature.* 4th ed. Ed. Michael Meyer. Boston: Bedford, 1997. 484-85. Print.

GLOSSARY: LITERARY TERMS

In the following glossary, examples appear in parentheses. Questions to help you determine the function of the term in a specific literary work appear in brackets.

alliteration: repetition of consonants, especially at the beginning of words or of stressed syllables. (Example: The tiny tot told a tall tale.)

allusion: a reference to something outside the work itself—to the Bible, to another literary work, to an event, to a common myth, etc. (Example: He strove as Samson to overcome his foes.)

analysis: the discovery of a work, determining what the parts of a work are, what purposes the parts serve, or how a specific aspect of the work functions in relation to the work as a whole.

anomaly: a deviation from the expected. (Example: Using "shroud" in a poem about birth is anomalous.)

assonance: repetition of identical or related vowel sounds, especially in stressed syllables. The word sound, not the spelling, is pertinent. (Example: How now brown cow?)

cacophony: use of harsh and unmusical sounds, discordancy. (Example: The jangled monkey jerked.)

characterization: the representation of a person or being.
[Who are the characters? What are their characteristics: mental, physical, behavioral, verbal? How do they see themselves? How do others see them? How do they react to others? How do others react to them? How do they think or reveal thought? Are they fully developed (*round*) or stereotyped (*flat*)?]

climax: the turning point of the plot, the outcome of the struggle. [When does it occur and what does it reveal? Is there an *epiphany*?]

conflict: the opposition of forces in the fiction. [Who is the main character (*protagonist*)? Who is the character who opposes the protagonist (*antagonist*)? Are the forces in opposition just characters, or do they represent larger ideas? What is the type of conflict: *person against person, person against society, person against god or fate, person against nature, person against self* (internal conflict)?]

consonance: repetition of consonant pattern, with changes in intervening vowels. (Example: A diller, a dollar, a duller scholar.)

criticism: determination of artistic quality and value of a work.

dénouement: the falling of the action after the climax of the fiction; the "untying of the knot" in which unsolved complications are resolved.

epiphany: moment at which a character perceives truth about self or others. [When does it occur? What truth is perceived?]

essay: work of nonfiction, usually meant to be read in one sitting.

euphony: a pleasant, melodious effect. (Example: "The tolling and the rolling of the bells." —Poe)

explication: explaining the work, line by line or paragraph by paragraph, etc., in words other than the original. (Example: The line by Dylan Thomas says, "Twenty-four years remind the tears of my eyes," and you, the reader, explicate the line by saying, "The speaker is twenty-four sad years old.")

fiction: literary work portraying imaginary events and characters. [What is the name of the work? Who is the author? When was it written?]

first person central: See *point of view.*

first person observer: See *point of view.*

first person secondary: See *point of view.*

flashback: a technique by which past events are told by the narrator as though the events were happening in the present. [When does the flashback begin? When does it end? What function does it serve in the work? Why is a flashback used instead of straight narration of events of the past?]

hyperbole: extravagant exaggeration, used either for serious or comic effect. (Example: He ate enough breakfast to feed an elephant.)

image: a sensory experience in words. [What are the overriding images? What senses do they involve?]

initiation:	a type of story in which a person moves from one stage of life development to another. [At what stage in life does the character begin? At what stage in life does the character end? What causes the character to change or grow? Is the initiation actualized or a failure?]
interpretation:	analysis which involves discerning what the work is about. [Possible interpretations include *literal, biographical, historical, sociological, psychological,* and *religious.* How do the symbols in the work function in each interpretation?]
metaphor:	a word which in ordinary use signifies one kind of thing, quality, or action that is applied to another without express indication of the relationship between them. (Examples: His name is mud. Her brother is a pain in the neck. Life is a song.)
meter:	rhythm pattern in poetry. [What kind of meter exists in the poem? Each rhythm unit, which consists of accented and unaccented syllables, is called a *foot,* which is the poetic equivalent to a measure of music. The standard feet are iambic (unaccented, then accented syllable, as – /), trochaic (/ –), anapestic (– – /), dactylic (/ – –), spondaic (/ /), and pyrrhic (– –). A one-foot line is called monometer, two feet is dimeter, three trimeter, four tetrameter, five pentameter, six hexameter, seven heptameter, etc.]
onomatopoeia:	use of words whose sounds seem to resemble the sounds they describe. (Examples: hiss, buzz, rustle, bang.)
oxymoron:	a paradoxical statement combining two terms that, in ordinary usage, are contraries. (Examples: bitter joy, pleasing pain)
paradox:	a statement that seems absurd and self-contradictory but that turns out to have a tenable and coherent meaning. (Examples: "He who is last will be first." "He who would save his life must lose it." —Bible)
personification:	a figure of speech in which either an inanimate object or an abstract concept is described as being endowed with human attributes, powers, or feelings. (Example: Justice is blind.)
plot:	action; what happens, the sequence of events. [Is the action told in perfect, chronological order? Is it told in *flashbacks?* Is it told in the present or past tense?]
point of view:	the position from which the fiction is told by the narrator. [Is it told in first person (I or we)? If so, is the narrator a major character (*first per-*

son central) or a minor character (*first person secondary*) character? Or does the narrator just tell what he or she sees (*first person observer*)? Is the story told in the third person (he or they)? If so, does the narrator seem to know *everything* (*third person omniscient*) or just certain character's thoughts (*third person limited*) or only the actions taking place, almost as a movie camera functions (*third person objective*)? How does the point of view color the story? Is the narrator reliable?]

rhyme (also *rime*): similar or identical sounds in accented syllables. [What is the rhyme scheme of the poem? Rhyme schemes are determined by putting a letter at the end of each line of the poem, the same letter for rhyming words, and are designated by those letters, as aabba or abcabc, etc. Rhyme may be end rhymes, as discussed previously, or internal rhyme, rhyme that occurs within a line of poetry, as "In mist or *cloud*, on mast or *shroud*" —Coleridge, "The Ancient Mariner"]

setting: the environment of the fiction, its location in time and space. [When did the story take place? Where did it take place?]

simile: a comparison between two essentially different items, expressly indicated by the terms *like* or *as*. (Example: A pretty girl is like a lovely tune.)

style: the use of language in the fiction to achieve desired effect. [What kinds of words, phrases, sentences, and paragraphs does the author use?]

symbol: something concrete in the work that suggests something abstract outside the work or recalls something else concrete in the work; an item in the work meaning more than its physical entity. [What could be the symbols in the work? What do they mean?]

theme: central or dominating idea of the work. [What does the work mean? What is it trying to teach or reveal? *Note:* Specific themes are always stated in a clause or a sentence. For example, a writer might make this statement: One theme of *Much Ado about Nothing* is that truth will prevail.]

third person limited: See *point of view*.

third person objective: See *point of view*.

third person omniscient: See *point of view*.

tone: the attitude of the writer to the subject. [Is the story or poem serious, comic, tragic, ironic, etc.?]

BUSINESS WRITING

Job Interviews

Sooner or later, you will face a job interview. An interview is the formal name for the exchange of information and impressions between you and a potential employer. So an interview is not simple conversation. It is serious business. It is not, however, the most difficult thing you will face in life, and you should not feel that it is. Preparation is the key to feeling confident (or, at least, not feeling petrified). For additional guidance and information, see an instructor in the business department or go to a Career Planning counselor. Following is a short list of interview tips:

1. Find out the time and place of the interview. Go alone.

2. Find out about the company. Some of the things you might need to know are the name and address, field or industry, kinds of clients or customers, location(s), growth and prospects.

3. Be on time for the interview.

4. Dress properly, neatly, and cleanly. Do some research, if possible, to determine the type of dress favored by those employed by the company and dress accordingly. Otherwise, wear subdued or neutral colors (navy blue, tan, gray, black) in business-type apparel. Look like you could start immediately. Never wear jeans, shorts, T-shirts, athletic shoes or other athletic gear, or sandals.

5. Greet the interviewer, preferably by name, as you enter the office.

6. Be enthusiastic. Talk positively and concisely.

7. Be poised. Be confident (but not arrogant). Be direct, not evasive. Maintain eye contact with the interviewer. Avoid irritating mannerisms. Do not smoke or chew gum.

8. Have some goals, preferably that do not include being a millionaire by the time you are twenty-five. Have clearly defined objectives and career plans. Interviewers look for people with a purpose.

9. Be interested in the company. Show that you are willing to learn about the company, but avoid seeming to shop for the best deal.

10. Know your qualifications. Carrying a résumé and a transcript is a good idea. Know that you can do the job. Know also that you may have to start at the bottom and work up: conceit, arrogance, and unrealistic expectations cause an interviewer to look elsewhere.

11. Do not stay too long. Once the interviewer has indicated the interview is over, leave quietly, courteously, and quickly.

12. Immediately after an interview, send a short, typewritten letter, thanking the interviewer for the opportunity and experience of the interview. This brings your name to the interviewer's mind and reinforces the effect of the interview.

Business Letters

Sometimes you need to write a business letter for one reason or another. No matter what the reason, the basic format is the same. Whether you write to complain that you found a spider in your cracker or whether you write to inquire if the computer part you need is stocked by that company, a business letter follows the same basic format. Only the body of the letter—what you want to say—differs.

Remember that all of the things you learned about writing in English class (spelling, grammar, format, etc.) are just as important in writing a business letter. The only thing you have to represent you to that consumer complaint department or manager (or prospective employer or senator or city official, etc.) is what you have typed in your letter. Make it impressive by making it correct and accurate.

Also remember these things:

1. Get to the point fast.

2. Use formal English. Keep the language simple. Do not try to impress with long, difficult words.

3. Consider the reader. Treat him or her with courtesy and respect. Be concise. Be clear.

4. Keep it neat. Keep it correct.

Be sure to use an envelope of the correct size for the letter. Usually a business-sized envelope looks neater and more professional than an envelope of smaller size.

Also be sure to fold the letter or document neatly for insertion. Usually, the correct procedure is to fold the bottom of the letter (or document) up a scant one-third of its length and the top of the letter (or document) down, over the first fold, a scant one-third of its length.

One of the kinds of business letters you may be most interested in is the letter of inquiry about a job opening or possible position. This letter of inquiry is also called a job application letter. (See the job application letter example.)

Example (Business Letters: Block Format)

> Your Street Address
> Your City, State and ZIP Code
> Date
>
> Name of the person you are writing to
> Title of this person
> Company name
> Company address (include ZIP)
>
> Salutation: (Be sure to address a specific person if possible.)
>
> Body of letter
>
> (Use proper spacing—one line between the return address and the "to" address, one line between the "to" address and the salutation, one line between the salutation and the body, one line between the body and the close, four lines between the close and the typed signature block. If the letter is short, center the letter on the page.)
>
> Sincerely yours,
>
> (Sign the letter in this block.)
>
> Your name

The U.S. Postal Service recommends an envelope format that allows machine reading, using block letters and no punctuation.

Example (Business Envelope)

> JOE GRADUATE
> 1600 SUCCESS RD
> CLAREMORE OK 74017
>
>   MR HOWARD H DRUCK
>   PERSONNEL DIRECTOR
>   CALCUTEX INDUSTRIES INC
>   1800 FINANCIAL BLVD
>   SUCCESS CITY OK 72233

Example (Job Application Business Letter: Block Format)

1600 Success Rd.
Claremore, OK 74017
April 17, 20—

Mr. Howard H. Druck
Personnel Director
Calcutex Industries, Inc.
1800 Financial Blvd.
Success City, OK 72233

Dear Mr. Druck:

The *Tulsa Daily World* recently reported that Calcutex Industries is building a new data processing center just north of Tulsa. I would like to apply for a position as an entry-level programmer at the center.

I am a recent graduate of Rogers State University in Claremore with a Bachelor of Science degree in Information Technology. In addition to taking required courses, I have served as a computer consultant at the college's computer center, where I helped train novice computer users. Since I understand Calcutex Industries produces both inhouse and customer documentation, my technical writing skills (as described in the enclosed résumé) may be particularly useful.

I will be happy to furnish any additional information you may need. I will contact your office Wednesday, April 24, 20—, to arrange for an interview. Please feel free to contact me (AC 918 555-1200) if there is a convenient time prior to that date.

Sincerely yours,

Joe Graduate

Joe Graduate

ENCL: résumé

RÉSUMÉS

With the job application letter, enclose a résumé. To begin compiling a résumé, take a self-inventory. Find the facts: gather information about education, interests, professional memberships, civic activities, volunteer activities, employment—include title(s), dates, company names, complete company addresses, and responsibilities. Decide what your three most notable attributes are. Are you loyal, dependable, conscientious, reliable, energetic, intelligent, trainable, and/or adaptable? Then write what you want from a career in less than twenty-five words. For example, you might want to "secure a position as office assistant with management possibilities."

The effective résumé reflects favorably on you and stimulates interest in you because it draws attention to your special abilities and reflects your qualifications. It attracts the eye with a professional appearance and is concise enough to be read quickly. It is completely accurate in spelling and grammar.

The effective résumé does *not* do any of the following:
- does not include information that works against you
- does not list every job you have had if the marginal jobs are not relevant
- does not include hobbies unless they are directly related
- does not include salary history
- does not include references
- does not include lies

The effective résumé uses effective words. Use positive words, words that show action. Use words such as *trained, coordinated, saved, supervised, demonstrated, led, innovated, conducted, installed, produced, initiated,* etc.

The effective résumé is tailored to the job you want to get. Do not slavishly follow a format if it is not appropriate to you or to the position you are seeking. The effective résumé sells you—in the best way possible. It may emphasize education, or perhaps experience, or maybe skills, etc. No matter what is emphasized, the purpose is the same: to show you at your best, to get you the job.

Example (Résumés)

GREGORY D. ABLEMAN
7809 Potter St.
Altmore, OK 77999
(918) 555-6548

JOB OBJECTIVE

Secure a position as automotive company representative and diagnostician to dealerships. Willing and eager to travel.

EDUCATION

B. A. in Liberal Arts
Rogers State University
May 20–

EMPLOYMENT HISTORY

Management	Service Manager: Managed the service department of an area Olds/Buick/GMC dealer. Supervised mechanics. Scheduled. Initiated policies, dealt with customers. Trained underqualified new employees. Improved relations with General Motors Corp. in warranty work. Fegs Motor Co., Altmore, OK 1/99–8/03
	Self-Employed. Ableman Auto, Altmore, OK 8/03-Present
Technical	MMM Transmission and Motor Co., Tryn, OK 9/92-1/99
	Sears Automotive Center, Yarkan, AK 5/92-8/92
	Hull Oldsmobile and Fiat, San Diego, CA 2/92-8/92
Sales	Self-employed. Engine part sales, Gregory, OK 1/90-1/92

OTHER TRAINING

Diesel Mechanics Certificate   Oklahoma State Tech

REFERENCES FURNISHED ON REQUEST

GREGORY D. ABLEMAN
7809 Potter St.
Altmore, OK 77999
(918) 555-6548

JOB OBJECTIVE   Secure a position as general manager in automotive dealership with several lines of automobiles.

EDUCATION   B. A. in Liberal Arts   Diesel Mechanics
             Rogers State University   Certificate
             May 20–   Oklahoma State Tech 1990

EMPLOYMENT

    MANAGEMENT:

    Self-Employed: Ableman Auto, Altmore, OK. Diagnose/repair all makes. 8/03-Present

    Service Manager: Managed the service department of an area Olds/Buick/GMC dealer. Dealt directly with customers. Scheduled jobs, trained and managed personnel. Initiated policies. Fegs Motor Company, Altmore, OK 1/99-8/03

    TECHNICAL:

    MMM Transmission and Motor Co., Tryn, OK. Mechanic/Assistant: Repaired and rebuilt transmissions. Handled office, customers, money for owner in his absence. 9/92-1/99

    Sears Automotive Center, Yarkan, AK. Mechanic: General and air conditioner repair. 2/92-8/92

    Hull Oldsmobile/Fiat, San Diego, CA. Mechanic: Repair, trouble shooting, diagnosis. 1/90-1/92

    SALES:

    Self-employed: Engine part sales, Gregory, OK. Sold, ordered, recorded, delivered products. 1/90-5/92

REFERENCES FURNISHED ON REQUEST

Now that you have the job, you must write to accept it. Please note that in an acceptance letter it is important to state the job title and salary you are accepting. Specify the date on which you will report to work, and do not forget to state your pleasure at joining the company.

Example (Letter of Acceptance: Block Format)

1600 Success Road
Claremore, OK 74017
April 30, 20–

Mr. Howard H. Druck
Personnel Director
Calcutex Industries, Inc.
1800 Financial Blvd.
Success City, OK 72233

Dear Mr. Druck:

I am pleased to accept your offer of a position as a trainee in the Programming Department at a salary of $1200.00 per month.

Since finals end on May 8, I plan to leave Claremore on Tuesday, May 12. I should be able to locate suitable living accommodations within a few days and be ready to report for work on the following Monday, May 18. Please let me know if this date is satisfactory to you. I may be reached at (918) 555-7890 for the next few weeks.

I look forward to a rewarding future with Calcutex.

Sincerely,

Joe Graduate

Joe Graduate

You may be called upon to write a letter of recommendation. What to say (and how to say it) often poses a real problem.

Example (Letter of Recommendation: Block Format)

2001 Success Road
Claremore, OK 74017
April 20, 20–

Mr. Howard H. Druck
Personnel Director
Calcutex Industries, Inc.
1800 Financial Blvd.
Success City, OK 72233

Dear Mr. Druck:

As her employer and former professor, I am happy to have the opportunity to recommend Susan Scholar to you. I have known Ms. Scholar for the last two years, first as a student in two of my classes and, for the last year, as a work-study assistant.

I have found Susan to be an excellent student, with a 3.95 grade point average. On the basis of her GPA and her pleasant and responsible attitude, Susan was offered and assumed unusual responsibility in the Composition Writing Lab. She has kept accurate and complete reports concerning students working in the lab. Her reports are well-written, meeting my requirements and more. She is courteous, helpful, pleasant, dependable, and very conscientious.

I strongly recommend Susan for her ability to work independently, to write clearly, and to organize her time efficiently. Please let me know if I can be of any further service.

Sincerely yours,

Ella Efficient

Ella Efficient
Professor of English

EE: jp

MEMORANDA

Memoranda, or memos, are useful in interoffice communications. Generally. The rules for memos are the same as those for letters. Keep it short. Make it clear. Use correct mechanics—grammar, punctuation, spelling, etc.

Memo form is very simple. The heading consists of four categories: to, from, subject, and date. After the body of the memo, which contains the information to be transmitted, there may appear a typist's notation, such as EH/dm. This notation means the memo was written by Evelyn Horton and typed by Dan Martin. The next section (headed Dist.) is the distribution section and lists those people who receive a copy of the memo in addition to the writer and the person to whom the memo is written.

Example (Memorandum)

TO: Dr. John North

FROM: Dr. Evelyn Horton

DATE: Aug. 15, 20–

SUBJECT: Slides for Aug. 25 Meeting

The plans for the Aug. 25, 20–, meeting are completed. Your department is in charge of furnishing the 50 slides showing distinctions between species of gram-negative and gram-positive bacteria. Slides should be labeled by number and accompanied by a list with corresponding numbers and description of those slides.

If you could have those to the presenter, Dr. H. Cummings, or me by Aug. 20, it would facilitate practice of the presentation. I would appreciate your attendance at practice on Aug. 24 at 4:00 p.m. in the Assembly Room. We need your comments on how the presentation can be improved.

Please let me know how you want your acknowledgment to appear on the program. The program will be useful to the participants, and they will all appreciate knowing who helped make this such a success.

EH/dm

Dist: Dr. H. Whitebird
Dr. G. Adams
Mr. N. Carracolough

SCIENCE FORMATS

A class in one of the sciences usually involves a laboratory, and that means laboratory reports. No, writing a lab report is not hard. Simply follow the instructions for the demonstration or the experiment, collect the data, and write up the results that you have found, using the report form required by the class. One suggested form follows.

EXAMPLE:

LABORATORY REPORT

NAME_____   PARTNER'S NAME_____

EXPERIMENT TITLE_____   DATE_____

PURPOSE: State what you are trying to do, find, verify, examine, measure, etc.

METHOD: a. Sketch the apparatus or circuit diagram.
b. Briefly describe what you did.

DATA: Record your observations and measurements (format may vary depending on data collected).

CALCULATIONS: Show all mathematical computations necessary to obtain your results.

GRAPHS: All graphs will be plotted on separate sheets of graph paper.

CONCLUSION: Make a statement, similar to the purpose, of what you found. References to calculations and graphs are appropriate here.

SOURCES OF ERROR: List measuring devices and techniques used to get your data that would cause the measurements to be less than 100% accurate.
Also include calculations of percent error and/or difference.

GRAPHS

Many times in a science lab you are required to make a graph as part of the demonstration of the collection of the data. Graphs are not complicated. Remember that you want the scale of the graph to be the largest possible that fits the graph paper and that everything should be clearly and completely labeled.

Example (Graph Form)

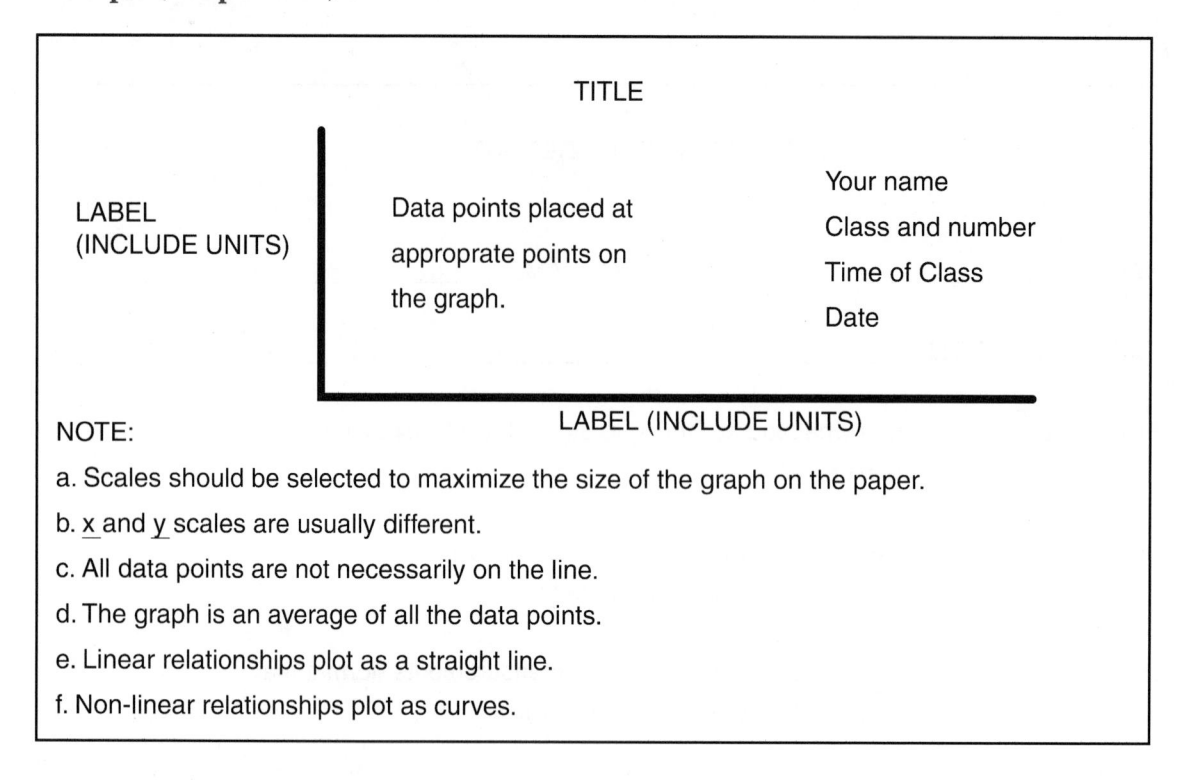

```
                            TITLE

                                              Your name
    LABEL        Data points placed at        Class and number
(INCLUDE UNITS)  appropriate points on        Time of Class
                 the graph.                   Date


                          LABEL (INCLUDE UNITS)
```

NOTE:

a. Scales should be selected to maximize the size of the graph on the paper.

b. x and y scales are usually different.

c. All data points are not necessarily on the line.

d. The graph is an average of all the data points.

e. Linear relationships plot as a straight line.

f. Non-linear relationships plot as curves.

Example (Graph)

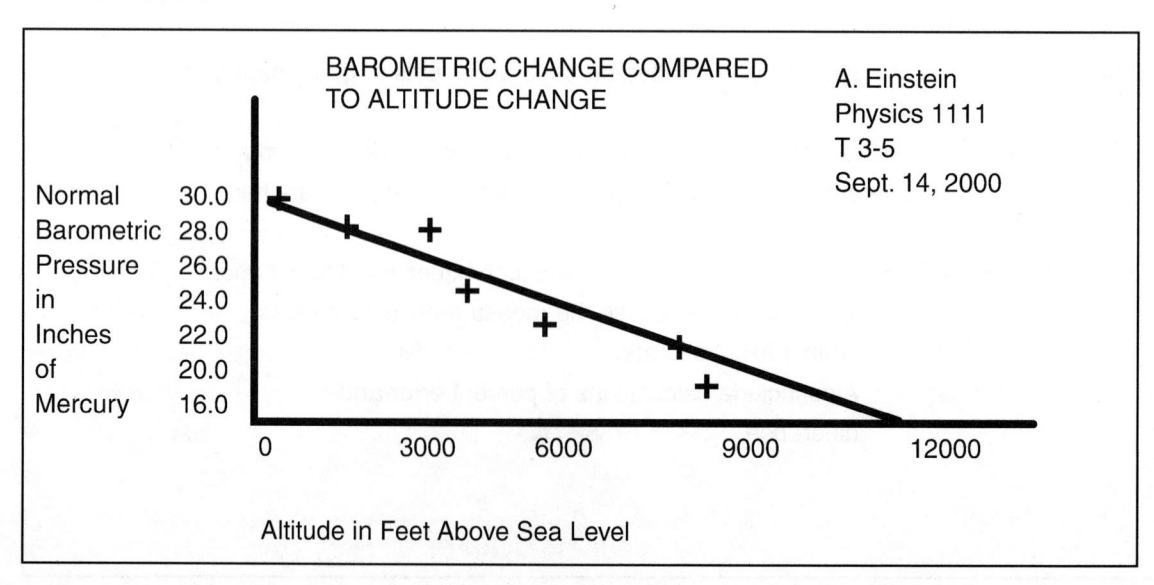

```
                  BAROMETRIC CHANGE COMPARED      A. Einstein
                      TO ALTITUDE CHANGE          Physics 1111
                                                  T 3-5
                                                  Sept. 14, 2000
Normal      30.0
Barometric  28.0
Pressure    26.0
in          24.0
Inches      22.0
of          20.0
Mercury     16.0
                 0      3000    6000    9000    12000

            Altitude in Feet Above Sea Level
```

LIBRARY DISCOVERY

A library may look like an imposing edifice on the outside (and, to some, it looks imposing on the inside, too), but, in fact, a library is a treasure chest, a cornucopia of intellectual delights. And you do not have to be an "intellectual" to use one. The library is available to all—with only a few skills needed to open the treasure chest and taste the fruits in the cornucopia.

The first skill needed is the courage to open the door. Once you have passed that point, everything else is easier. Look around and investigate the landscape. How is the library arranged? What furniture is where? Where are the fattest books? Where do the newspapers rustle and the magazines crackle? Where do the globes spin? Where do the microfilm and microfiche machines fill the air with their distinctive acrid odor? Where do the computer stations connect to the electronic world?

After you become familiar with the library's physical plant, investigate the resources. A casual glance shows you that the library has many books. How do you, overwhelmed by the sheer volume of volumes, choose which book to pick off the shelf? You can, of course, just browse around and pick up books at random until you find one that interests you. But this is probably most effective when you just want to read for pleasure. And, even then, it is most effective when you want to read fiction for pleasure. What if you want to find a book on a specific subject, or with a particular title, or by a certain author? Go to the card catalog!

Card Catalog

Some libraries have card catalogs that are made up of cards. Some libraries have computer or online catalogues. In this case, the works available in book form in the library appear on a computer screen. Either online or in print, books are catalogued by author, title, and subject. No matter which of the three you know, you can find information about a book and discover the other information you need to locate the book.

Remember, when looking up the title, that the title is alphabetized by the first word of the title that is not *a*, *an*, or *the* (unless the article is an integral part of the title). After you find a listing for a book, you have to understand how to find the book. You must understand the call number based on the Dewey Decimal System number or the Library of Congress Number.

One way to catalog books is the Library of Congress system, which classifies all books, fiction and nonfiction. Each book is assigned a letter corresponding to a subject category—like *P* for *Language and Literature*. Subject categories can be subdivided by adding another letter. Then each book receives an individual number. A book of 19th-century American literature might have the Library of Congress call number *PS 3319*. To find the books, look along the shelves (also called stacks) to find the correct area for the call number for which you are looking. This is not difficult, because the books are shelved in alphabetic and numerical order.

Another way to catalog books is by the Dewey Decimal system, a ten-category system based on subject. Novels and short stories are labeled fiction and found in a separate, alphabetized section. The Dewey Decimal categories are the following:

000–099	Generalities: Facts and Information, including encyclopedias, bibliographies, periodicals, facts, world records, journalism, handbooks, etc.
100–199	Philosophy and Psychology, including philosophy, psychology, conduct, supernatural, etc.
200–299	Religion, including religion, mythology, theology, etc.
300–399	Social Sciences, including sociology, political science, law, economics, occupations, communications, education, etc.
400–499	Language, including language (including foreign language) study, dictionaries, grammar, writing, etc.
500–599	Natural Sciences and Mathematics, or Pure Science, including mathematics, astronomy, physics, chemistry, earth and life sciences, botany, zoology, etc.
600–699	Technology (Applied Sciences), including engineering, home economics, medicine, agriculture, aviation, invention, manufacturing, building, etc.
700–799	The Arts, including architecture, art, photography, music, recreational and performing arts, sports, etc.
800–899	Literature and Rhetoric, including poems, short stories, plays, literature of the United States and the world (as well as untranslated literature of other languages), etc. Does not include novels or short stories, which are found on the fiction shelves.
900–999	Geography and History, including geography, history, biography, travel, etc.

Each category is further divided. Science, for example, has the following categories:
500–509 General Science,
510–519 Mathematics,
520–529 Astronomy,
530–539 Physics, etc.

And then these categories are subdivided:
511 Arithmetic,
512 Algebra,
513 Geometry,
514 Trigonometry, etc.

The categories are then further divided into subcategories shown by numbers after the decimal point. A letter at the end of the number or on the second line of the number designates the first letter of the last name of the author. This combination of numbers is the Dewey Decimal system call number.

Example (Finding a Book Source on a Topic)

- **Dewey Decimal System**

A book titled *Technology and the Changing Family* is about family and is catalogued in the Dewey Decimal system in the Social Science category. The author's name is Ogburn. The book has the number 301.42 as the first line of the Dewey Decimal system call number and OG2 as the second.

A book titled *Open Marriage* by O'Neill is also on the subject of family and is catalogued in the Social Science category. The Dewey Decimal System call number is 301.42 on the first line and ON2 on the second.

A book on television and feminism is edited by Rory Dicker and Alison Piepmeier and titled *Catching a Wave: Reclaiming Feminism for the 21st Century*. The Dewey Decimal system call number is 305.42 C284.

- **Library of Congress System:**

A book on television and morality is written by Gregory Stevenson and titled *Televised Morality: The Case of Buffy the Vampire Slayer*. The Library of Congress call number is PN1992.77.B84 S74 2003.

A book on television and feminism is edited by Rory Dicker and Alison Piepmeier and titled *Catching a Wave: Reclaiming Feminism for the 21st Century*. The Library of Congress call number is HQ1426.C284 2003.

- **All Systems:**

To find the books, look along the shelves (also called stacks) to find the correct area for the call number for which you are looking. This is not difficult because the books are shelved in numerical order.

What if you cannot find what you want in the card catalog? If it is simply a matter of not finding the exact subject heading for which you are looking, perhaps you can choose to look under another word that is close in meaning to the one with which you started. Or you may have to go to a broader category.

Example (Finding a Book Source on a Topic)

- If you have been looking for information on the Iditarod Dog Sled Race and you know it takes place on the Iditarod Trail in Alaska, you would probably start looking for all of the easy choices, such as *Iditarod* and *dog sled*, and you may even go to *racing* and *Alaska*. Under *racing*, there is nothing about racing dogs, and under *Alaska* is information on population and geography. What now? Go to a broader category. Look under *dogs*. Surely there is some relevant information you can use in one of the books about dogs. But that may not be enough.

- You may have to ask a librarian to use the *Library of Congress Subject Headings*. This index gives you lists of alternative choices of words under which to look.

If a source is just not available in the library, you may want to investigate interlibrary loan. Most libraries can obtain books and other material from other libraries. All you have to know is the name and author of what you want. But that is just what you were looking for! What now? To discover the names of authors and of works, find one of the specialized indexes. (See the section on special helps and articles from magazines and newspapers: indexes.) Or you might go to a computer database. (See the section on computer and Internet sources.)

ARTICLES FROM MAGAZINES AND NEWSPAPERS: INDEXES
Indexes

What if what you want to find is not a book? What if you want to find a current or topical item that has not had time to become the subject of a book? Or what if you just want the latest information? Go to the magazine and newspaper indexes, many of which are available in databases of various kinds and some of which are still available in hard copy in small libraries.

The library probably does not have all of the magazines indexed. Check the availability of magazines by looking for a list of periodicals or by asking a librarian. (Remember that the interlibrary loan service applies to periodicals as well as books.)

Some magazines are on the periodical display shelves. Earlier issues may be bound and found on the bound periodical shelves. Or they may be available on microfiche or on microfilm.

NON-PRINT

What if you are looking for nonprint sources? Many libraries have audio tapes, audio books, video cassettes, and compact discs listed alphabetically in the catalog.

Library Discovery

SPECIAL HELPS

Where do you look for special help? You may, of course, look in an encyclopedia for information. It is not customary, or advisable, to use a general encyclopedia in doing research at the college level. After all, the authors and editors of the encyclopedia are doing the research for you in that case. But it is both feasible and advisable to go to a general encyclopedia for easily accessible background information on a subject in which you are interested. Some special encyclopedias, encyclopedias on specific subject areas, are listed in the appropriate subject sections.

Never forget the wealth of information available in the simple dictionary (some of which are not so simple). The largest dictionaries are those called unabridged dictionaries, which are full dictionaries, not abridged (cut down) versions.

Some dictionaries are specialized dictionaries, such *as Funk and Wagnall's Standard Handbook of Synonyms, Antonyms, and Prepositions.*

Some general reference books, such as yearbooks and almanacs, can be helpful. These books are useful sources for factual information on dates, lists, events, etc. These include the *World Almanac and Book of Facts.*

If you need information on geography (which can include information on economics, agriculture, biology, ecology, political divisions, and weather, in addition to the locations of mountain ranges and rivers), look for an atlas. Atlases are divided into two general categories—historical and general.

General atlases give information on geographic data of the year published, such as economic, political, agricultural, and other data. Some general atlases include the *Oxford Atlas of the World, Times Atlas of the World,* and *Macmillan World Atlas.* Historical atlases show the world of different eras: for example, *The Times Atlas of the Second World War.*

Business indexes contain various kinds of information. One of these indexes may tell you company names, product lines, major personnel (by name and position), addresses, subsidiaries, parent companies, net worth, capital, etc. Try *Thomas Register* or *Standard and Poor's Register of Corporation Directors and Executives.*

If you need information on a person in history, literature, or politics, look in one of the biographical references, which include information about contemporary or past notables. These references include *Current Biography* (outstanding personalities of our time), *The Dictionary of American Biography* (distinguished Americans no longer living), *The Dictionary of National Biography* (distinguished English people no longer living), *The New Century Cyclopedia of Names* (more than 100,000 proper names, including persons, places, events, literary works and characters, works of art, mythological and legendary persons and places), *Webster's Biographical Dictionary* (biographies of famous people through the ages), *Who's Who* (distinguished living British and Commonwealth persons—includes parents, schooling, spouse, children, accomplishments, etc.), *Who Was Who* (distinguished dead British and Commonwealth persons), *Who's Who in America* (distinguished living Americans), *Dictionary of Scientific Biography, Notable Twentieth-Century Scientists, New Grove Dictionary of Music and Musicians,* and *Notable American Women 1607–1950.* Biographical references solely about authors are also available: *Contemporary Authors, European Authors 1000–1900* by Kunitz and

Colby, *World Authors* by Wakeman, *American Authors 1600–1900* by Kunitz and Haycraft, *British Authors Before 1800* by Kunitz and Haycraft, *American Writers* by Unger, *Twentieth-Century Authors* by Kunitz and Haycraft, *Dictionary of Literary Biography, Magill's Cyclopedia of World Authors*, and *Dictionary of American Biography*.

Other literary reference books include some specialized works: *Bartlett's Familiar Quotations* (lists of famous authors and their quotations; lists of quotations and their sources); *Granger's Index to Poetry* (lists of titles, authors, first lines of poems, titles of books containing poems); *Home Book of Quotations, Classical and Modern; Untermeyer's Modern British Poetry; Encyclopedia of Poetry and Poetics.*

Other specialized reference books include information from specific subject areas.

COMPUTER AND INTERNET SOURCES

What if you want even more information than you are finding? You might want to investigate some of the major databases and/or the Internet. Library computers are connected to the Internet; you can search an enormous volume of material for the subject in which you are interested. In addition to websites, libraries have access to electronic databases. Those databases have either article abstracts, full-text articles, or both. Some databases include unpublished material, doctoral dissertations, and conference presentations, in addition to journal articles. Databases can be a valuable source for anyone doing extensive research on a subject.

Databases contain information on business, general reference material, psychology, pharmacology, physiology, linguistics, law, social work, anthropology, health, astronomy, law, religion, history, psychology, humanities, current events, sociology, communications, general sciences, books, newspapers, education, conferences, and other topics too numerous to mention.

LIBRARIANS

Librarians know everything. Well, that is not quite true. Librarians can find out anything. And that is true. A librarian by training knows where to look to find odd, unusual, or specialized subjects. A librarian by nature is curious and tenacious. When you need help, ask a librarian!

> *When you need help, ask a librarian!*

MECHANICS

This large section is concerned with the technical aspects of writing, those picky "English things" like punctuation, grammar, and spelling that make papers easier to read and, thus, life easier to live.

USAGE

Choosing which words to use depends largely on the situation in which you find yourself. Some forms of usage are not appropriate when formal written or spoken English is required but may be acceptable at another time or place.

Formal English is that form of the language that is appropriate in all situations (except maybe a party with the Hell's Angels). Formal English follows certain usage conventions; that is, some ways to speak and write are acceptable and some are not. Formal English is usually required in college speaking and writing.

Colloquialisms are expressions acceptable in informal use only. An example of a colloquialism is referring to a father as "Pa."

Regionalisms are usages known only in certain areas. In Mississippi, people "carry" their grandmothers to the market instead of taking them. In Louisiana, people "make" groceries at Safeway instead of buying them. In Maine, people drink "tonic" instead of "pop," "soda," or "Coke."

Slang is a form of language used only among certain groups and is usually of short duration. Slang labels people as "in" or "out" of certain groups, depending on their use of the terms. Those who belonged to the drug culture of the 1950s talked knowledgeably and esoterically about "grass" (not Bermuda) so that eavesdroppers or casual overhearers would not be aware of the subject under discussion. Of course, slang quickly becomes outdated when "everyone" can use the terms and knows their meanings. Then slang changes. Outdated slang sounds very strange.

Non-standard or illiterate usages are below the standard for use by even minimally educated people. Saying "He done gone to the store; I seen him go" is non-standard.

Informal English is English used between friends or on occasions when it is not necessary to be especially formal. It is much like a sweat suit, which is fun and comfortable but would not be worn to a job interview.

Non-idiomatic English is English that is used improperly, not because it is incorrect by the rules of grammar but because English speakers do not use the language in that manner. A non-idiomatic expression would be to say that someone "went at" the store instead of "went to" because *at* is usually not used after the word *went*.

Archaic or obsolete words or phrases are no longer used but appeared in earlier writing and speaking. People no longer appear "betimes"; they now appear quickly.

Poetic usage is found in poetry or poetic prose. Using "o'er" instead of "over" is poetic.

Dialect is a continuing pattern (including pronunciation, grammar, and vocabulary) of speech or writing used in particular areas. It is related to regionalism but is not restricted to one or two words in a conversation. It is a pattern that is used overwhelmingly in the area or by the group.

Professional or occupational dialects include specialized terms, abbreviations, etc., applicable mainly to certain jobs or occupations.

SENTENCE STRUCTURE

Effective sentences reflect clear thinking. Clumsy or ill-structured sentences imply that the idea has not been clearly thought out. Thus, not only must you know what you think you want to say, but you must also decide how to say it so that the reader has a clear idea of what you mean.

Following are common errors.

1. A sentence fragment or incomplete sentence is a sentence that does not contain all the necessary parts (subject and verb) or that does not make complete sense when standing alone.

   EXAMPLE (incomplete sentence)
   I went to the store. Following the marvelous lesson on sentence structure in my English class.

   - The first part of this example, "I went to the store," is complete because it has a subject and a verb and it makes complete sense when read alone. The second part does not have a subject and a verb and it does not make sense when read without the preceding sentence.

   EXAMPLE (complete sentence)
   I went to the store following the marvelous lesson on sentence structure in my English class.

2. A run-on sentence merges two or more sentences together without proper terminal punctuation or beginning capitalization. A comma splice, which is a kind of run-on sentence, hangs two or more sentences together with a comma between them.

EXAMPLE (run-on sentence)
When we go to the zoo, we hope to see the baby elephant its mother died from a twisted intestine and the baby is orphaned.

EXAMPLE (comma splice)
The baby elephant is very small, it is not as big as a pony yet.

EXAMPLE (correct sentences)
When we go to the zoo, we hope to see the baby elephant. Its mother died from a twisted intestine, and the baby is orphaned.
The baby elephant is very small. It is not as big as a pony yet.

PARALLEL CONSTRUCTION

The use of parallel construction enhances writing because it lends clarity, elegance, and symmetry. Wonderful! So what is parallel construction?

Parallel construction is using words, phrases, or clauses in series in a similar fashion, both grammatically and logically. Parallelism, as parallel construction is also called, coordinates words, phrases, or statements in similar grammatical construction. This means paralleling noun with noun, verb with verb, phrase with phrase, and statement with statement.

Consider the following famous quotation by Julius Caesar: "I came; I saw; I conquered." Caesar uses three simple verbs, in parallel construction, to tell about the things he did. The parallel construction makes what he said memorable. Suppose he had said, "I came to Gaul. I saw all those barbarians sitting around on all that undefended land. So I decided to conquer them and did." In that case, people may have remembered what he did, but hardly what he said about it.

When you have two or more items in a list, a series, a contrast, a choice, a statement of equivalence, a formal definition, a statement of evaluation, or a comparison, you should put all of the items into the same grammatical form.

EXAMPLE (parallel construction):

- **List**
  "I have nothing to offer but blood, toil, tears, and sweat."   —Winston Churchill (four nouns)

- **Series**
  Let every nation know, whether it wishes us well or ill, that we shall pay any price, bear any burden, meet any hardship, support any friend, oppose any foe to assure the survival and success of liberty." —John F. Kennedy (five object-verb combinations)

- **Contrast**
  "On all these shores there are echoes of past and future: of the flow of time, obliterating yet containing all that has gone before." —Rachel Carson (two participles)

- **Series plus contrast**
  "Rather than love, than money, than fame, give me truth."
  —Henry D. Thoreau (four nouns)

- **Choice**
  "We must indeed all hang together, or most assuredly, we shall all hang separately."
  —Benjamin Franklin (two clauses)

- **Comparison**
  "A living dog is better than a dead lion."
  —Ecclesiastes 9:4 (two noun phrases)

Conjunctions play a part in the formation of parallel construction. Correlative conjunctions are defined as words or phrases used in pairs to join words, phrases, or clauses. Correlatives include *both/and, not only/but also, either/or, neither/nor*, and *whether/or*.

When using a pair of correlatives, be sure that the word or word group following the first member of the pair is parallel with the word or word group following the second.

EXAMPLE (parallel construction):

Janet Rostek not only got the leading role of Fanny Brice, but also played the part brilliantly.
Windsurfing is both exciting and dangerous.
Janie could not decide whether to start college right after high school or to get a job first.

AGREEMENT

Agreement of subject with verb and of pronoun with antecedent noun is a common problem.

The two general rules are
- Make every verb agree with its subject in both person and number.
- Make every pronoun agree with its noun antecedent in person and number.

The difficulty is to follow the rules. Following are the specifics that make it possible to follow those rules.

VERB/SUBJECT

1. When two or more subjects are joined by *or* or *nor*, the verb agrees with the nearer subject.

   EXAMPLE: Neither you nor (she) is going to go.

2. When two or more subjects are joined by *and*, use a plural verb unless the two subjects are considered a unit.

   EXAMPLE: (You and she) are going to go.
   BUT (Milk and cereal) is his favorite breakfast.

3. When a verb is separated from its subject, ignore the words of separation.

   EXAMPLE: (One) of the four boys is going to get selected.

4. A linking verb agrees with the subject, not the subject complement.

   EXAMPLE: The most interesting (item) is the bridles.
   AND (It) is miles to the next town.

5. Singular pronouns and collective nouns both take singular verbs unless the members of the collective noun group are acting or are considered as individuals or individual items.

   EXAMPLE: (Everyone) is trying for a scholarship.
   The (board of directors) has voted yes to the merger.
   (Four dollars) is all I have.
   BUT The (dollars) are on the table.
   The (board of directors) are arguing over the merger outcome.

6. Singular nouns that look plural still take a singular verb. Literary titles and words as words take singular verbs.

   EXAMPLE: (Mumps) is a disease for which there is now a vaccine.
   AND (*Christmas Stories*) is an edition of Dickens's short stories about Christmas.
   AND (Mass) is used with several meanings in different areas.

7. *There* is never a subject.

   EXAMPLE: There is one (way) to do this project.
   AND There are two (ways) to do this project.

8. Verbs after words like *who, which,* and *that* agree with the antecedent noun.

   EXAMPLE: He is one (person) who has the list.
   AND He is one of the (people) who have the list.

PRONOUN

1. A word such as *this, that, these,* and *those* agrees with the nouns it modifies.

   EXAMPLE: This sort of class is helpful.
   AND These sorts of classes are helpful.

2. Following the same logic as subject/verb rule 5, pronouns agree with the sense of the antecedent noun.

   EXAMPLE: The board of directors has made its vote.
   AND The board of directors have not finished their argument.

3. Keep pronouns in person agreement; do not shift to *you.*

   EXAMPLE: I like films when I get interested in the action.
   NOT I like films when you get interested in the action.

4. Singular pronouns agree with singular nouns, such as

   | person | woman | everybody | everyone | neither | either |
   | somebody | someone | anybody | man | one | each | anyone |

   EXAMPLE: The man has his own desk.
   AND Somebody has taken his pencil.

   When a singular antecedent may be either masculine or feminine, you may use the masculine pronoun because it has been considered to be neuter; however, it is not neuter politically, so the best alternative is to use both pronouns or change the entire sentence to plural to avoid using "sexist language."

   EXAMPLE: A person has his own desk.
   OR A person has his or her own desk.
   OR People have their own desks.

5. Using the same logic as verb/subject rules 1 and 2 above, for antecedent nouns joined by *and,* use a plural pronoun; for antecedent nouns joined by *or,* use a pronoun agreeing with the nearest antecedent noun.

EXAMPLE:	The cat and the dog are eating their food.
AND	The cat and the dogs are eating their food.
AND	George or the boys are bringing their car.
AND	The boys or George is bringing his car.

Capitalization

1. Capitalize the first word of every sentence, including a quoted sentence. If the quotation is interrupted, do not capitalize the second part unless it is also a complete quoted sentence.

EXAMPLE:	The boy wailed, "A dog has bitten me!"
AND	"A dog," the boy wailed, "has bitten me!"

   a. Do *not* capitalize the first word of an indirect quotation.

EXAMPLE:	The boy wailed that the dog had bitten him.

   b. Do *not* capitalize the first word of a fragmentary quotation.

   EXAMPLE: Although the Carpenter told the Oysters to go on home, they could not go because the Carpenter and the Walrus had "eaten every one."

   c. Do *not* capitalize the first word of a sentence in parentheses within another sentence.

EXAMPLE:	Alice (did you know her?) did not appreciate the story about the oysters.

2. Capitalize the first word of a line of poetry (unless, as in some modern poetry, the poet has not capitalized the first word of the line).

   EXAMPLE:
   "It seems a shame," the Walrus said,
       "To play them such a trick,
   After we've brought them out so far,
       And made them trot so quick!"
   The Carpenter said nothing but
       "The butter's spread too thick!"
           —Lewis Carroll, "The Walrus and the Carpenter"

3. Capitalize first word of phrases or words used as sentences.

EXAMPLE:	Not on your life.	Yes, of course.	Certainly.

4. Do not capitalize the first word of a formal question or statement following a colon unless the formal question or statement is quoted or unless the colon introduces a series of sentences.

> **EXAMPLE**: The problem is simple: we haven't the money.
> *AND* Because the Oysters were tired, the Walrus was sad: "The Carpenter said nothing. . . ."
> *AND* Discuss the following items: How do the Oysters travel? Who are the other characters? When does the meal take place? What is its accompaniment?

5. Capitalize the first word of numbered enumerations that form complete sentences and of phrasal lists and enumerations twhose items occupy separate lines. Do not capitalize phrasal lists or enumerations that are prepared as part of the text.

> **EXAMPLE**: Be sure to ask these questions: (1) When did the patient last eat? (2) What was eaten? (3) What quantity was ingested? (4) What ffect was first noticed?
> *AND* A short story has these elements:
> > Character
> > Setting
> > Plot
> > Point of view
> > Theme
>
> *AND* A short story has these elements: (1) character, (2) setting, (3) plot, (4) point of view, and (5) theme.

6. Capitalize the first word and the last word and all important words in a title.

> **EXAMPLE**: "The Walrus and the Carpenter"   *Alice in Wonderland*

7. Capitalize the first word of each item in a formal outline.

> **EXAMPLE**: I. Capitalization
> > A. First word of a sentence
> > B. First word of a title
> > C. Last word of a title

8. Capitalize the first word of a letter salutation and the first word of the complimentary close.

> **EXAMPLE**: Dear Mary,   Dear Sir: Love,   Sincerely,   Very unhappily,

9. Capitalize proper nouns and all words made from them. Do *not* capitalize common nouns.

   EXAMPLE: Mary woman Tulsa city David man May month
   Lion's Club club Great Dane dog Rogers State College college

   a. Capitalize abbreviations if the full form is capitalized.

   EXAMPLE: Dec. December   Capt. Captain

   b. Do *not* capitalize general terms referring to degrees. Capitalize names of academic degrees following a person's name. Capitalize abbreviations for degrees.

   EXAMPLE: Martin Shawn, Doctor of Divinity   Dr. James Fotinblach
   Julia Sheppard, M.S.W.   working for an associate's degree
   received an A.A. degree

   c. Do *not* capitalize names of academic disciplines unless they are part of course titles or are proper nouns.

   EXAMPLE: He did especially well in math and English.
   AND   That course is Humanities 1223, the first humanities course.

   d. Do *not* capitalize directions unless they refer to a specific section of the country.

   EXAMPLE: Reporters traveled south on I20 to cover primaries in the South.

   e. Do *not* capitalize words of family relationship unless they are used as part of a name.

   EXAMPLE: I call my grandfather on my father's side Grandfather Ames and my grandfather on my mother's side Grandpa.

   f. Capitalize a title or position only when it is used preceding a person's name.

   EXAMPLE: The president of the United States was President Reagan; the queen of England was Queen Elizabeth.

10. Capitalize words in a memorandum following a heading as if the words appeared in a title.
    EXAMPLE: SUBJECT: The Writing of Memos
    TO: All Memo Writers

NUMBERS

1. With certain exceptions, write as words numbers which can be written as one word Other numbers should be written as numerals. **Exceptions:** Dates, addresses (except for "one"), highway route numbers, etc., are written as numerals.

EXAMPLE:	She owns forty horses and 176 sheep.
AND	The farm is on U.S. 40 at Exit 11A, and the address is PO Box 1177, Clinton, OK, until May 11, 1999, when it will become One Bayshore Road, Arapaho, OK 77337.

2. Approximate or round numbers should be written out.

   EXAMPLE: Almost five thousand people attended the play.

3. Numbers that begin a sentence should be spelled out. (If the sentence looks odd or awkward with the number spelled out, restructure the sentence so that the number appears internally.)

EXAMPLE:	Four thousand ninety attended.
OR	The group numbered 4,090 people.

4. Hyphens are used in spelled-out numbers between *twenty-one* and *ninety-nine*.

5. Hyphens are used in written-out fractions used as modifiers.

   EXAMPLE: When he cut the slices, each child got one-eighth pie.

6. Numbers are not divided at the end of a line.

7. Roman numerals should appear as uppercase letters (except for the designation of a scene in a play) unless the original quoted source uses lowercase letters for the numerals.

   EXAMPLE: Richard has an ironic speech in Richard II, Act I, scene i, lines 139-141, according to critic Don DeLoon on page vii in the forward to his book *Shakespeare's Great Shakes*.

8. With some exceptions (year dates, check numbers, binary numbers, telephone numbers, etc.), whole numbers of five or more digits are punctuated with commas in groups of three, counting from the right. Punctuation of whole numbers of four digits is optional.

EXAMPLE:	A.D. 1255	Check No. 135667	line 8
	command 11011	population of 1,233,544,651	
OR	population of 1,333		
OR	population of 1333	10,876 cans of spaghetti sauce	(918) 555-1345

PUNCTUATION

In the past, writing was characterized by full and detailed punctuation. Today we realize that, just as a speaker who hems and haws and pauses too long is hard to understand, too much punctuation interferes with the flow of reading. You will have few punctuation problems if you use a mark of punctuation for only one of two reasons:

- Meaning demands it.
- Conventional usage requires it.

If a sentence is not clear, punctuation will not help it. If you find yourself struggling with the punctuation of a sentence, ask yourself if the problem is your arrangement of phrases or choice of words. The problem can often be eliminated by rephrasing the sentence.

END MARKS

1. A statement is followed by a period.

   EXAMPLE: A statement is followed by a period.

2. An abbreviation or initial is followed by a period.

   EXAMPLE: Mr. A. B. Cloe, born 1925 A.D., has entered college.

3. A question is followed by a question mark.

   EXAMPLE: What is a person like you doing in a place like this?

   a. Use the question mark after a direct question only. Do not use the question mark after a declarative sentence containing an indirect question.

   EXAMPLE: Did she enroll in the summer, fall, or spring?
   AND He asked if she went to school too.

   b. Orders and requests are often put in the form of a question, even when no real question is intended. Such a question may be followed by a question mark or a period.

EXAMPLE:	Will you please turn that report in now.
OR	Will you please turn that report in now?

   c. A question mark should be placed inside quotation marks when the quotation is a question. If the whole item is a question, the question mark should be placed outside the quotation marks.

EXAMPLE:	She asked, "Is that biology lab?"
AND	Did she ask, "Is that lab"?

4. An exclamation is followed by an exclamation mark.

EXAMPLE:	Of course I made an A on the exam!

   a. An interjection at the beginning of a sentence is almost always followed by a comma.

EXAMPLE:	Yes, I will get the scholarship!

   b. An exclamation mark should be placed inside quotation marks when the quotation itself is an exclamation. Otherwise, it should be placed outside the quotation marks.

EXAMPLE:	The murderer said, "I'm going to kill you!"
AND	That wonderful actor exclaimed, "Hands up"!

   c. Do not use an exclamation mark unless a statement is obviously emphatic.

EXAMPLE:	What a party!
NOT	The party was a little fun!

COMMAS

Next to end marks, the comma is the most frequently used mark of punctuation, grouping words that belong together and separating those that do not. It is also used in conventional ways that have little to do with meaning.

1. Use commas to separate items in a series. Under circumstances where the meaning of the phrase cannot be misunderstood, it is not necessary to put a comma before the last *and* in a series. However, it is best to include the comma prior to the last *and* in the series

EXAMPLE:	RSC offers programs in accounting, education, and business.

Mechanics

2. Use commas to separate two or more adjectives that modify the same item. **Hint:** If you can say *and* between the two adjectives, put in the comma.

    EXAMPLE: A course of study leading to an associate's degree will enable a studious, interested student to more easily achieve his lifetime goals.

3. Use a comma before *and, but, or, nor, for, yet, so* when they join independent clauses.

    EXAMPLE: We came to party, but we stayed to study.

4. Use a comma to set off nonessential clauses and nonessential participial phrases.

    EXAMPLE: The radio station, which is staffed by college students seeking broadcast experience, has become a vital part of the community experience.

5. Use a comma after certain introductory elements:

    a. Words such as *well, yes, no,* and *why* when they begin a sentence.

    EXAMPLE: Yes, you can get an excellent background for engineering and science courses at this university.

    b. An introductory participial phrase.

    EXAMPLE: Watching the viewers carefully, the art student was pleased that his first exhibit was such a success.

    c. A succession of introductory prepositional phrases.

    EXAMPLE: In the building at the edge of the campus, RSC houses the horse management facilities.

    d. An introductory adverbial clause.

    EXAMPLE: As the end of the play approached, the actors gave even better performances.

6. Use commas to set off expressions that interrupt the sentence:

    a. Appositives.

    EXAMPLE: The junior college, a community-based college offering the first two years of study, is the ideal place to begin college.

b. Words in direct address.

EXAMPLE: Gene, you need to see your advisor before enrolling.

c. Parenthetical expressions.

EXAMPLE: I believe, even though the course may not be required, that you need to take typing.

7. Use a comma in certain conventional situations:

   a. To separate items in dates and addresses.

   EXAMPLE: She was born in Guy, Oklahoma, on May 8, 1950, in the local hospital.

   b. After the salutation of a friendly letter and after the closing of any letter.

   EXAMPLE:

   > Dear Mom,
   >   Thank you for the money! Now I can buy a Valentine in the bookstore and eat dessert.
   >   Love,
   >   Jim

   c. After expressions that introduce direct quotations.

   EXAMPLE: Thoreau said, "Rescue the drowning and tie your shoestrings."
   AND   "Rescue the drowning," Thoreau said, "and tie your shoestrings."

8. Do not use unnecessary commas.

   EXAMPLE: Do, not, put, commas, just, anywhere.

Mechanics

COLONS

1. Use a colon to mean "note what follows:"

   a. Use a colon before a list of items, unless the list immediately follows a verb or preposition.

   EXAMPLE: RSC offers these options: Associate of Arts, Associate of Science, Certificate of Achievement, and Associate of Applied Science.
   NOT RSC offers: Associate of Arts, Associate of Science . . .
   NOT RSC has options in: Associate of Arts, Associate of . . .

   b. Use a colon before a long, formal statement or quotation except when the quotation immediately follows a verb or preposition.

   EXAMPLE: In "The Bear" Faulkner unites man, bear, and wilderness:
   > He had left the gun; of his own will and relinquishment he had accepted not a gambit, not a choice, but a condition in which not only the bear's heretofore inviolable anonymity but all the old rules and balances of hunter and hunted had been abrogated. (157)

   NOT Faulkner says:
   > He had left the gun; of his own . . .

   NOT In "The Bear" Faulkner unites man and wilderness in:
   > not a gambit, not a choice, but . . .

   c. Use a colon between independent clauses when the second clause explains or restates the idea of the first.

   EXAMPLE: A student makes a choice: he chooses to study or not to study.

2. Use a colon in certain conventional situations:

   a. Between the hour and the minute in clock time.

   EXAMPLE: It is 5:45 p.m.

   b. Between the chapter and verse numbers in referring to passages in the Bible.

   EXAMPLE: Read John 3:16 in the New Testament.

   c. After the salutation in a business letter.

   EXAMPLE: Dear Mr. James:
   > Your shipment dated Monday . . .

SEMICOLONS

The semicolon has often been described as a weak period or a strong comma; in other words, it is part period and part comma. The most common use of the semicolon is to indicate a close relationship between two independent clauses.

1. Use a semicolon between independent clauses not joined by *and, but, for, or, nor,* <u>or *yet*</u>.

    EXAMPLE: Work turned in on time receives full credit; work turned in late receives partial credit; work not turned in at all receives no credit.

2. Use a semicolon between independent clauses joined by the word or phrase *accordingly, also, besides, consequently, furthermore, hence, however, indeed, instead, moreover, nevertheless, otherwise, similarly, still, therefore, thus, for example, for instance, that is,* or *in fact*.

    EXAMPLE: I have taken only a few courses; nevertheless, I know that I will finish my degree.

3. A semicolon (rather than a comma) may be needed to separate independent clauses if there are commas within any of the clauses.

    EXAMPLE: The humanities classes, although required, seem to be favorites of the students; and students often comment on how much they have learned.

APOSTROPHES

1. To form the possessive of singular and plural nouns and indefinite pronouns, use an apostrophe.

    a. To form the possessive case of a singular noun, add an apostrophe and *s*.

    EXAMPLE: cat   cat's dish   car   car's bumper

    b. To form the possessive case of a plural noun ending in *s*, add only the apostrophe.

    EXAMPLE: horses   horses' manger   helpers   helpers' apron
    commanders   commanders' baton   heroes   heroes' tales

    c. Indefinite pronouns in the possessive case require an apostrophe and *s*.

    EXAMPLE: anybody   anybody's guess   somebody   somebody's book

d. In hyphenated words, names of organizations and business firms, and words showing joint possession, only the last word is possessive in form.

EXAMPLE: John and Mary   John and Mary's boat
              son-in-law   son-in-law's talent
              Rogers State College   Rogers State College's class

e. When two or more persons possess something individually, each of their names takes the possessive form.

EXAMPLE: John and Mary   John's and Mary's clothes
              Tom and Jerry   Tom's and Jerry's traps

f. The words *minute, hour, day, week, month, year*, etc., when used as possessive adjectives, require apostrophes. Words indicating amounts in cents or dollars, used as possessive adjectives, require apostrophes.

EXAMPLE: year   year's end   cent   cent's worth

g. Use the apostrophe and *s* to form the plurals of letters, numbers, and signs, and of words referred to as words.

EXAMPLE: one *l*   two *l*'s   one *   three *'s   one *3*   four *3*'s
              one *you* seven *you*'s

2. Personal pronouns in the possessive case do not require an apostrophe.

   EXAMPLE: her   her job   his   his class   its   its claws
                 their   their car

3. Use an apostrophe to show where letters have been omitted in a contraction or in dialect.

   EXAMPLE: can not   can't   you are   you're
                 "She'll be comin' 'round the mountain...."

HYPHENS

1. Use a hyphen to divide a word at the end of a line.

   EXAMPLE: Sheila has found it almost impossible to become a published author this year.

2. Use a hyphen with compound numbers from *twenty-one* to *ninety-nine* and with fractions used as adjectives.

   EXAMPLE: Only the fortyfirst draft was acceptable.

3. Use a hyphen with the prefixes *ex-, self-, all-*; with the suffix *-elect*; and with all prefixes before a proper name or proper adjective.

   EXAMPLE: Ex-President Jones is the president-elect of his bridge club; he will take office in mid-October.

4. Hyphenate a compound adjective when it precedes the word it modifies.

   EXAMPLE: That well-dressed woman swatted the best-known actor here with her umbrella.

5. Use a hyphen to prevent confusion or awkward constructions.

   EXAMPLE: semi-invalid   re-cover a floor   re-form a line
                  re-mark a paper

QUOTATION MARKS

1. Use quotation marks to enclose a direct quotation—a person's exact words.

   a. A direct quotation begins with a capital letter unless the quoted material is only a phrase.

   EXAMPLE: My grandmother used to say, "You children don't pay any more attention to me than to the wind ablowing."
   AND   Faulkner said Boon had "the heart of a horse."

   b. When a quoted sentence is divided into two parts by an interrupting expression such as *she said* or *I asked*, the second part begins with a small letter unless the second part begins another complete sentence.

   EXAMPLE: "Boon was four inches over six feet," William Faulkner wrote, "and he had the mind of a child and the heart of a horse and the ugliest face I ever saw."

Mechanics

    c. A direct quotation is set off from the rest of the sentence by commas or by a question mark or an exclamation mark unless the quoted material is only a phrase.

EXAMPLE: She asked, "Have you already fulfilled the General Education requirements?"
AND She felt she was looking "through a glass darkly."

    d. When used with quotation marks, other marks of punctuation are placed according to the following rules:

        (1) Commas and periods are always placed inside the closing quotation marks.

EXAMPLE: "I want to take biology," he said, "because it will be useful to me in understanding both myself and my ecology."

        (2) Semicolons and colons are always placed outside the closing quotation marks.

EXAMPLE: She said, "Yes, I'll go to the Scholar's Dance with you"; however, that was before she caught the flu.
AND Some companies understand "rush order": they begin order processing upon receiving the invoice.

        (3) Question marks and exclamation marks are placed inside the closing quotation marks if they belong with the quotation; otherwise they are placed outside.

EXAMPLE: She asked, "Did he go?"
AND Did she ask, "Did he go"?

    e. When a quoted passage consists of more than one paragraph, place quotation marks at the beginning of each paragraph and at the end of the entire passage. Do not put quotation marks at the end of any paragraph except the last.

    f. Use single quotation marks to enclose a quotation within a quotation.

EXAMPLE: Faulkner writes about "a little dog, nameless and mongrel and many-fathered, grown, yet weighing less than six pounds, saying as if to itself, 'I can't be dangerous, because there's nothing much smaller than I am.'"

    g. When you write **dialogue** (two or more persons carrying on a conversation), begin a new paragraph every time the speaker changes.

EXAMPLE: Beauty and the Beast might well have had this conversation:
"I liked you even as the Beast," said Beauty.
"I know," replied the Beast.
"But you have changed only in appearance."
"Yes, am I not better to look at?"
"You're not only better to look at; you'll be easier to take out in public."

2. Use quotation marks to enclose titles of chapters, articles, other parts of books or magazines, short poems, short stories, and songs.

EXAMPLE: "Lion: A Dog" is one of Faulkner's short stories.
AND "Amazing Grace" is both a hymn and a folk song.

3. Use quotation marks to enclose slang words, technical terms, and other expressions that are unusual in standard English.

EXAMPLE: In the past some students referred to courses as "Mickey Mouse" if the courses were easy.

UNDERLINING/ITALICIZING

1. Use italics for titles of books, periodicals, newspapers, works of art, ships, etc.

EXAMPLE: *Claremore Daily Progress* (newspaper)   *Pieta* (sculpture)
Sports Illustrated (magazine)   the *Nautilus* (ship)
Bolero (musical selection)   *Mona Lisa* (painting)
The *Challenger* (shuttle)   *The Shining* (book)
the *Congressional Limited* (train)

2. Use italics for words and letters referred to as such and for foreign words.

EXAMPLE: She would choose only the *crème de la crème*.

AND In formal writing avoid contractions such as *isn't* and *doesn't*.

3. Use italics to emphasize words or phrases.

EXAMPLE: Notify the employee *in writing* if his job performance is not satisfactory.

4. Use italics to indicate a word that re-creates a sound.

EXAMPLE: The students scream *whee* when escaping from a classroom.

PARENTHESES

Use parentheses to enclose informative or explanatory matter that is added to a sentence but is not considered of major importance.

EXAMPLE: That school year (1987-88) was my first year on my own.

1. Be sure any material contained in the parentheses can be omitted from the sentence without changing the meaning and construction of the sentence.

2. Punctuation marks belong outside the parentheses unless the material punctuated lies entirely within the parentheses.

EXAMPLE: In the cartoon the only dialogue of the lavender moose ("He went that way!") serves to accent his character.

AND The years when they were away (1986-88), although financially difficult, were almost a relief.

BRACKETS

1. Use brackets to enclose explanations within parentheses.

   EXAMPLE: Many traitors (Ullum Oak Meenen [named for his grandfather] among them) were hanged from this tree.

2. Use brackets in quoted material when the explanation is not part of the quotation.

   EXAMPLE: In his discussion, the author states that "any year, and especially that year [1514], would have been difficult for the peasants of Royolan."

ELLIPSIS

1. Use an ellipsis (three spaced periods) to designate omitted material in a direct quotation.

   EXAMPLE: *The quoted material as stands reads like this:*
   "If we place a penny on a bottle edge (and any bottle edge will do) and it falls, what will we do?"

   The quotation in the writer's text in MLA format might read like this:
   "If we place a penny on a bottle edge . . . and it falls, what will we do?"

2. If the material includes more than one sentence, or if the material includes the end of a sentence, the ellipsis mark will consist of four spaced periods—the ellipsis and the final period.

   EXAMPLE: *The quoted material reads like this:*
   "I wanted a dog, a dog of surpassing strength, ugliness, and power, a dog that would slay on command, a dog that would slay on my command. Dog. Yes, a real dog."

   The quotation in the writer's text might read like this:
   "I wanted a dog, a dog of surpassing strength, ugliness, meanness and power, a dog that would slay on command. . . . Yes, a real dog."

3. If the quoted material begins in the middle of a sentence, it is not necessary to use the ellipsis at the beginning of the quoted material unless the beginning word starts with a capital letter.

   EXAMPLE: *The quoted material reads like this:*
   "A necessary list of Roman numerals is included."
   The writer's text in MLA might read as follows:
   The book says a "list of Roman numerals is included."

   OR   The book says that a table of ". . . Roman numerals is included."

DASHES

1. Use the dash to indicate an abrupt break in thought.

   EXAMPLE: How many classes—how many people—have failed because they would not work to fulfill their expectations?

2. Use a dash to set off parenthetical material.

   EXAMPLE: Only one person—the student—can determine what was learned.

3. Use a dash to mean *namely, in other words, that is*, and similar expressions that precede explanations.

   EXAMPLE: I want a horse—I want to take horsemanship classes.

SPELLING

Inaccurate spelling is a common problem. It is not one with which you have to live. Spelling skills can be improved. You need to be aware of whether you have difficulty with spelling and be willing to work on this problem. Getting a good dictionary and being willing to use it is one technique; having other people check your work is another.

The following are some simple techniques for improving your spelling skills.

1. Try to visualize how the word looks on the page. See if the visualization agrees with the word.
2. Practice pronouncing and spelling troublesome words that you commonly use.
3. Take care to distinguish between words that are similar in sound and/or spelling. Be conscious of these as you are writing.

    EXAMPLE: its/it's   lose/loose   to/too/two   your/you're
                         cote/coat   idea/ideal   whose/who's   reign/rain
                         there/their/they're

4. Use any memory devices that can help you remember words.

    EXAMPLE: Emma is in a dilemma.
                       Always put a dent in the superintendent.
                       The principal should be your pal; a principle never can be.

5. Memorize these spelling rules (remembering, of course, that they will not apply in all cases and that you will just have to remember those exceptions).

    a. Remember this old, old—but still useful—little rhyme:
    When the sound is like EE,
    Put i before e—
    Except after c.

    EXAMPLE:
    - *i* before *e:*   chief   grief   relief   belief   field   niece
    - except after *c:* receive   conceit   deceive   ceiling
    - unless the word doesn't sound *EE*: eight   their   veil   counterfeit   foreign

    b. When adding a suffix, drop a final silent *e* if the suffix begins with a vowel or with *y*.

    EXAMPLE: type+ing = typing   hope+ed=hoped
                       fame+ous = famous   scare + y = scary

(1) Keep the *e* when the suffix does not begin with a vowel.

EXAMPLE: grate + ful = grateful force + ful = forceful
safe + ty = safety love + less = loveless
lone + ly = lonely

(2) Keep *e* if *e* comes after *c* or *g* in the base word and the added suffix begins with *a* or *o*.

EXAMPLE: notice+able = noticeable courage+ous = courageous

(3) Keep the *e* to avoid confusion with other words.

EXAMPLE: singe+ing = singeing (to avoid confusion with *singing*)
dye+ing = dyeing (to avoid confusion with *dying*)

c. Change a final *y* to *i* before any suffix except *ing*.

EXAMPLE: happy + ness = happiness cry + ed = cried
BUT cry + ing = crying

d. Double a final consonant before a suffix beginning with a vowel (including *y*) if the consonant ends a word of one syllable and is preceded by a single vowel, or if the consonant ends an accented syllable of the root word and is preceded by a single vowel.

EXAMPLE: hop+ed = hopped occur+ed = occurred control+ed = controlled
BUT hoop+ed = hooped boat+er = boater offer+ed = offered

e. To form most plurals add *s* to the singular word.

EXAMPLE: dog dogs textbook textbooks

(1) When making a word plural creates a new syllable, add *es* to the singular word.

EXAMPLE: fox foxes church churches

(2) When the final *y* rule (see rule 5c) applies, add *es*.

EXAMPLE: fly flies fraternity fraternities

(3) For a few nouns, change the final *f* or *fe* to *v* and add *es*.

EXAMPLE: calf calves knife knives

Mechanics

(4) For a few nouns ending in *o,* add *es.*

EXAMPLE: hero heroes   potato potatoes

(5) To make a singular compound noun plural, add *s* or *es* to the end if the word has no hyphen. If the word is a hyphenated word, add the *s* or *es* to the noun portion.

EXAMPLE: cupful cupfuls   strongbox strongboxes   son-in-law sons-in-law

(6) For some nouns of foreign origin, use the foreign plural.

EXAMPLE: alumnus alumni   stimulus stimuli   datum data
synopsis synopses   crisis crises
axis axes   hypothesis hypotheses

WHEN IN DOUBT, LOOK IT UP!

SPACING PUNCTUATION MARKS

1. A dash as a sign of a break in thought is typed as two hyphens with no spaces between.

   EXAMPLE: This is a dash—a kind of interruption.

2. A dash in place of an omitted word is four unspaced hyphens. This is the only kind of dash that is preceded, and followed, by a space.

   EXAMPLE: To fill the blank, place the word —— there.

3. An ellipsis is three spaced periods, with spaces before and after the first period. A four-period ellipsis (signifying the omission of quoted material that includes at least one mark of end punctuation) begins with an unspaced mark.

   EXAMPLE: *The quoted text reads like this:*
   "A baby mouse in a tree in the woods lay quietly in the nest of cotton balls, newsprint, shredded Styrofoam and lace."
   The replicated text reads like this:
   "A baby mouse . . . lay . . . in the nest. . . ."

4. When a slash separates two quoted lines of poetry, leave a space before and after.

   EXAMPLE: One child's verse begins, "Jack and Jill went up the hill / To fetch a pail of water."

5. When a slash joins two words in an alternative relationship or as a span of time, use no space before or after the slash.

   EXAMPLE: It's a case of either/or not and/or.

6. Leave one space after a period, question mark, exclamation mark, colon, four-dot ellipsis, comma, semicolon, closing quotation mark, closing parenthesis, or closing bracket.

   EXAMPLE: This is a sentence. Yes! One space after question mark, period, colon . . . . One, two, what do we do? We act; we write. "Create," we say. We (quietly) scream.

7. Leave no space before or after a dash, hyphen, or an apostrophe within a word.

   EXAMPLE: A dash–a mark of punctuation–is used by Fea-Smith when he's writing informally.

8. When an apostrophe ends a word, leave no space before any following punctuation.

   EXAMPLE: When singing, "We're Goin'; We're Gone," remember to drop the final *g* in *going*.

9. Do not begin a line with any punctuation from the preceding line. Do not leave punctuation from a following line on the previous line.

   WRONG EXAMPLE: It is **wrong** to say and mean the lines I'll go
       NEVER ⟶ , I'll follow, under any circumstances.
       DO THIS!

   WRONG EXAMPLE: It is also **WRONG** to say anything that can be
       misconstrued by a listener who overhears   **NEVER**
       and this is the truth). ⟵ **DO THIS!**

10. Do not continue an ellipsis from one line to the next.

    WRONG EXAMPLE: When you write and leave out words in a ⟵ **NEVER**
        quotation from a text or other written work. .   **DO THIS!**
        ., don't do this.

Mechanics

COMMON MISTAKES NEVER TO MAKE!

NEVER	ALWAYS	NEVER	ALWAYS
grammer	grammar	gonna	going to
thier	their	could of	could have
haf to	have to	alot	a lot
suppose to	supposed to	writting	writing
theirself	themselves	hisself	himself
off of	off		

ALWAYS In titles, *is* is an important word and must be capitalized.

NEVER SAY   He is prejudice.
SAY INSTEAD   He is prejudiced.

IMPORTANT DISTINCTIONS

loose = not tight   choose = to select   except = excluding   they're = they are
lose = to misplace   chose = selected   accept = to receive   their = belonging to them
                                                                                                                        there = a place

you're = you are   it's = it is
your = belonging to you   its = belonging to it

REMEMBER: DO NOT USE CONTRACTIONS IN FORMAL WRITING.

ABBREVIATIONS AND SYMBOLS USED ON GRADED AND MARKED PAPERS

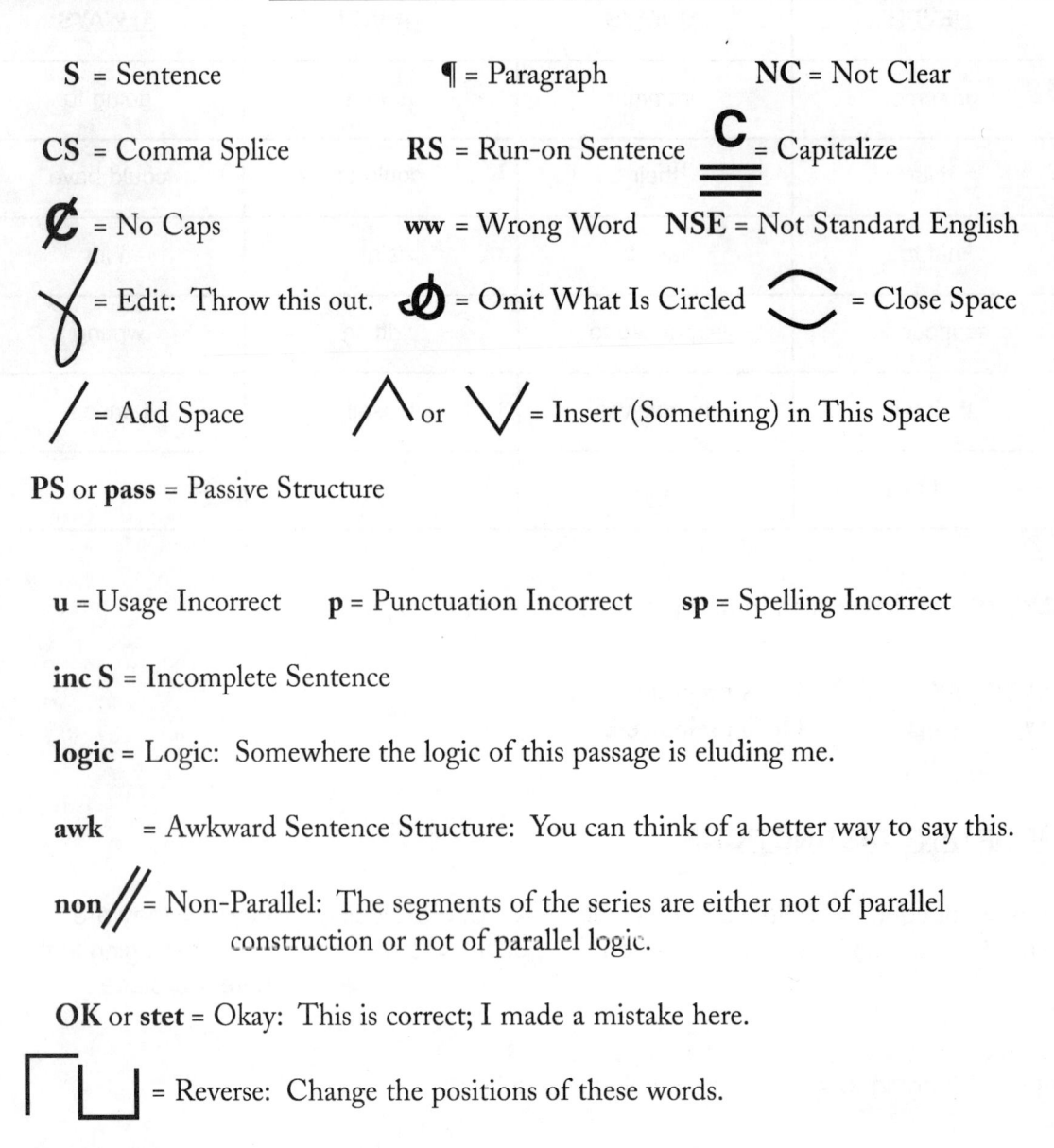

    S = Sentence   ¶ = Paragraph   **NC** = Not Clear

    CS = Comma Splice   **RS** = Run-on Sentence   ☰ = Capitalize

    ¢ = No Caps   **ww** = Wrong Word   **NSE** = Not Standard English

    ✓ = Edit: Throw this out.   ⊘ = Omit What Is Circled   ⌒ = Close Space

    / = Add Space   ∧ or ∨ = Insert (Something) in This Space

PS or **pass** = Passive Structure

    u = Usage Incorrect   **p** = Punctuation Incorrect   **sp** = Spelling Incorrect

inc S = Incomplete Sentence

logic = Logic: Somewhere the logic of this passage is eluding me.

awk = Awkward Sentence Structure: You can think of a better way to say this.

non // = Non-Parallel: The segments of the series are either not of parallel construction or not of parallel logic.

OK or **stet** = Okay: This is correct; I made a mistake here.

⌐⌙ = Reverse: Change the positions of these words.

- Two symbols are used for mistakes of all kinds. If a word is circled, it is incorrect somehow: incorrect spelling, incorrect tense, etc. If a line is checked, there is a mistake in it somewhere. Just find it. If you cannot find your mistake or do not understand it, ask and the instructor will explain.
- **Remember:** You cannot do better if you do not know what you have done right or wrong on a paper. So, if in doubt about what is marked or said, **ask**!

APPENDIX A: STUDENT MODELS

The following model student papers are in different documentation formats. These models are above-average papers, but may or may not represent "A" work.

Papers in **MLA format** are shaded, like this:

Essays

- **NOTE:** The following paper is written in MLA format. Papers in MLA format have a blue background.

Jane Martin
Comp III
Analogy Essay
February 18, 1998

The Subtle Fist

    Nora Helmer of Henrik Ibsen's "A Doll House" is no stranger to me. For some, she may seem too accommodating and naïve to be believed; but, for me, she is all too real. When I think of her, I am filled with feelings of pity, shame, and disgust. I feel pity for the way that her own innocence is used against her, shame at her willingness to be so easily manipulated, and disgust at the reflection I see when I look at Nora. For when I am forced to look at her, it is my own reflection that I see; then I am forced to admit that I, too, was the victim of a subtle fist.

    Innocence can be a pitiful thing indeed. Nora proves this by willingly giving up any notion of self to be her beloved Torvald's wife. At first, she probably does not see the harm in giving in to her husband's demands for control. She might even think that Torvald's controlling manner is sweet and thoughtful, that he has a touching conviction to take care of her. She could not know in the infancy of their relationship how much this eagerness to compromise would cost her. Just as Nora, I went straight from being my father's daughter to being my first husband's wife. I never felt as though I was in control of my own life as my parents were strict and protective. Therefore, my relationship with my boyfriend did not seem unnatural when he began asserting his authority over me. I did not know until after my ten-year marriage ended that I, as an individual human being, did have this thing called power.

    After a time, however, innocence does wane. Nora begins realizing that she has a right to make some choices for herself. The first endeavor on her own is to secretly acquire a loan to take Torvald on an extended vacation for his health. Torvald would never allow such an action, as he feels going into debt reduces one's status in life. Nora keeps this secret for years before she gets the courage to defy again. She begins sneaking macaroons, telling little white lies, and fantasizing about telling Torvald "to hell and be damned!" (Ibsen 1079). Her bravery, however, is quite confined, as only a couple of people know of her little acts of defiance. I must admit, though, that her concealed courage is greater than any I ever possessed under the control of my captor. I spent every day of ten years living as if I were walking on eggs. I was always so afraid that I would do or say something to offend or upset my first husband that I could never even entertain thoughts of rebellion. I was afraid that if I angered him, he might leave; and how could I ever live without him?

    Nora finally sees her husband as he truly is. Upon this revelation, she realizes that she must begin to find herself and make her own way in this life. She does not yet realize that leaving is the easy part. When people wrap so much of themselves into another human being, they do not realize how little of a person exists without the other. My first husband's manipulation was so complete that I became a mirror image of him. I did only the things he liked to do. I associated only with the people that he found suitable. I worked only at jobs that received his consent. I readily changed my clothes if he, for any reason, did not approve. Obviously, this was not a happy way to live, but I thought that it was easier than the alternative of leaving the man I loved so dearly. When after more than ten years of marriage, my first husband left me, I was utterly lost. I had committed every particle of my being to this man and this marriage, so much so that without it, I threw only the shadow of a person. I had no identity, no substance, without him.

My memory of this time is still so painful that even now, five years and what seems a lifetime later, I rarely can speak his name. I refer to him only as "What's-his-name." Some may think this a bit childish and bitter, but when I speak his name, I feel as if a part of the power that I suffered so to gain is compromised by his memory. Only one who has felt the kind of devastation and humiliation that was my life, and was Nora Helmer's life, can understand the vehemence with which I protect this priceless treasure that is called independence.

[*Note:* **The Works Cited page is generally a separate page from the rest of the paper and is paginated as the next page in the series.**]

Works Cited

Ibsen, Henrik. "A Doll House." *The Compact Bedford Introduction to Literature: Reading, Thinking, and Writing.* 4th ed. Ed. Michael Meyer. Boston: St. Martin's, 1997. 1069–75. Print.

Gay 1

Rick W. Gay
Comp II 9:30 MWF/Sesso
Essay #2 – April 6, 1998

To Serve Man

As mankind's quest for power takes him ever deeper into the realm of the unknown, the danger of unforeseen consequences grows ever greater. As the protagonist in Mary Shelley's *Frankenstein* learns, some knowledge is best left unknown. An endeavor being possible does not guarantee it being ethical (Kreyche 82). Even eminent scientist Freeman J. Dyson worries that the growing use of high technology will only exacerbate friction between upper and lower social classes, thereby creating greater problems than the ones it solves (Pennar 84). As Orlin Damyanov puts it, "We have unparalleled knowledge and power over nature and yet this faces us with moral dilemmas and responsibilities for which we are ill-prepared." It seems that with each solution that people produce to improve lives, a vast number of new problems occur.

Problem begets solution. Solutions begets new problem. Thus, technology perpetuates and guarantees its own necessity. But, if technology cannot advance the whole of humanity, then it is only creating more social strife (Kreyche 82). Like Frankenstein's monster, technology has become a colossal entity with dangerous and unforeseen powers.

Technology's basic mandate is to raise the quality of life, but each step forward is both wondrous and frightening. While medical science makes people healthier, it creates a higher level of stress, anxiety, and worry. Alcohol consumption is down; smoking is down; careful diet and exercise is up. However, despite all medical statistics, Americans do not see themselves as healthier (Tenner 26). Political scientist Aaron Wildavsky describes it as "doing better but feeling worse" (Tenner 26). In short, progress in medical technology has created a great anxiety about personal health.

Advances in medicine have made treatments generally less invasive, but this has not brought peace of mind to the populace. As medical techniques become more complicated, they demand a higher degree of skill and education from the operator. This increases the possibility of mistakes and miscalculations due to human error. And, of course, the high cost of sophisticated equipment and technical training is passed on to the patient (Tenner 27). This adds to the general feeling of worry associated with any major medical procedure. Giant medical centers, with darkened rooms full of impersonal machines used to test every pore of the human body, give rise to visions of a mad scientist's laboratory.

Technological breakthroughs have certainly raised the standard of living around the world, but this too produces an unfortunate consequence (Tobias, Popcorn, and Celente 41). As modern science lengthens the average lifespan, mortality rates fall and birth rates continue. The population becomes larger, which contributes to increasing levels of mental illness, depression, and anti-social behavior: "Humans are designed to function best psychologically in the open, grassy spaces our ancestors inhabited. Stark, stony urban landscapes, replete with an ever-present backdrop of traffic and airplane noise, stress our psyches in subtle but real ways" (Tobias, Popcorn, and Celente 41). It is not surprising that Los Angeles, one of the most densely populated cities in the U.S. has approximately two thousand practicing psychologists per square mile (Tobias, Popcorn, and Celente 41).

Overpopulation places great stress not only on society but on the environment. Technological progress allows more people to survive, but it does not provide their sustenance. The growing crowd exacerbates the problem of depleting natural resources. The exponentially multiplying populace demands an ever-increasing amount of food and energy, but it also takes up more land that would be used to generate these products (Tobias, Popcorn, and Celente 40). It is simple arithmetic. The amount of arable farmland decreases each year. Grassland for stock diminishes as well. The oceans provide a finite number of fish. As demand continues to rise, greater strain is placed on supply. Agriculture still manages to increase output by approximately one percent per year, but this is clearly a precarious situation (Tobias, Popcorn, and Celente 41). Through increased pollution, overcrowding, food and water shortages, and, of course, traffic, this technologically-induced population explosion will ultimately reduce the quality of human life.

Technology has helped give the world peace, but this too is not without consequence. The world's arsenal has evolved from weapons to doomsday devices. As weapons have increased in destructive power, world leaders have become less likely to actually use them. The threat remains that a nuclear incident could be instigated by terrorists or some country's irrational leader even if global thermonuclear war is unlikely. Today's technology has relegated warfare to conventional skirmishes in small politically-unstable areas. Technology creates peace; peace leads to overpopulation. Man's proclivity to war has always been a primary means of population control, but technology has limited its effectiveness. The most highly-populated countries are hesitant to instigate conflict with each other for fear that a limited engagement could escalate to a nuclear confrontation. Thus, millions of deaths may have been avoided: "One might even argue that the misery that would have resulted from these unfought wars is less than the suffering from prolonged, worldwide famine" (Tobias, Popcorn, and Celente 41).

Man's quest for knowledge is not always beneficial to society. Technology has certainly brought great wonders, but it has created a complicated society. Science has given humans a life less physically demanding and more mentally stressful. In endeavoring to cure the world's ills, people have produced overcrowding, anxiety, and the possibility of famine. The same technology that made humanity more powerful erodes social ties. The world has not improved; it has gained a new set of problems.

In fact, we can learn an important lesson from *Frankenstein*. The social and psychological problems attributed to technology are a product of people's experimentation. Technology is a monster that carries its own curses. Some believe the monster is truly benign, but even they harbor a few fears. People have a deep and innate concern about the vast power unleashed as compared to their own mortality. This speaks of an ancient fear, fear not of technology itself but of people's ability to control it. In the end, Shelley's protagonist pays the ultimate price for his lack of foresight when his own creation destroys him. One can only hope the same fate does not befall humanity.

[*Note:* The Works Cited page is generally a separate page from the rest of the paper and is paginated as the next page in the series.]

Works Cited

Damyanov, Orlin. "Technology and Its Dangerous Effects on Nature and Human Life as Perceived in Mary Shelley's *Frankenstein* and William Gibson's *Necromancer*." Web. 9 Mar. 1998.

Kreyche, Gerald. F. "Does the Future Have a Future?" *USA Today Magazine* Nov. 1996: 82. Print.

Pennar, Karen. "Science's Great Dream-Spinner." *Business Week* 20 Oct. 1997: 84-92. Print.

Tenner, Edward. *Why Things Bite Back: Technology and the Revenge of Unintended Circumstances.* New York: Knopf, 1996. Print.

Tobias, Michael, Faith Popcorn, and Gerald Celente. "What's Next?" *Psychology Today* Feb. 1995: 34-42. Print.

Tobias, Michael, Faith Popcorn, and Gerald Celente. "What's Next?" Psychology Today Feb. 1995: 34-42.

Earlene Bradshaw
Composition 2
TR 12:30
Research Paper

Midwifery in the United States

For as long as women have been having babies, there have undoubtedly been other women caring for them and encouraging them during the birth process. Midwives have been mentioned in literature since recorded history. In the second book of the Bible, possibly written during the reign of Rameses II in the thirteenth century B.C., we read, "the king of Egypt spoke to the Hebrew midwives . . ." (Exodus 2:12). Even today, those involved in the occupation known as "midwifery" continue to play important roles in women's healthcare in much of the world.

As people migrated from Europe to the colonies, midwives were kept busy delivering babies for the settlers. The use of midwives as primary caretakers of pregnant women continued from the time Pilgrims settled in Plymouth Rock until the latter part of the 1800s, when a shift in healthcare began: "Between 1750 and 1852, women in the United States had four choices for childbirth: physicians, Indian doctors, herbalists, and midwives. A review of deliveries during the Colonial period showed that 2% of urban physicians had obstetrical cases and rural doctors had none" (Ament 2). Journals and other records indicate that most women chose midwives to deliver their babies. During the latter part of the 1800s more men began to train as physicians; their training included obstetrics; they began to deliver babies that would ordinarily have been delivered by midwives: "In the early years of this century, midwives attended about 40% of births in the United States, but by the early 1950s, that proportion had fallen to just over 3%" (Gabay 12). I am training for a career in midwifery; as a Certified-Nurse Midwife, I will be part of the group of healthcare professionals that will raise the percentage of midwife-attended births in the United States. Even though training for midwives has greatly improved, and even though there is a multitude of proof that midwives continue to have excellent birth results and patient satisfaction, there are many barriers to midwifery in the United States today.

In the early years in the United States, midwives had little or no formal training. Instead, they learned by watching and assisting experienced midwives called "grannies or lay midwives." These types of midwives, grannies, and lay midwives "existed in the United States, but . . . are virtually nonexistent today" (Hyder 5). While there are still people who do not feel they need formal training to become midwives, more women and men are realizing the necessity for quality training. During the past three decades, training for midwives is on the rise. Currently, "there are 43 major colleges and universities across the country offering a certificate or masters [sic] degree in nurse-midwifery. In addition, a community-based program allows students flexibility in graduate education, utilizing independent study and community resources" (U.S. Department of Health 12).

Today, training is intense and licensing is based on graduation from the training as well as passing a national examination similar to that of Registered Nurses: "Certified Nurse-Midwives (CNMs) are Registered Nurses (RNs) who complete training to become certified in nurse-midwifery by the American College of Nurse-Midwifery. In the US, CNMs care for 5% of all births and 95% of all births delivered by midwives" (Hyder 5).

There are many reasons why women who have used midwives are satisfied with the results: personal care, excellent birth outcomes, and cost, to name a few. As early as 1925, a ". . . White House Conference on Child Health reported, . . . the record of midwives surpasses the record of physicians for normal deliveries. . . . Midwives took better care of the expectant mothers because they waited patiently and let nature take its course'" (Ulrich 108). According to the Congressional Office of Technology in 1986,

> these health care professionals managed routine pregnancies safely and as well as or better than physicians. Midwives were less likely to prescribe drugs or rely on technology. They had more interactions with the patients, who spent less time in the waiting room and had shorter hospital stays. Also, the patients receiving care from nurse-midwives tended to be more satisfied with their care. (Ulrich 108)

Another reason for patient satisfaction is that Nurse-Midwives usually know their patients and the patients' families well. They spend time teaching expectant mothers how to care for a newborn: how to bathe a baby, how to get the home ready for baby, birthing techniques and positions, how to breast-feed, and so on. They are available to answer questions and therefore ease stress and worry before and after the baby is born.

The majority of Nurse-Midwives have excellent records in birth outcomes. Detailed records are kept on many aspects of childbirth, including cesareans (C-sections) and Low Birth Weight (LBW) infants: "Many retrospective studies have shown that CNMs have a lower C-section rate than physicians . . . [for example] the C-section rate for six nurse-midwife services in Minnesota in 1982-1983 was 8.6% compared with the state's rate of 14.6%" (Ulrich 108). Those types of comparisons are reflected in many states over several years' studies. Concerning LBW infants: "Women who receive insufficient prenatal care are twice as likely to have LBW infants. They are also more likely to have premature infants, stillborn deliveries, or babies who die in the first year of life" (Ulrich 106). Because of the personalized, diligent care given by midwives, expectant mothers are more apt to take vitamins, eat well, and get sufficient rest. This in turn produces babies who are generally healthier, more likely to be carried to full term, have higher birth weights, and have fewer troubles during delivery.

Cost is an extremely important consideration when monitoring birth outcomes. In the issue of LBW infants, "The National Committee to Prevent Infant Mortality . . . estimated the lifetime cost of caring for a LBW infant to be $400,000. Avoiding one LBW infant would save between $14,000 and $30,000 a year" (Ulrich 106). Another startling statistic concerns unnecessary C-sections: "We estimate that 473,000 of the 966,000 cesareans performed in 1991 (49.0 percent) were unnecessary, costing American society more than $1.3 billion" (Gabay 30). There is a growing number of professionals who see the all-around benefits of a return to midwife-attended births in the United States: for mothers, for infants, and for America's pocketbook.

In spite of the many positive results, there are several formidable barriers to midwifery in the United States. These include public perception, physician opposition, and lack of training programs. Negative perception concerning midwifery can be traced back to Europe; there were times when the very lives of midwives were in danger:

> In 1484, Pope Innocent VIII made an official declaration against the crime of midwifery, which was codified in a volume called *Malleus Maleficarium*. This book became expert testimony and was utilized by European judges and magistrates for over 300 years. Women were tried and executed as directed by this book. . . . Witch hunters of the middle ages referred to midwives as 'crones', and 'hags'. Not coincidentally, American physicians of the 19th and 20th centuries use these same terms when discussing this continent's midwives. Comments made . . . include: '[She] is pestiferous . . . the typical old hag, gin-fingering, gin-drinking . . . her mouth full of snuff and her fingers full of dirt. (Granju 2-3)

These stereotypical remarks have plagued midwives through the years; it has proven a difficult task to overcome the perception these remarks generate.

Professional jealousy over clients is another barrier in the struggle between physicians and nurse-midwives: "Unfortunately, physicians often view CNMs as competition for clients. If CNMs . . . assist with the care of private physicians' clients, there is a potential for real competition" (Ament 9). Often when a patient realizes the quality of care the midwife gives, she will request the midwife to assist her in delivery rather than the physician. This raises a green-eyed monster in the hearts of the doctors, who use it as "proof" that midwives are out to steal their reputation, as well as their clients. There are reported cases of physicians taking midwives to court attempting to rid the country of these troublemakers: "The obstetrical community deemed out-of-hospital birth 'child abuse' at one point . . ." (Murray 10).

Training for midwives, or the lack of it, is another challenge facing women and men who desire to become Certified Nurse-Midwives. Because public perception of midwives is still somewhat negative, physicians continue to be in greater demand than midwives. It is difficult for students desiring financial aid to receive grants or loans to attend training schools.

Despite the barriers, there is a growing number of physicians who see the value of midwives in obstetrics. Patients are demanding the medical profession to legitimize midwives as healthcare professionals. Many women are choosing the services of midwives rather than physicians for care during pregnancy and delivery. These women appreciate the complete, personalized healthcare they receive from the CNMs. Accredited schools of midwifery are beginning to receive Federal funding.

I have attended the births of four of my grandchildren. It has been wonderful for me to be included in the birthing process. I held my daughter and daughters-in-law as they gave birth to their precious babies. As a trained birthing coach, I was able to comfort, encourage, and even scold these new mothers as the babies were born. Upon completion of the training I am now taking, I will be a Certified Nurse-Midwife and will be able to help many other young women during their pregnancies. I will help them prepare for their new babies; I will teach them how to keep healthy during and after pregnancy, and I will help during the actual delivery of their little ones.

The reputation of Certified Nurse-Midwives is definitely on the rise. Should this trend continue, it will be considered an honor to be a nurse-midwife, even in the United States.

[*Note:* **The Works Cited page is generally a separate page from the rest of the paper and is paginated as the next page in the series.**]

Works Cited

Ament, Lynette A., and Lisa Hanson. "A Model for the Future: Certified Nurse-Midwives Replace Residents and House Staff in Hospitals." *Nursing and Health Care Perspectives* 19.1 (Jan.-Feb. 1998): 26-34. Web. 24 Feb. 2000.

King James Version Study Bible. Nashville: Thomas Nelson, 2002. Print.

Gabay, Mary, and Sidney M. Wolfe. "Nurse-Midwifery: The Beneficial Alternative." *Public Health Reports* 112.5 (Sep.-Oct. 1997): 386-45. Web. 24 Feb. 2000.

Granju, Katie A. "Midwives Under Fire." *Special Delivery* 22.2 (Summer 1999): 1-8. Web. 24 Feb. 2000.

Hyder, Leah. "Routine Midwifery Care: Why Not Here?" *The Network News* 23.4 (Jul. 1998): 1-6. Web. 24 Feb. 2000.

Murray, Elisa. "Birth Rights." *Eastsideweek* 19 Nov. 1997: 10-11. Print.

Ulrich, Susan. "Revisiting an 'Old' Solution to the High Costs of Maternity Care." *Medical Interface* Oct. 1994: 106-18. Print.

United States Department of Health and Human Services. Office of Inspector General. *A Survey of Certified Nurse-Midwives 1992*. 1992. Print.

Renetta Harrison
Composition II/Cinema
Film Analysis Essay
October 30, 1997

A View Out a Rear Window

The film *Rear Window* is a very voyeuristic suspense film starring James Stewart, Grace Kelly, Thelma Ritter, and Wendell Corey. James Stewart is the main character, Jeff, confined to his apartment with a broken leg. Grace Kelly portrays his girlfriend, Lisa. Thelma Ritter plays Stella, the nurse who comes to check on Jeff each day. Jeff is a traveling photographer who gazes out his apartment window to pass the time. He becomes obsessed with watching his neighbors, especially Mr. and Mrs. Thornwall. Lisa and Stella also develop interest in watching when Jeff explains the suspicious behavior of Mr. Thornwall. The remainder of the film deals with the three of them trying to prove their suspicions to Jeff's friend, Detective Doyle, played by Wendell Corey. Alfred Hitchcock is the brilliant and creative director of this film. Hitchcock is famous for his creative use of *mise en scene* in films of suspense and mystery. *Rear Window* is a perfect example of his creativity. This film consists of more than just a few *mise en scene* elements. In my opinion, the five most prominent elements in *Rear Window* are character proxemics, angles, shots and camera proxemics, lighting key, and framing.

First, character proxemics are useful tools in many of the scenes in Hitchcock's *Rear Window*. One example is the scene with Lisa and Stella gazing out the window while Jeff is on the phone with Mr. Thornwall, trying to get him to leave his apartment. Hitchcock places Lisa in the foreground, facing front, and Stella in the midground. This character placing shows the viewer that Lisa is the more important character of the two. Also, Lisa walks in front of Stella when leaving the room, blocking Stella from view. This action is meant to draw the viewer's attention to Lisa and possibly set up the importance of her in an upcoming scene. Another good example of Hitchcock's use of character proxemics to create a mood is the scene in which Mr. Thornwall leaves his apartment. In this particular scene, the viewer is watching through Jeff's camera lens and sees a medium shot of Mr. Thornwall walking from right to left and disappearing behind a brick wall. This action of walking right to left on screen denotes a conflict. The viewer later discovers that Mr. Thornwall is on his way to Jeff's apartment for a confrontation. Hitchcock uses character proxemics in almost every scene in this film to emphasize a point for the viewer.

Second, Hitchcock uses a variety of angles in *Rear Window* to place significance on an article or person. He mostly uses an eye-level angle when shooting scenes in which the viewer sees Jeff. For example, in the scene with Jeff talking on the phone to Mr. Thornwall, the viewer sees Jeff at eye level, as if the viewer were in the room with Jeff. This involves the viewer more intimately with Jeff. Hitchcock uses a high angle in the scene of Jeff watching Lisa and Stella dig in the flower bed below his window. This gives the viewer the feeling of being in the room beside Jeff and looking down at the girls with him. Another high angle shot is of Jeff in his wheelchair hiding in the shadows of his apartment listening to Mr. Thornwall approach his door. These instances are of high angle shots, one of Mr. Thornwall standing over Jeff before attacking him, and again when Jeff is struggling to get away from him. This creates a foreboding mood and depicts Mr. Thornwall as a menace. Hitchcock implements several different angles in this film in order to entangle the viewer in the action.

Third, shots and camera proxemics are very important aspects Hitchcock uses in this film. He uses extreme close-ups to emphasize the great importance of certain objects in *Rear Window*. An example of this is in the scene with Jeff watching Lisa and Stella digging. The viewer sees a shot through Jeff's camera lens of the girls' feet, panning to the empty hole dug. This places great importance on the fact that there is nothing in the hole. Next, the camera pans up to a close-up of Stella shaking her head, stressing the fact of there being nothing in the hole. Hitchcock uses full shots to long shots of Jeff's neighbors in their windows. These shots show that the neighbors are not directly involved or intimate with Jeff. Use of medium shots of Jeff, Lisa, and Stella creates a more friendly relationship between the three. Several shots of the three of them gazing out the window toward Mr. Thornwall's apartment are good examples. Hitchcock uses a very interesting long shot of both Lisa in Mr. Thornwall's apartment and the neighbor below, Ms. Lonely Heart, in her bedroom. In this shot, Lisa is snooping around Mr. Thornwall's apartment and Ms. Lonely Heart is about to attempt suicide. Jeff and Stella are watching out Jeff's window and are concerned about Ms. Lonely Heart, who is about to take a handful of sleeping pills. Jeff picks up his phone and dials the police department. At the same time, Mr. Thornwall arrives back home. Jeff and Stella have been concentrating on saving Ms. Lonely Heart and now do not have time to call and warn Lisa of the danger. This shot is meant to agitate the viewer and create an uncomfortable feeling of not being able to help Lisa escape. I found myself wanting to shout out to Lisa that Mr. Thornwall was back and to get out. Hitchcock frequently uses shots and camera proxemics to rivet the viewer's attention to the film.

Fourth, Hitchcock uses lighting to define the mood of a scene or film. In *Rear Window*, he uses low key lighting to emphasize a dark, foreboding atmosphere. The prim example of this use is in the scene of the conflict between Jeff and Mr. Thornwall. In this scene the viewer sees only silhouettes of Mr. Thornwall and Jeff. This use of low key lighting lends an eerie feeling to the scene. Another example of Hitchock's use of lighting is the scene in which the viewer sees Jeff in the light as he wheels himself backwards into the shadows of his apartment. Seeing Jeff in the shadows of his apartment gives the viewer the illusion that Mr. Thornwall will not be able to see him. Also, it sets a mysterious, disoriented mood for the scene. Another lighting key Hitchcock uses is masking. In *Rear Window* he uses masking when the viewer sees shots of Jeff's view of his neighbor's windows at night. Their windows are brightly lit, but the surrounding building is blacked out. This allows the viewer to concentrate on what he or she sees through each window. Primarily low key lighting is used throughout this film; however, other lighting aspects are occasionally implemented for effect.

Finally, framing is the major *mise en scene* element Hitchcock uses in *Rear Window*. He uses framing to include the viewer in the action of this film. In most of *Rear Window* Hitchcock utilizes a window for a framing effect. The window framing effect gives the viewer the feeling of actually looking out of or into a window. This film's setting is Jeff's apartment and the view out his window. Therefore, Hitchcock shows several scenes of Jeff in his window and then shows what he is seeing out of his window. One scene includes shots of Jeff by his window with his camera and binoculars, watching Lisa and Stella dig in the flower garden. Also, Hitchcock uses window framing in the shots of Lisa snooping in Mr. Thornwall's apartment. Another abundant framing aspect he uses in *Rear Window* is iris framing. This framing effect gives the viewer the feeling of actually looking through a camera or binocular lens. Iris framing is evident in the scene where Jeff is looking out his window through his camera at the girls' digging. The viewer sees Jeff's actual view through his camera zoom lens, complete with the rounded shadow effect around the edges of the shot. Hitchcock uses iris framing throughout this film as a transition to a close-up shot of an important person or item. In the scene of the girls digging, the camera pans a shot of their feet, the hole, and then finally Stella's face, using iris framing. This style of framing is Hitchcock's way of enabling the viewer to become much more involved and intimate in the film. He uses window and iris framing frequently in *Rear Window* to draw the viewer's total attention.

Rear Window is an excellent film in which to observe many *mise en scene* elements. Alfred Hitchcock is a director who uses many different elements in his films. The elements in *Rear Window* are abundant and usually easy to read. Hitchcock's use of character proxemics in this film allows the viewer to distinguish each character's importance. His uses of angles and shots lend emphasis to every scene. In addition, the lighting key defines the mood of the film, and framing personally involves the viewer. All of these elements create the suspense and mystery for which Hitchcock is so famous.

[*Note:* **The Works Cited page is generally a separate page from the rest of the paper and is paginated as the next page in the series.**]

Works Cited

*Rear Windo*w. Dir. Alfred Hitchcock. Screenplay by John Michael Hayes. Perf. James Steward and Grace Kelly. Paramount Pictures, 1954. DVD.

Rick W. Gay
Composition II
Literary Analysis
06 March 1998

In the Name of Love

On its surface, Andre Dubus' "Killings" may look like just another tale of murder and revenge, but closer examination reveals a much deeper theme. The murders in this story are not incited by hatred or vengeance. They are brought on by emotion that is not usually considered malevolent. Both Richard and Matt are driven to extremes by their strong sense of family. These killers cite love as their motive.

With the statement "He was making it with my wife," Richard Strout believes he is justifying his murder of Frank (67). Despite legal separation, divorce proceedings, and his involvement with another woman, Richard still feels the obligation to protect his loved ones. This instinct to defend his territory causes him to perceive Frank as an interloper. Strout begins his defense on the civilized end of the spectrum, but when all attempts to warn off the intruder fail, he moves toward violence. Eventually he sees only one solution. To preserve his love of family, Richard Strout kills Frank.

Matt feels the same protective instincts. The love of a parent for a child is enormously strong but as the child matures, parents must make concessions. When Ruth complains of Frank's relationship with Mary Ann, Matt defends it saying, "She probably loves him. . . . Why can't we just leave it at that?" (65). He does not entirely approve of his son's liaison but his parental protectiveness is giving way to confidence in Frank's judgement. Matt believes that love justifies even questionable actions. Even his respect for the law is eventually overcome by this love for his family.

Matt cannot endure his wife's pain at seeing their son's murderer free on bail. "She sees him all the time. It makes her cry," he says, confiding his anguish to a friend (62). His inability to prevent Frank's death only intensifies his desire to shield his wife from further misery. Even the probability of Richard's eventual imprisonment is not enough to relieve Ruth's suffering. Matt is motivated to remove the source of her pain. His elaborate preparations for the murder are not for his own sake, but to protect Ruth from the misery she would surely endure if her husband were to be incarcerated. Matt murders Richard for love of family.

Both of these men take another human life for essentially the same reason. But the manifestation of love takes a decidedly different form with each killer. Richard loves his family, and yet he commits murder in the living room right before their very eyes. The repercussions of his action will undoubtedly have a profound effect on his entire family for the rest of their lives. Matt, on the other hand, goes to great lengths to limit his family's exposure to the unsavory event. With one outside party involved, and Ruth present in spirit only, Matt succeeds in shielding his family as much as possible. Richard's crime can be argued as a spur of the moment decision, and thus would fall to the lesser charge of manslaughter. Conversely, Matt's crime is obviously premeditated, making it indisputably first degree murder. Despite the fact that Matt has committed the worse offense, his circumstances and distraught state of mind are more likely to elicit sympathy from a jury. In short, emotion can cause bizarre behavior.

The compelling force behind all criminal activity is nothing more than primitive human emotions. Although religious zealots would be quick to point out the Seven Deadly Sins as the source of all men's troubles, there is more to consider. Man is a hopelessly emotional creature, and his judgements are not always built on the foundation of right and wrong. Pride, lust, envy, anger, greed, gluttony, and sloth may be responsible for the bulk of mankind's problems, but another variable figures prominently into the equation. Criminal behavior is not exclusively generated by the dark side of man's psyche. Some crimes are motivated by love.

[*Note:* The Works Cited page is generally a separate page from the rest of the paper and is paginated as the next page in the series.]

Works Cited

Dubus, Andre, "Killigns." *The Compact Bedford Introduction to Literature.* 4th ed. Ed. Michael Meyer. Boston: Bedford Books, 1997. 61-73. Print.

Rodgers 1

Anna Rodgers
Composition II
Literary Analysis
MWF 9:30
Nov. 12, 1993

The Woman's Place

Throughout history, women's roles have been portrayed as inferior, if not downright subservient, to men's. Even in a story that has a heroine instead of a hero, there is usually a man around that has some measure of power over her, romantic or otherwise. These submissive roles are especially prevalent in literature written before the dawning of the women's liberation movement of the 1960's. The play by Susan Glaspell, "Trifles," and the short story "Boys and Girls" by Alice Munro both make a comment on how women tend to be portrayed and also give a glimpse into how that portrayal makes them feel. In both stories the point is made that anything a woman does is subject to an attitude of amused derision from a man, that the work women do is less important than the work men do, and that women are capable of only the most trifling of thoughts and emotions.

The words and actions of the women in these two stories receive amused, occasionally derisive, comments from the men. In Glaspell's play, there are several instances in which the men make fun of what the women are doing, such as looking at and discussing the quilt Mrs. Wright was working on (181). They also laugh at and put down some of the women's comments, especially when the women try to defend Mrs. Wright in any way (179). When the young girl in "Boys and Girls" lets Flora, the horse, escape, she does so out of strong feelings she has about the shooting of the horse. Rather than trying to understand her actions or praising her for acting on her convictions, her father simply demeans and dismisses her with the single comment, "Never mind. . . . She's only a girl" (Munro 835).

The work that the women do is regarded as unimportant compared to the work men do. Unfortunately, the women occasionally seem to share this opinion. There are several references in Glaspell's play to the unimportance and (men assume) easiness of the tasks women perform. The lawyer makes degrading remarks about the poor job Mrs. Wright seems to do of keeping her house up. He even kicks her pans around the kitchen floor, showing how little respect he has for the work she has done. When Mrs. Hale tries to defend her, he dismisses her reaction as the result of her simply being loyal to her own sex (179). Mrs. Peters, in an example of how women tend to accept the judgments of men, tries to explain away their rude behavior as due to the fact that "They've got awful important things on their minds" (181). The young girl in Munro's story describes her mother's work as "endless, dreary, and peculiarly depressing" while the work her father does is "ritualistically important" (828). The work that women are capable of is further demeaned when the mother and father discuss the fact that only after her little brother gets a little older and starts working with her father will he have "a real help" (827). In fact, the mother may be jealous of the freedom her daughter has to work at men's tasks instead of women's (829).

Not only is the work women do regarded as without merit, so is most of what they think and feel. In "Trifles" the men act as if the fact that Mrs. Wright is worried about her preserves is ridiculous compared to the fact that she is being held for the murder of her husband, the men saying, "Well, can you beat the women! Held for murder and worryin' about her preserves!" (Glaspell 178). It does not occur to them that Mrs. Wright worked hard to put them up and that if she is not convicted, she will need them to get through the winter. The statement is also made that "women are used to worrying over trifles" (Glaspell 179). When the men overhear the ladies discussing how they think Mrs. Wright might be planning to finish her quilt, they speak to the women in a patronizing, amused tone. In fact, any time the men bother to bring their attention to the ladies at all it is as if they are "turning from serious things to little pleasantries" (Glaspell 183). The women, however, do not see anything amusing about spending their time "with little things" while they wait for the men to finish what they are doing (Glaspell 181). That women are considered incapable of deeper thoughts is evinced in the fact that the sheriff is not the least bit worried about what things they have gotten into and what they have chosen to take to Mrs. Wright in jail (Glaspell 185).

In both stories, men seem to regard the women as somehow less than men, based on things as irrelevant as the types of work women do, the topics that occupy the minds of women, and the fact they are women. This is probably the attitude that existed in society at the time the stories were written and is an attitude that even the raised consciousness of our current society has not lost. Both authors seem to be making a statement about how the attitude makes women feel. Both authors seem to think it is an incorrect way to regard women. In "Trifles" the men's disregard for the women's mental abilities turns against them in that the women basically solve the murder, but are able to hold back the damning evidence by using the men's attitude as a way to camouflage what they know (Glaspell 185). Conversely, in Munro's story of a young girl learning exactly what it means to be a girl, her reactions to how she is treated show how damaging to the girl's self esteem it can be to be forced into the small box of acceptable actions and behaviors men deemed as the woman's place in society.

[*Note:* The Works Cited page is generally a separate page from the rest of the paper and is paginated as the next page in the series.]

Works Cited

Glaspell, Susan. "Trifles." *Literature for Composition: Essays, Fiction, Poetry, and Drama*. Ed. Sylvan Barnet, Morton Berman, William Burto, and Marcia Stubbs. New York: HarperCollins, 1992. 176–185. Print.

Munro, Alice. "Boys and Girls." *Literature for Composition: Essays, Fiction, Poetry, and Drama*. Ed. Sylvan Barnet, Morton Berman, William Burto, and Marcia Stubbs. New York: HarperCollins, 1992. 825–835. Print.

Stephen Ryan
Native American Literature
M/W/F 10:00
Research Paper 2

In the Reservation of My Mind: Exploring Sherman Alexie

Native American literature continues to explode on the popular consciousness, with such famous writers as Joy Harjo and Leslie Marmon Silko continuing to gain in popularity and notoriety as the years go by. One of the most popular and, in many ways, most controversial Native American authors writing today is Sherman Alexie. Sherman Alexie, most well known for his poetry, has branched out into the world of novel-length fiction and even into the realm of motion pictures. Obviously, for an artist to continue to stretch himself into various means and methods of storytelling speaks of a great passion for the art produced. Sherman Alexie is very obviously a passionate writer who believes in the things that he says and does. In the arena of art theory,

Alexie has just as many strong ideas as he does in other areas and, not surprisingly, he articulates them strongly and unflinchingly.

In his "General Commentary," Sherman Alexie talks about heroes. He states that he has always had as his heroes people who were "just decent people . . . my writing is somehow just about decency" (Caldwell 2). Great art, then, is about decency. Great art is about the people who, against all odds, continue to hold their ground against a tide of selfishness and degradation and maintain their decency. In "The Trial of Thomas Builds-the-Fire," Alexie tells the story of a single Indian man who stands his ground in a court of law and tells his stories, unwilling to be silenced. Though Thomas Builds-the-Fire is punished, sentenced to two concurrent life terms in prison for his stories, still he stands and refuses to change, as evidenced by the closing line of the story: "Thomas closed his eyes and told this story" (Alexie, *Lone Ranger* 103). In this way, Alexie's story helps, in his own words, to "even the score" (Caldwell 2), by showing the unflinching determination and rigid beliefs of one man.

Alexie also believes that Native American writers should write "about the way we live" (Caldwell 3). Alexie states that Native American writers, especially, should be true to their real lives, writing "from their own lived experiences, not some nostalgic and romanticized notion of what it means to be Indian" (Caldwell 3). Alexie fulfills this particular bit of his theory quite well, writing many poems that could certainly be autobiographical. In his ironically titled "An Unauthorized Autobiography of Me," Alexie tells of many events from his own childhood, such as a music class in school (*One Stick Song* 15) and a winter when, after failing to pay the electric bill, Alexie's family lived without heat (*One Stick Song* 14). Alexie does not restrict his writing to such extremely personal events, however, but also writes about larger events and ideas that can apply to all Native Americans, such as Alexie's *Indian Killer*, in which Alexie shows the plight of the modern day urban Indian in a story intended to represent true Indian experiences in a modern city. Alexie states that he believes Native American writers should write out of the experiences that they have gathered in their lives, and it is certainly easy to see that Alexie practices what he preaches.

Sherman Alexie confronts many dangerously controversial issues in his works and never shies away from that conflict. He does, however, hold that the author who dares to condemn something must make sure that his or her own life bears out the standard taken: "If you're writing about racism, I don't think you should be a racist. If you're going to write about sexism and exploitation, then I don't think you should be sleeping around. If you're going to write about violence and colonialism, then I don't think you should be doing it to your own family" (Caldwell 3). Alexie, then, speaks with a bitter sarcasm in "Open Books," when he writes, "Thank God he wrote love poems to his son / even as he beat the boy bloody into corners. / Let us now celebrate the poet who wrote odes / to her husband on the skin of her lover's back" (*One Stick Song* 31). Sincerity and honesty are important to Sherman Alexie, and Alexie reviles the artist who condemns with his mouth while partaking in private.

Alexie also discusses the dangers of art: "Part of the danger of being an artist of whatever color is that you fall in love with your wrinkles . . . then you don't want to get rid of them . . . . We can write about pain and anger without having it consume us" (Caldwell 4). Alexie certainly delves deeply into his own pain to find material for his writing. In "One Stick Song," Alexie enumerates the tragedies that have shaken his personal life: "and I will sing of my sister / asleep when her trailer burned / o, bright explosion, crimson and magenta / o, burned sister, scarlet skin and white ash" (*One Stick Song* 38). Alexie dwells, not only on his sister, but on a tremendous number of relatives: father, mother, grandfather, grandmother, aunts, uncles and cousins, all of whom gave pain when they passed from Alexie's life. In another poem, "Sugar Town," Alexie focuses page after page on his father and the struggle with diabetes. Alexie digs deeply into his own private pain and anger for his poetry. Whether or not Alexie has managed to walk the fine line of drawing on and using his pain without falling prey to the dangers of treading too closely to that pain and anger, only Alexie himself could say; and on that point, he is very closemouthed.

Alexie believes the art of storytelling is tied very deeply to the art of lying, saying, "The nature, in my opinion, of storytelling in general . . . is that fiction blurs and nobody knows that the truth is" (West 6). Alexie explores this aspect of fiction and poetry writing and art in a poem already referenced once—"Open Books." Alexie tells in the opening section of reading a poem about a canyon and being impressed with the artist's descriptions. Upon talking with the artist's son, Alexie discovers the truth: "Hell, we never / even got close to the actual / canyon . . . Later on, my mother and I went out / for hamburgers while my father sat in the room / and wrote that goddamn poem" (*One Stick Song* 29–30). It might be stretching the point to call a storyteller a glorified liar, but the point Alexie makes is well taken. In "Soon to be a National Geographic Special," Alexie pushes the boundaries of truth even farther in the opening lines, when he tells us, "All the Indian boys in the world / gathered into one red Toyota Celica / or perhaps it was just Steve, Tom and me / though, truthfully speaking, it wasn't Tom / at all" (*One Stick Song* 62.) Sherman Alexie then recounts a true event from his youth, but only after he has lied twice in the first stanza. From claiming that all the Indian boys in the world occupy the car, he shifts quickly to give the reader three distinct names and then almost immediately retracts one of those names, only to finally reach the truth, or at least, what he finally says is the truth. This holds true in *Indian Killer* as well, where Alexie, if he does not actively lie, at least withholds truth of any kind, leaving it up to the reader to draw his or her own conclusions about the identity of the killer. If "lying" is part of art, then Sherman Alexie is truly an artist, for he has taken the method of "lying" to new stylistic heights.

Alexie certainly, however, sees art as a medium for uncovering the dark sides of society. Alexie discusses the recurring theme of the absent father within his writings and then springboards to a discussion of the problems that cross racial barriers: "Brown artists . . . write about fathers who physically leave and don't come back. White artists deal with fathers who leave emotionally, who sit in the chair in the living room but are gone" (West 7). Art, then, should illuminate the darker aspects of society that cross racial boundaries, not just those that are particular to a certain ethnic group. Alexie certainly does this with his theme of the absent father, as he states above, but he does not confine his cross-cultural writings to that theme. In *Indian Killer*, Alexie addresses the issue of adoption, not only with his Native American character, John Smith, but also with the white character, Jack Wilson. Alexie discusses the effects of not truly knowing origin in some detail. This is an issue that not only Native Americans face, but all people. Alexie might write from the perspective of the Native American, but he addresses issues that are larger than any single ethnic group, issues faced by all.

As an artist, Alexie also takes a stance somewhat reminiscent of Wagner's. When asked about his work on film, Alexie responds that he gave input on "everything—casting, costumes, sets, editing" (West 9). Much as Wagner did with his operas, Alexie attempts to keep his finger in every aspect of his storytelling. A true artist does not leave any aspect of his work up to outside influences, Alexie would say, but maintains creative control throughout the process. Alexie, having forged his theory while working alone on his poetry and fiction, does not let it go, even in the intricate and involved world of filmmaking.

A great deal of art theory can be derived by looking at those that Alexie credits as his major influences. Alexie names, as his five primary influences, "my father, for his nontraditional Indian stories, my grandmother for her traditional Indian stories, Stephen King, John Steinbeck and The Brady Bunch" (West 10). The first two influences Alexie illuminates himself. His grandmother and father, respectively, taught Alexie that Native Americans are tied to a tradition of the past, but also that they can work with and tweak that tradition. Alexie lives up to their influences. In "A Drug Called Tradition," Alexie discusses the ways in which tradition influences the lives of Native Americans today, even as Native Americans adapt that tradition and change it to suit their own needs (*Lone Ranger* 12). This is also a theme in *Indian Killer*, which deals with some Native characters, such as Reggie Polatkin, who are non-traditional in some ways and yet traditional in others.

By referencing Stephen King and John Steinbeck, Alexie intimates that his theory is somehow tied to their writings. In the writings of Stephen King, one finds ordinary people thrust into extraordinary circumstances. In the writings of Steinbeck, everyday people struggle for life in the hard passages of the world. Both of these themes can be traced in Alexie's writings. In the previously mentioned "The Trial of Thomas Builds-the-Fire," Alexie paints a picture of a modern setting in a courtroom that quickly trades in the mundane for the bizarre, as the title character finds himself convicted for murders convicted over a century previous (*Lone Ranger* 93). Also, one could again turn to *Indian Killer*, in which Alexie approaches racial issues through the avenue of a serial killer who may or may not have supernatural powers, including wings and the ability to make himself or herself invisible.

Alexie, however, is not averse to showing simple and everyday struggles and portraying them as struggles so large and important as to be almost mythic. In "Tiny Treaties," Alexie presents a situation so simple as to be almost boring: a walk down a highway in the midst of snowstorm (*First Indian* 56). Yet, for Alexie, this simple walk becomes a symbol for racial understanding and tolerance and, in the final analysis, becomes a powerful statement about the state of society. Ordinary people in ordinary situations can become very important under the hand of the master, and Alexie is certainly the master at this aspect of writing.

Alexie also cites as the fifth of his five great reference points, a television show. Specifically, Alexie gives credit to *The Brady Bunch*. As Alexie says later in the same interview, "I think a lot of Indian artists like to pretend that they're not influenced by pop culture or Western culture, but I am, and I'm happy to admit it" (West 10). Alexie acknowledges popular culture as his heritage of, using it in many different ways to inform his art. Alexie's most intriguing foray into popular culture comes with "Reservation Drive-In," which features a paragraph of writings on five different films, ranging from *Rocky* ("Do you remember those Yakima Indian boys played the theme song from *Rocky* ninety times straight one summer day") to *Enter the Dragon* ("Suddenly the Indian boy is Bruce Lee. Maybe he's only the Bruce Lee of the reservation playground, kicking every other child aside on his climb to the top of the slide") (*First Indian* 16). Another tie to *The Brady Bunch* lies in Alexie's love for an almost obscenely large cast, such as occurs in *Indian Killer*.

Alexie states that his work should "bridge the cultural distance between the characters . . . and the non-Indian audience" (West 10). Despite the anger and pain inherent in much of Alexie's work, his final goal is to see the great gap between races and cultural groups bridged in some small way. In many ways, Alexie's work does do this, by using dominant popular culture as a touchstone and by addressing larger questions that cross boundaries of race, as mentioned before.

Alexie also wants to find a way to "speak to the audience through my characters in a way that will give them something to hold onto as they're hearing and seeing something brand new" (West 10). Great art, then, should communicate something new and different to the audience and take them to places they have never been before and show them ways to think that they have never thought of before. In his poems, Alexie takes certain events and gives them a new spin, such as in "Split Decisions," in which Alexie dissects the Muhammad Ali–Joe Frazier fight and injects sociological statements and lines of thought into the event (*First Indian* 88). In "A Reservation Table of the Elements," Alexie shows that even tragic events are not immune to his new perspective: "Crazy Horse / never died. / Don't you know / he was the one / who climbed on top / of the Hindenburg / and lit / a match?" (*First Indian* 39). It is in these new perspectives that Alexie often offends the unprepared reader who finds in these statements simply inflammatory insults, rather than thought-provoking allegorical ramifications. As Alexie himself states, "I always want to be on the edge of offending somebody" (West 11). In this area, certainly, Alexie has succeeded with flying colors.

When discussing the uses of humor, Alexie states that humor is "really just about questioning the status quo" (West 11). Even a glance at the titles of some of Alexie's work can make this plain, as with his "An Unauthorized Autobiography of Me," which takes two opposing terms and puts them next to each other with no shame (Alexie, *One Stick Song* 13). That particular piece shows even more questioning:

"Sherman," says the critic, "How does the oral tradition apply to your work?"

"Well," I say, as I hold my latest book close to me, "It doesn't apply at all because I typed this. And when I'm typing, I'm very, very quiet." (Alexie, *One Stick Song* 16)

Alexie employs humor, in this way, to tweak the notion that all Native American literature ties directly to the oral tradition of ancient history. Humor, in Alexie's hands, is effective in the usual ways: it makes the reader laugh. Beyond that immediate response, however, lies a deeper purpose. The humor is often thought-provoking and significant, making statements about society and preconceived notions. Comedy often does not receive the recognition it deserves. In the hands of a talented individual, humor can be a powerful tool, just as it is in the hands of Alexie.

In a day when many artists are close-mouthed about the things they do and the reasons they have for doing them, Sherman Alexie stands as a great example of an artist who is not afraid to say what he believes in. His art theory is prominent in his interviews and can most often be seen directly in the art he produces. Alexie purports to be an artist to whom sincerity is very important. It is fitting then, that his art theory should coincide with his art as well as it does. The art of Sherman Alexie is easy to appreciate. Upon studying his art theory, however, it becomes even easier to understand the vision that drives Alexie and the means that he is willing to employ to see his vision come to life.

[*Note:* The Works Cited page is generally a separate page from the rest of the paper and is paginated as the next page in the series.]

Works Cited

Alexie, Sherman. *First Indian on the Moon*. New York: Hanging Loose Press, 1993. Print.

——. *Indian Killer*. New York: Warner Books, 1996. Print.

——. *The Lone Ranger and Tonto Fistfight in Heaven*. New York: The Atlantic Monthly Press, 1993. Print.

——. *One Stick Song*. New York: Hanging Loose Press, 2000. Print.

"General Commentary by Sherman Alexie." *Modern American Poetry: An Online Journal and Multimedia Companion to* Anthology of Modern American Poetry, Oxford University Press, 2000. Ed. Cary Nelson. 28 June 1998. Web. 15 Jan 2003.

West, Dennis. *Sending Cinematic Smoke Signals: An Interview with Sherman Alexie*. 30 Sep 1999. Cineaste Publishers. Web. 11 March 2003.

- **Note:** APA guidelines are similar to MLA guidelines but do have some major differences.
  - Papers in APA format submitted for a class use a 1 inch margin.
  - Pages are numbered consecutively, beginning with the title page.
  - Every page contains a running head, a shortened form of the title, instead of the writer's last name.
  - An abstract (a short summary) of the paper may be required as the document's second page.
  - Quotations of less than 40 words appear as part of the running text; quotations of more than 40 words are inset five spaces and double-spaced, using no quotation marks.
  - Section headings may be appropriate. If so, they are centered; subsection headings are left-justified and underlined.
  - The References list (the APA equivalent of the Works Cited page) is a separate page of the manuscript, numbered consecutively with the rest.

APPENDIX B: PRINCIPLES OF READER RESPONSE AND REVIEW

Writers who are interested in a good product tend to revise extensively. In fact, it's possible to throw out an entire draft and start over. Revision is based on a number of factors. A writer might revise to include additional material. A writer might revise to make his or her audience and/or purpose more clear. A writer might revise to make the structure stronger. A writer might revise because, as he or she writes, his or her ideas change. Finally, a writer revises for correct grammar and mechanics and to make the document as elegant as possible.

As a peer reviewer, it is your job to help the writer determine what needs revision. You might want to help the writer brainstorm for more ideas or help the writer with clarification. If you disagree with the ideas expressed, help the writer with the areas of disagreement so the writer can strengthen the arguments.

A peer reviewer is a reader. It is the reviewer's job to function as a reader so the writer can determine what he/she needs to revise to make the points more clear.

ESSAY RESPONSE FORMS

During the semester, you may want to check your essays against a checklist before those essays are submitted in final copy for grading. Forms that you might use to aid you in the review process follow.

ESSAY RESPONSE FORM

Subject
1. Is the subject sufficiently narrowed for an essay of the assigned length?
2. List two or three other narrowed topics that might be used for an essay on this general topic.

Introduction
1. Does the introduction sufficiently catch your attention and make you want to read the paper?
2. Does the introduction lead logically to the thesis?
3. What suggestions could you make for improving the introduction?

Thesis
1. Where is the thesis? Is it in the appropriate place?
2. Does it fit the requirements of a thesis?

Development
1. List the segments of the thesis that you are trying to develop.
2. What are the strongest segments?
3. What other segments within the range of the thesis could have been included?

Conclusion
1. What method of conclusion are you using?

2. To what degree do you feel the discussion is "rounded off" by the conclusion paragraph or paragraphs?

Each Body Paragraph
1. What is the topic sentence?
2. What is the principal method of development?
3. What is the order in the paragraph, the logical connection between the sentences?
4. What other ordering of the sentences might work?
5. Evaluate the completeness of the paragraph. To what extent do you feel satisfied with the paragraph's development?
6. What one or more pieces of development might you include?
7. Are there transitional elements in the paragraph? List obvious attempts at transition. Are they successful and smooth?

Whole Essay
1. What is your level of interest in the essay as it is written?
2. Do the mechanics interfere with your reading of the essay?
3. Do you make unnecessary use of the indefinite "you"?
4. Is there careless shifting of tone?

ESSAY RESPONSE FORM

The answer to each section must be YES before you go to the next section.
1. Read the paper. Does the paper make sense? YES/NO If the answer is NO, where does the paper not make sense and what do you need to do to make the paper make sense?
2. Find the thesis statement. Is it clear? YES/NO If the answer is NO, what do you need to know to make it clear?
3. Are there topic sentences in the paragraphs in the body of the paper? YES/NO If the answer is NO, what do you need to know to make a clear topic sentence for each paragraph in the body?

    Do the topic sentences support the thesis statement? YES/NO If the answer is NO, what would make the topic sentences support the thesis statement?

    Are the topic sentences supported by the information in the paragraph, such as three or more specific items of support or one long example? YES/NO If the answer is NO, what do you need to see in the paragraph to have a fully supported topic sentence?
4. Does the introduction of the paper lead up to the thesis statement? YES/NO If the answer is NO, what do you need to see in the introduction paragraph to lead up to the thesis?

    Does the conclusion of the paper summarize the main points, restate the thesis, state the significance of the information in the paper, or otherwise provide closure for the paper? YES/NO If the answer is NO, what do you need to see in the conclusion to really end the paper?
5. Are the mechanics accurate? YES/NO If the answer is NO, what corrections need to be made?

    If the paper is documented, is the documentation accurate in the paper and on the Works Cited page? YES/NO If the answer is NO, what corrections in documentation need to be made?

ESSAY RESPONSE FORM

The answer to each section must be YES before you go to the next section.
1. Read the paper. Does the paper make sense? YES/NO If the answer is NO, where does the paper not make sense and what do you need to do to make the paper make sense?
2. Find the thesis statement. Is it clear? YES/NO If the answer is NO, what do you need to know to make it clear?
3. Are there topic sentences in the paragraphs in the body of the paper? YES/NO If the answer is NO, what do you need to know to make a clear topic sentence for each paragraph in the body?

    Do the topic sentences support the thesis statement? YES/NO If the answer is NO, what would make the topic sentences support the thesis statement?

    Are the topic sentences supported by the information in the paragraph, such as three or more specific items of support or one long example? YES/NO If the answer is NO, what do you need to see in the paragraph to have a fully supported topic sentence?
4. Does the introduction of the paper lead up to the thesis statement? YES/NO If the answer is NO, what do you need to see in the introduction paragraph to lead up to the thesis?

    Does the conclusion of the paper summarize the main points, restate the thesis, state the significance of the information in the paper, or otherwise provide closure for the paper? YES/NO If the answer is NO, what do you need to see in the conclusion to really end the paper?
5. Are the mechanics accurate? YES/NO If the answer is NO, what corrections need to be made?

    If the paper is documented, is the documentation accurate in the paper and on the Works Cited page? YES/NO If the answer is NO, what corrections in documentation need to be made?

ESSAY RESPONSE FORM

The answer to each section must be YES before you go to the next section.
1. Read the paper. Does the paper make sense? YES/NO If the answer is NO, where does the paper not make sense and what do you need to do to make the paper make sense?
2. Find the thesis statement. Is it clear? YES/NO If the answer is NO, what do you need to know to make it clear?
3. Are there topic sentences in the paragraphs in the body of the paper? YES/NO If the answer is NO, what do you need to know to make a clear topic sentence for each paragraph in the body?
   Do the topic sentences support the thesis statement? YES/NO If the answer is NO, what would make the topic sentences support the thesis statement?
   Are the topic sentences supported by the information in the paragraph, such as three or more specific items of support or one long example? YES/NO If the answer is NO, what do you need to see in the paragraph to have a fully supported topic sentence?
4. Does the introduction of the paper lead up to the thesis statement? YES/NO If the answer is NO, what do you need to see in the introduction paragraph to lead up to the thesis?
   Does the conclusion of the paper summarize the main points, restate the thesis, state the significance of the information in the paper, or otherwise provide closure for the paper? YES/NO If the answer is NO, what do you need to see in the conclusion to really end the paper?
5. Are the mechanics accurate? YES/NO If the answer is NO, what corrections need to be made?
   If the paper is documented, is the documentation accurate in the paper and on the Works Cited page? YES/NO If the answer is NO, what corrections in documentation need to be made?

ESSAY RESPONSE FORM

The answer to each section must be YES before you go to the next section.
1. Read the paper. Does the paper make sense? YES/NO If the answer is NO, where does the paper not make sense and what do you need to do to make the paper make sense?
2. Find the thesis statement. Is it clear? YES/NO If the answer is NO, what do you need to know to make it clear?
3. Are there topic sentences in the paragraphs in the body of the paper? YES/NO If the answer is NO, what do you need to know to make a clear topic sentence for each paragraph in the body?
   Do the topic sentences support the thesis statement? YES/NO If the answer is NO, what would make the topic sentences support the thesis statement?
   Are the topic sentences supported by the information in thc paragraph, such as three or more specific items of support or one long example? YES/NO If the answer is NO, what do you need to see in the paragraph to have a fully supported topic sentence?
4. Does the introduction of the paper lead up to the thesis statement? YES/NO If the answer is NO, what do you need to see in the introduction paragraph to lead up to the thesis?
   Does the conclusion of the paper summarize the main points, restate the thesis, state the significance of the information in the paper, or otherwise provide closure for the paper? YES/NO If the answer is NO, what do you need to see in the conclusion to really end the paper?
5. Are the mechanics accurate? YES/NO If the answer is NO, what corrections need to be made?
   If the paper is documented, is the documentation accurate in the paper and on the Works Cited page? YES/NO If the answer is NO, what corrections in documentation need to be made?

RESPONSE SHEET FOR ESSAYS

Explain each "No" answer and mark the paper.
1. Does the paper support the thesis?   Y N
2. Does the paper have logical sequencing?   Y N
3. Does each topic sentence relate to the thesis?   Y N
4. Are the topic sentences clearly defined in the paragraphs?   Y N
5. Do the sentences in the paragraph all relate to the topic sentence?   Y N
6. Does the paper have correct format?   Y N
    a) Paragraphs   Y N
    b) Documentation
        Does the paper contain information from sources?   Y N
        Is this information in the form of paraphrases/summaries/quotations?   Y N
        Is each quotation connected to the text? (No quotation can stand without words from the essay writer—that's you—to introduce it.)   Y N
        Has all information from sources been documented?   Y N
        Is the documentation exactly in accordance with MLA format?   Y N
        Is there a Works Cited page?   Y N
        Does the Works Cited page contain the number of sources required by the assignment/ subject/length of the paper?   Y N
        Do each of the Works Cited entries exactly correspond to MLA format requirements?   Y N
    c) Manuscript   Y N
7. Are the sources appropriate to the topic of the paper?   Y N
8. Do the citations in the paper correlate to the listing on the Works Cited page?
    Does each Works Cited entry appear at least once cited in the text or as a parenthetical citation in the text?   Y N
9. Does the Works Cited page correlate to the citations in the paper?
    Does each source that appears in the text or as a parenthetical citation in the text appear as a Works Cited entry?   Y N
10. Does the tone fit the subject matter?   Y N
11. Is the paper easy to read? Is it interesting?   Y N
12. How could the paper be improved?
13. Additional Comments

Forms

RESPONSE SHEET FOR REPORTS

Explain each "No" answer and mark the paper.
1. Is the format correct for each section? Y N
    a. Correct bibliographic data Y N
    b. Title of the work in the first sentence of the summary paragraph Y N
    c. Sufficient number of sentences to cover and develop the topic in each paragraph Y N
2. Does the summary convey the necessary information? Y N
3. Does the evaluation address the work and its strengths and weaknesses? Y N
4. Does the personal reaction reveal engagement with the work? Y N

RESPONSE SHEET FOR PARAGRAPHS

Each Expository Paragraph
1. The topic sentence is _____
2. The principle method of development (the mode) is _____
3. The development order is _____
4. An alternative developmental ordering might be _____
5. Evaluate the completeness of the paragraph. To what extent do you feel satisfied with the paragraph's development? _____
6. What one or more pieces of development might you include?
7. Are there transitional elements in the paragraph? Yes/No Explain.
   List obvious attempts at transition.
   Are they successful and smooth? Yes/No Explain.
8. Does the paragraph interest you?
9. Is the manuscript prepared in accordance with manuscript guidelines? Yes/No Explain.

READER RESPONSE FORM

Writer: Prepare two or three questions for the respondent. You might ask about some aspect of the essay with which you want help or that you especially like or dislike.

Respondent:
1. First read through the entire paper. Note in the margin "good" when you come across particularly strong or interesting writing. Place a question mark next to any item you find confusing, that needs more explanation, or that does not seem to fit.

2. Read through the paper again carefully and answer the following questions:
   a. Does the title catch your interest and tell you what the paper is about?
   b. Does the introduction engage your interest and lead you to the thesis?
   c. What kind of essay is the paper designed to be? Does the essay fulfill the requirements for that kind of essay? For example, does a descriptive essay appeal to all five senses? Does a classification essay divide the topic into categories and then define how those categories are limited? Does a cause and effect essay show you the clear cause-effect relationship? If the paper contains an analogy, is the analogy clear? Does an argument essay present an argument, address both sides, and appropriately prove the writer's side? Does an expository essay use examples on which to base the reader's view of the topic?
   d. What is the thesis of the paper? What does the thesis say that makes you want to read the rest of the paper? What is new or interesting about the thesis?
   e. Is the evidence sufficient to prove the writer's point? How could the evidence be improved? What evidence or material should the writer add? For each argument, are the lines of reasoning clear? Where could the reasoning be made clearer? Are alternative views addressed and then disproved?
   f. Does the writer seem knowledgeable? Credible? Trustworthy? Does the writer appeal to the audience's values, intelligence, imagination, emotion? How could that appeal be strengthened?
   g. What strategies could the writer use to improve the essay? What changes in words, sentences, or sentence structure might the writer make to increase the effectiveness or to improve the accessibility of the essay?
   h. What points need clarification or expansion? Where might the writer improve the essay by explaining more or more clearly? Where might the writer add examples?
   i. Is the essay organized appropriately for presentation of the topic? Might the writer move paragraphs or thoughts around to improve clarity or effectiveness?
   j. Does the conclusion bring closure? Does it complete the essay? How might it be improved?
   k. Sum up the strengths and weaknesses of the essay. Make at least one comment in each category.

3. Respond to the writer's questions. Carefully consider what the writer has asked and try to make helpful comments in response to that question.

4. Finally, read the paper again, carefully noting any problems in grammar, spelling, mechanics, documentation, etc. Place a check or bar in the margin for each problem you find, one check or bar per problem.

WRITER REFLECTION FORM

To improve your skills as a writer, it is important to think critically about the process as well as the product that you have produced.

First, gather all the material that you used in creating the document: pre-writing, organizational plans, drafts, reader response or reaction forms, etc.

Then, write reflectively about the process you went through as you created the document.

1. Write one-half to one page about the process you used as you created the document.

2. Write one page about a problem you had while you worked on the essay. Tell how you solved that problem and what you learned while working on it.

    a. For example, if you were writing a descriptive essay, did you have trouble making sure you addressed all five senses? If you were writing an expository (informative) essay, did you have trouble finding examples to support your point? If you were writing a research essay, did you have trouble designing a thesis that was interesting and informative? Did you have trouble with the documentation or with the appropriate use of quotations?

    b. How did you find out you had the problem? Did you find it yourself by having difficulty originally or did a peer reviewer call it to your attention?

    c. How did you solve that problem? Did you work on wording? Did you go to a peer? A tutor? The instructor? How useful were the tactics you used to solve the problem?

    d. What did you learn from working on this problem?

WRITER REFLECTION FORM

To improve your skills as a writer, it is important to think critically about the process as well as the product that you have produced.

First, gather all the material that you used in creating the document: pre-writing, organizational plans, drafts, reader response or reaction forms, etc.

Then, write reflectively about the process you went through as you created the document.

1. Write one-half to one page about the process you used as you created the document.

2. Ask yourself the following questions and answer them in approximately one page.

    a. What could you have improved in your paper?
    b. What worked?
    c. What did not work?
    d. What would you do differently, now that you have had the experience of writing this paper?
    e. What was the hardest part of the assignment for you?
    f. What was the easiest part of the assignment for you?
    g. What was the most satisfying part of the assignment for you?
    h. What was the least satisfying part of the assignment for you?

3. Finally, draw a conclusion from this process and the process of doing the original assignment: what did you learn from the original assignment and from the reflection?

WRITER REFLECTION FORM

As you look over a body of work, consider the following:
1. In which areas of writing do you consider you've shown most improvement? What are your strengths as a writer? What are your weaknesses?
2. Rate each essay or other work in the body according to the grading rubric that follows, using 1-5. Support the rating that you give each work.
3. Choose an item from the body of work that you believe you could revise most successfully. Plan a strategy for revision.
4. Choose one section (a paragraph, an introduction, etc.). Include the original and the revised versions and explain why you chose to make the revisions you did.
5. After completing steps 1-4 above, assemble the answers into a full document of approximately two pages (500 words). That means each of the four steps should be a paragraph or more.

GENERAL RUBRIC FOR PAPERS, SCALE OF 1-5[1]

(Rubrics, scaled 1-5, furnished by Jim Ford.)

Students will demonstrate mastery of course material and stated goals under the following guidelines.

5   The paper displays mastery of the following communication skills. All work is rich, smooth, and significant; it is free of mechanical errors; and it shows stylistic finesse. The paper demonstrates excellence in all areas. The paper is intriguing and thought-provoking. Arguments are logical and persuasive. Ideas are well articulated and presented in original ways.

4   The paper is significantly more than competent. The paper should be free of mechanical errors. The paper engages the reader, and shows evidence of significant critical and creative thinking. The student displays excellence in critical analysis or artistic creation, if not both. Arguments show careful thought and are basically persuasive. Ideas are presented in original ways.

3   The paper is generally competent, with few errors. The paper shows evidence of significant progress, and as a whole gets the job done. The paper provides evidence of some critical and creative thought. The student may display excellence in either critical analysis or artistic creation. Arguments are present and show some thought. Ideas are present and developed, if not particularly original or well articulated.

2   The paper is barely competent. The paper may have mechanical errors and/or lack significance. The paper may provide evidence of the student's ability to communicate but not reveal skill. Evidence of critical and creative thinking is marginal. The paper displays adequate critical and creative thinking, but not much more than that. Arguments and ideas are asserted without much critical thought. Little originality is evident. This is a rote or hasty paper.

1   The paper is inadequate. There are frequent errors. The paper is superficial and lacks organization. Evidence of critical and/or creative thinking is largely absent. The paper shows little or no method or planning. Work seems thrown together with minimal critical or creative thought.

---

[1] Narrative rubrics with 1-5 scores are furnished by Dr. Jim Ford.

GENERAL RUBRIC FOR PROJECTS, SCALE OF 1-5
Rubric for Evaluating Capstone Portfolio and Project

Written, Oral, and Visual Communication

5   Both the project and the portfolio display mastery of these communication skills. All work is rich, smooth, and significant; is free of mechanical errors; and shows stylistic finesse. The portfolio demonstrates strength in all three areas, and excellence in at least two of the three (written, oral, visual).

4   Both the project and the portfolio are significantly more than competent. The project should be free of mechanical errors. The portfolio demonstrates significant ability in all three areas, and excellence in at least one of the three (written, oral, visual).

3   Both the project and the portfolio are generally competent, with few errors. The portfolio shows evidence of significant progress, and as a whole gets the job done.

2   Both the project and the portfolio are barely competent. The project may have mechanical errors and/or lack significance. The portfolio may provide evidence of the student's ability to communicate in one of the three areas, but at least one other skill is not evident.

1   Either the project or the portfolio (or both) is inadequate. There are frequent errors. The project itself is superficial and lacks organization.

Critical and Creative Thinking

5   Both the project and the portfolio are intriguing and thought-provoking. Arguments are logical and persuasive. Ideas are well articulated and presented in original ways.

4   Both the project and the portfolio engage the reader, and show evidence of significant critical and creative thinking. The student displays excellence in either their critical analysis, or their artistic creation, if not both. Arguments show careful thought, and are basically persuasive. Ideas are presented in original ways.

3   Both the project and the portfolio provide evidence of some critical and creative thought. The student may display excellence in either their critical analysis, or their artistic creation, and are competent with both. Arguments are present and show some thought. Ideas are present and developed, if not particularly original or well articulated.

2   Evidence of critical and creative thinking is marginal. The project and portfolio display adequate critical and creative thinking, but not much more than that. Arguments and ideas are asserted without much critical thought. Little originality is evident. This is a rote or hasty project and/or portfolio.

1   Evidence of critical and/or creative thinking is largely absent. Either the portfolio or the project (or both) shows little or no method or planning. Work seems thrown together with minimal critical or creative thought.

Ability to Critique Own Work

5   The reflective paper is insightful and nuanced. The student articulates a deep awareness of the strengths and limitations of both the portfolio and the project. The reflective paper critically examines the various works in the portfolio and the project. The student illuminates the key decisions that shaped the final version of the project and portfolio, weaving the entire work into a coherent narrative.

4   The reflective paper is coherent and engaging. The student articulates some awareness of the strengths and limitations of both the portfolio and the project. The reflective paper critically examines the various works in the portfolio and the project. The student discusses the key decisions that shaped the final version of the project and portfolio, and provides some narrative of the overall process.

3   The reflective paper is basically coherent. The student articulates some awareness of the strengths and limitations of either the portfolio, or the project, if not both. The reflective paper critically examines some aspects of the portfolio and the project. The student discusses the key decisions that shaped the final version of the project and portfolio; the larger narrative is present, although it is largely undeveloped and/or unpersuasive.

2   The reflective paper is problematic at best. The student articulates minimal awareness of the strengths and limitations of either the portfolio or the project, but not both. The reflective paper fails to critically examine either the portfolio or the project. The student discusses the final version of the project and portfolio without providing much insight into the overall creative process. If a narrative is presented at all, it is unoriginal and poorly articulated.

1   The reflective paper is weak. The student fails to provide a meaningful discussion of the strengths or limitations of the portfolio and project. The reflective paper shows little or no method or planning. Work seems thrown together with minimal critical or creative thought.

Understanding of Western Cultural Heritage/Appreciation of Diversity of Perspectives on Human Condition

5   Based on one of the items in the portfolio and/or on the capstone project, the rater finds the item insightful and nuanced. The student articulates a deep awareness of Western/world culture and an appreciation of varying perspectives on the human condition.

4   Based on one of the items in the portfolio and/or on the capstone project, the rater finds the item significantly more than competent. The student articulates some awareness of the Western/world culture and an appreciation of varying perspectives on the human condition.

3   Based on one of the items in the portfolio and/or on the capstone project, the rater finds the item generally competent. The student articulates some awareness of the Western/world culture and some appreciation of varying perspectives on the human condition, although they are largely undeveloped and/or unpersuasive.

2   Based on one of the items in the portfolio and/or capstone project, the rater finds the item barely competent. The item may lack significance: articulating only a narrow awareness and minimal insight into Western/world culture and narrow or minimal appreciation of varying perspectives on the human condition.

1   Based on one of the items in the portfolio and/or capstone project, the rater finds the item fails to show even minimal awareness of Western/world culture; the item fails to reveal even a narrow or minimal appreciation of varying perspectives on the human condition.

GRADING SHEET

CONTENT (0-25 points)

Excellent	25 points	no improvement necessary
Very Good	24, 23	writer's own truth, original perception; narrow enough to be clearly and completely developed by specifics; appropriate to audience/purpose; substantive; thorough development of thesis; relevant to topic; creative
Good	22, 21	has many of characteristics of truth/perception/appropriateness, development, relevance, but lacks thoroughness, freshness, creativity
Average	20, 19	some perception of subject; adequate range; limited development; mostly relevant to topic-lacks detail; reasonably well developed, but lacking completeness; good content, but lacking organization
Fair-Poor	18, 17, 16	limited perception of topic; little substance; little development
Very Poor	15-11	little perception of the subject; non-substantive; not pertinent to subject; not enough to evaluate

ORGANIZATION (0-15)

Excellent	15	no improvement necessary
Very Good	14, 13	fluent expression; ideas clearly slated/supported; succinct; well organized; logical sequencing; cohesive
Good-Average	12, 11	organized but predictable; obvious/mechanical organization; occasional blurring of purpose
Fair	10	focus blurred; poor beginning/ending; weak movement, repetition, paragraphing, proportion; lacking transitions
Poor	9, 8	ideas confused/rambling; lacks logic/sequence; not focused/no main point
Very Poor	7, 6	doesn't communicate; no organization; too little to evaluate

VOICE, TONE, DICTION (0-15)

Excellent	15	no improvement necessary
Very Good	14, 13	sophisticated range; precise word choice/usage; word form mastery; appropriate tone; effective figurative language
Good-Average	12, 11	adequate range; somewhat vague; occasional errors of word form, choice, use; clichés; slang; redundancies; little or no figurative language
Very Poor	8, 7	meaning confused or obscured; inappropriate use of language

SENTENCE STRUCTURE (0-15)

Excellent	15	no improvement necessary
Very Good	15, 14	sentence variety; mastery of compound-complex structure/tense/ parallelism/agreement/number/ word function/pronouns/prepositions
Good-Average	13, 12, 11	undistinguished; generally unified/correctly constructed—few slips in unity or clarity, some dull sentences; generally lacking in positive qualities
Fair/Poor	10, 9	occasional lack of unity/clarity; sentences noticeably thin and immature, repetitious patterns, wordy structures
Poor	8, 7	marked lack of unity or clarity
Very Poor	6, 5	communication seriously impeded by lack of unity/clarity

PUNCTUATION (10-0) one point deduction for each error
USAGE, MECHANICS (10-0) one point deduction for each error
SPELLING/READABILITY (10-0) one point deduction for each error: Manuscript form, carelessness, excessive errors also affect this area.

Note: Documented papers (papers assigned that should be documented) may lose additional points if incorrectly documented. For example, a paper might lose 10–20 points if it lacks correct Works Cited format and 10–20 points if it lacks internal, parenthetical documentation, etc.

NAME _____
CONTENT (0-25 points)
Excellent 25 points
Very Good 24, 23
Good   22, 21
Average   20, 19
Fair to Poor 18, 17, 16
Very Poor 15, 14, 13, 12, 11
ORGANIZATION (0-15)
Excellent to Very Good 15, 14, 13
Good to Average   12, 11
Fair   10
Poor   9, 8
Very Poor   7, 6
VOICE, TONE, DICTION (0-15 points)
Excellent to Very Good 15, 14, 13
Good to Average   12, 11
Very Poor   8, 7
SENTENCE STRUCTURE (0-15 points)
Excellent to Very Good 15, 14
Good to Average   13, 12, 11
Fair to Poor   10, 9
Poor   8, 7
Very Poor   6, 5
PUNCTUATION (10-0) _____
One point deduction for each error
USAGE, MECHANICS (10-0) _____
One point deduction for each error
SPELLING/READABILITY (10-0) _____
One point deduction for each error
Manuscript form, carelessness,
excessive errors may also affect this area.

NAME _____
CONTENT (0-25 points)
Excellent 25 points
Very Good 24, 23
Good   22, 21
Average   20, 19
Fair to Poor 18, 17, 16
Very Poor 15, 14, 13, 12, 11
ORGANIZATION (0-15)
Excellent to Very Good 15, 14, 13
Good to Average   12, 11
Fair   10
Poor   9, 8
Very Poor   7, 6
VOICE, TONE, DICTION (0-15 points)
Excellent to Very Good 15, 14, 13
Good to Average   12, 11
Very Poor   8, 7
SENTENCE STRUCTURE (0-15 points)
Excellent to Very Good 15, 14
Good to Average   13, 12, 11
Fair to Poor   10, 9
Poor   8, 7
Very Poor   6, 5
PUNCTUATION (10-0) _____
One point deduction for each error
USAGE, MECHANICS (10-0) _____
One point deduction for each error
SPELLING/READABILITY (10-0) _____
One point deduction for each error
Manuscript form, carelessness, excessive
errors may also affect this area.

NAME _____
CONTENT (0-25 points)
Excellent 25 points
Very Good 24, 23
Good   22, 21
Average   20, 19
Fair to Poor 18, 17, 16
Very Poor 15, 14, 13, 12, 11
ORGANIZATION (0-15)
Excellent to Very Good 15, 14, 13
Good to Average   12, 11
Fair   10
Poor   9, 8
Very Poor   7, 6
VOICE, TONE, DICTION (0-15 points)
Excellent to Very Good 15, 14, 13
Good to Average   12, 11
Very Poor   8, 7
SENTENCE STRUCTURE (0-15 points)
Excellent to very good 15, 14
Good to Average   13, 12, 11
Fair to Poor   10, 9
Poor   8, 7
Very Poor   6, 5
PUNCTUATION (10-0) _____
One point deduction for each error
USAGE, MECHANICS (10-0) _____
One point deduction for each error
SPELLING/READABILITY (10-0) _____
One point deduction for each error
Manuscript form, carelessness, excessive
errors may also affect this area.

NAME _____
CONTENT (0-25 points)
Excellent 25 points
Very Good 24, 23
Good   22, 21
Average   20, 19
Fair to Poor 18, 17, 16
Very Poor 15, 14, 13, 12, 11
ORGANIZATION (0-15)
Excellent to Very Good 15, 14, 13
Good to Average   12, 11
Fair   10
Poor   9, 8
Very Poor   7, 6
VOICE, TONE, DICTION (0-15 points)
Excellent to Very Good 15, 14, 13
Good to Average   12, 11
Very Poor   8, 7
SENTENCE STRUCTURE (0-15 points)
Excellent to Very Good 15, 14
Good to Average   13, 12, 11
Fair to Poor   10, 9
Poor   8, 7
Very Poor   6, 5
PUNCTUATION (10-0) _____
One point deduction for each error
USAGE, MECHANICS (10-0) _____
One point deduction for each error
SPELLING/READABILITY (10-0) _____
One point deduction for each error
Manuscript form, carelessness, excessive
errors may also affect this area.

NAME _____
CONTENT (0-25 points)
Excellent 25 points
Very Good 24, 23
Good   22, 21
Average   20, 19
Fair to Poor 18, 17, 16
Very Poor 15, 14, 13, 12, 11
ORGANIZATION (0-15)
Excellent to Very Good 15, 14, 13
Good to Average   12, 11
Fair   10
Poor   9, 8
Very Poor   7, 6
VOICE, TONE, DICTION (0-15 points)
Excellent to Very Good 15, 14, 13
Good to Average   12, 11
Very Poor   8, 7
SENTENCE STRUCTURE (0-15 points)
Excellent to Very Good 15, 14
Good to Average   13, 12, 11
Fair to Poor   10, 9
Poor   8, 7
Very Poor   6, 5
PUNCTUATION (10-0) _____
One point deduction for each error
USAGE, MECHANICS (10-0) _____
One point deduction for each error
SPELLING/READABILITY (10-0) _____
One point deduction for each error
Manuscript form, carelessness, excessive errors may also affect this area.

NAME _____
CONTENT (0-25 points)
Excellent 25 points
Very Good 24, 23
Good   22, 21
Average   20, 19
Fair to Poor 18, 17, 16
Very Poor 15, 14, 13, 12, 11
ORGANIZATION (0-15)
Excellent to Very Good 15, 14, 13
Good to Average   12, 11
Fair   10
Poor   9, 8
Very Poor   7, 6
VOICE, TONE, DICTION (0-15 points)
Excellent to Very Good 15, 14, 13
Good to Average   12, 11
Very Poor   8, 7
SENTENCE STRUCTURE (0-15 points)
Excellent to Very Good 15, 14
Good to Average   13, 12, 11
Fair to Poor   10, 9
Poor   8, 7
Very Poor   6, 5
PUNCTUATION (10-0) _____
One point deduction for each error
USAGE, MECHANICS (10-0) _____
One point deduction for each error
SPELLING/READABILITY (10-0) _____
One point deduction for each error
Manuscript form, carelessness, excessive errors may also affect this area.

NAME _____
CONTENT (0-25 points)
Excellent 25 points
Very Good 24, 23
Good   22, 21
Average   20, 19
Fair to Poor 18, 17, 16
Very Poor 15, 14, 13, 12, 11
ORGANIZATION (0-15)
Excellent to Very Good 15, 14, 13
Good to Average   12, 11
Fair   10
Poor   9, 8
Very Poor   7, 6
VOICE, TONE, DICTION (0-15 points)
Excellent to Very Good 15, 14, 13
Good to Average   12, 11
Very Poor   8, 7
SENTENCE STRUCTURE (0-15 points)
Excellent to Very Good 15, 14
Good to Average   13, 12, 11
Fair to Poor   10, 9
Poor   8, 7
Very Poor   6, 5
PUNCTUATION (10-0) _____
One point deduction for each error
USAGE, MECHANICS (10-0) _____
One point deduction for each error
SPELLING/READABILITY (10-0) _____
One point deduction for each error
Manuscript form, carelessness, excessive errors may also affect this area.

NAME _____
CONTENT (0-25 points)
Excellent 25 points
Very Good 24, 23
Good   22, 21
Average   20, 19
Fair to Poor 18, 17, 16
Very Poor 15, 14, 13, 12, 11
ORGANIZATION (0-15)
Excellent to Very Good 15, 14, 13
Good to Average   12, 11
Fair   10
Poor   9, 8
Very Poor   7, 6
VOICE, TONE, DICTION (0-15 points)
Excellent to Very Good 15, 14, 13
Good to Average   12, 11
Very Poor   8, 7
SENTENCE STRUCTURE (0-15 points)
Excellent to Very Good 15, 14
Good to Average   13, 12, 11
Fair to Poor   10, 9
Poor   8, 7
Very Poor   6, 5
PUNCTUATION (10-0) _____
One point deduction for each error
USAGE, MECHANICS (10-0) _____
One point deduction for each error
SPELLING/READABILITY (10-0) _____
One point deduction for each error
Manuscript form, carelessness, excessive errors may also affect this area.

RECOGNIZING LOGICAL FALLACIES

(or "What you should NEVER do when presenting an argument")

Renèe Cox

Read the essay below. Find and label the logical fallacies in the argument (the sentences are numbered for easy reference). Discuss how the fallacies weaken the writer's claims and how the writer should have/could have presented a stronger, more logical case.

[1] The gun control debate is really just a matter of the right of the American people to defend themselves and defend their property. [2] But many people, who seem to have no sense of reality and no sense of what it means to be an American, are fine with the idea of guns being completely controlled by the government and being taken away from decent people.

[3] Senator Scott Hayes, a Republican serving the state of Tennessee, understands this; he is a great sportsman and hunter and speaks against gun control several times a year in Washington. [4] On the other hand, Senator Daniel Chance has spoken in favor of gun control several times in the past decade, but considering the political party he serves, we should not be surprised. [5] However, since Senator Chance is the one who is now under investigation for hiring illegal aliens, I do not think we should take his opinions very seriously. [6] Thankfully, we have political watchdogs like Ridge Linton, who just two months ago on his late night radio show, made the following comment: "It's as simple as this, people. A government that would deny its own people the right to defend themselves is a government that echoes of fascist Germany, and I tell you I want no part of a nation like that." [7] Linton has been talking about political issues on the air for almost fifteen years; he knows what he is talking about.

[8] Some people say they are OK with gun control as long as it is handled responsibly and as long as people's individual rights are not trampled on, but they need to realize there is no middle road—there is complete, absolute gun control, or there is no gun control at all. [9] The people who are in favor of gun control are in favor of seeing all American's civil rights revoked, including the right of self-defense. [10] They believe that guns kill people, but all they need to do is remember the bumper sticker: "guns don't kill people—people kill people." [11–14] And just because a person owns a gun does not mean he is going to go out and shoot somebody. My family has owned guns for our whole lives, and we have never shot anyone. I do not know a single person in my whole family or circle of friends who is violent or who is a threat because he has a gun. Just from my own personal experience, it is easy to see that owning guns does not make a person more likely to be violent.

[15–16] But all this squawking and debating over gun control is not even necessary, because the United States Constitution solves everything. All the citizens of the United States are given the right to own handguns and hunting weapons in the Second Amendment, which was part of the Bill of Rights, ratified in December of 1791. [17] The fathers of our country knew that Americans deserved that right, and all true Americans believe that we still deserve it. [18] As for those who do not believe we deserve it, we should take a few minutes to imagine how the nation would be if gun control succeeds. **[19]** As the saying goes, "if guns are outlawed, only outlaws will have guns." **[20–22]** Innocent people will not have any way to stay safe from criminals who would kill them. Fathers and husbands will not be able to protect their wives from rapists. Men who do not make much money will not have the right to hunt and bring home food for their hungry children. **[23–24]** Is this really how we want life to be in our country? We have to stand up for our constitutional rights. **[25]** Either we find a way to keep gun control laws from being passed, or we lose everything.

APPENDIX C: OTHER DOCUMENTATION STYLES

In addition to APA and MLA documentation, documentation styles include the *ACS Style Guide* (for chemistry documents), the *Chicago Manual of Style* (for general documents), the *Columbia Guide to Online Style* (for online sources), the *Complete Guide to Citing Government Documents* (for citing government documents), *Scientific Style and Format: The CBE Manual for Authors, Editors, and Publishers* (for documents in the biological sciences), and Turabian's *A Manual for Writers* (for general documents). Some fields also have their own style guides. Always check with the person requesting the paper to determine which style is appropriate for the paper.

ENDNOTE/FOOTNOTE FORMAT: SAMPLE DOCUMENTATION EXAMPLES

Works Cited Page

- **Note:** For MLA-format Works Cited examples, see the main section on the research paper. For page setup, see "Manuscript Preparation."

Endnotes or Footnotes

Book with one author.
   [3] Charles Dickens, *Great Expectations* (New York: Rinehart, 1948): 134. Print.

Book with more than three authors, with an edition after the first, and with several volumes.
   [8] Walter Blair, et al., *The Literature of the United States*, vol. 1, 3rd ed., 3 vols. (Glenview: Scott Foresman, 1969) 322. Print.

Article, signed, appearing on only one page, in a magazine/journal with volume and issue number, with part of the title in quotation marks.
   [13] Richard Wolkomir, "For the 'Tied Up' Businessman," *Smithsonian* 17.12 (March 1987): 192. Print.

Article in a magazine/journal with no volume number, appearing on more than one page, inclusive pages, from a magazine/journal published bi-monthly.
   [7] Daphne Gail Fautin, "The Anemone Is Not Its Enemy," *National Wildlife* Oct.–Nov. 1987, 22–25. Print.

Online source.
   [6] Erica Recomp, "Computers and Film Focuses," 1 May 1998, Web, 15 Aug. 1996..

Subsequent References

[5] Dickens 136.
[9] Blair et al. 11.
[13] Wolkomir 192.
[9] Fautin 25.
[8] Recomp.

Index

abbreviations
    punctuation for, 145
    used on graded papers, 162
absolutes, 13
abstracts, 47
ACS Style Guide, 211
active voice, 14
actors, 103
agreement
    of pronoun with antecedent noun, 138, 140–141
    of verb/subject, 138, 139–140
alliteration, 113
allusion, 98, 113
analogy, 32–33
analysis
    defined, 113
    literary criticism and, 91–92, 95–100
analysis development, 35–36
annotated bibliographies, 78
annotating, of text, 3
An Officer and a Gentleman (film), 105
anomaly, 98, 113
APA (American Psychological Association), 184
    citation for quotations, 87
    References, 61, 62, 68–70
apostrophes, 149–151, 160
archaic words/phrases, 136
argumentation development, 36–37
articles
    documentation of sources for, 61–70
    reports and reviews on, 50–51
assonance, 113
atlases, 133
audience
    planning process and, 10
    writing hints and, 13
audio tapes/books, 132
authors, 14

"Behind the Formaldehyde Curtain" (Mitford), 9
bibliographies
    annotated bibliographies, 78
    APA format, 61, 62, 68–70
    "bib cards," 60
    choosing resources and, 60–61
    documentation and, 61–62
    MLA format, 60–67
biographical interpretation, 100
biographical references, 133–134
body paragraphs
    revision of, 37
    in three-section essays, 11–12
books, documentation of sources for, 61–70
brackets, 83–87, 155
brainstorming, 6
business indexes, 133
business writing
    business letters and, 118–120
    job interviews and, 117–118
    memoranda and, 126
    résumés and, 121–125

cacophony, 113
call numbers, 129, 130
camera directors, 104
capitalization, 141–143
card catalogs, 129–132
cataloging systems, 129–132
    Dewey Decimal System, 129, 130, 131
    Library of Congress system, 129, 131
Cat People (film), 104
cause and effect development, 35–36
characterization, 113
Chicago Manual of Style, 211
choice, parallel construction and, 138
chronological order, 14–15, 23–24
classification development, 33–35
climax, 96, 113
close-up, 105
coherence, 23–25
college essays
    organization for, 11–12
    patterns of development for, 27–37
colloquialisms, 135
colons, 148
Columbia Guide to Online Style, 211
commas, 146–148
compact discs, 132
comparison
    development, 31–32
    parallel construction and, 138
Complete Guide to Citing Government Documents, 211

complete sentences, 136–137
computer sources, for research, 134
conclusion
    revision of, 37
    in three-section essays, 11–12
conflict, 97–98, 113
consonance, 114
context, of poetry, 109
continuity, 104
contractions
    avoiding in formal writing, 161
    style and, 13
contrast
    comparison development and, 31–32
    parallel construction and, 138
controlling ideas. *see* main ideas
credibility, of sources, 71–72
criticism
    defined, 114
    literary criticism and, 91–92, 101–103
critiques, 52
cutting, 105

dashes, 156, 160
databases, 71, 134
definition development, 29
dénouement, 96, 114
description development, 28
Dewey Decimal System, 129, 130, 131
dialect, 136
dialogue, 153–154
Dickens, Charles, 100
dictionaries, 133
difference, grouping by, 31–32
directors, 103–104
division development, 33–35
docu-drama, 96
documentation styles, 211–212. *see also* APA (American Psychological Association); MLA (Modern Language Association)

editing, 37
editors, 104
electronic communication (e-mail), 58–59
ellipsis
    breaks in, 160
    for quotations, 83–87, 155–156
emoticons, 59
emotion, poetry and, 109, 110
encyclopedias, 60
end marks, 145–146, 160
endnotes, 211–212
entertainment writing, 9
envelopes, for business letters, 118, 119
epiphany, 96, 114
Essay Response Forms, 185–186, 187, 189
essays. *see also* reader response and review
    defined, 114
    reports and reviews on, 50–51
    revision of, 37
essay tests, 52–58
    examples, 55–56, 57, 58
    steps for, 52–55
E.T. (film), 104, 105
euphony, 114
evaluations, 51–52
"Eveline," 98
example development, 28–29
exclamation marks, 146
explication, 114
exploratory writing, 9

fade-in/fade-out, 105
Faulkner, William, 98
fiction, 95–96, 114
field notes, 2–3
film analysis, 103–108
final drafts, 88
first drafts, 79
    APA citation and, 87
    citing literary texts and, 82–83
    long quotations and, 86–87
    quotations and, 79–82
    special punctuation for quotations and, 83–85
    summarizing and paraphrasing, 86
first person central, 99, 114
first person observer point of view, 99, 114
first person secondary point of view, 99, 114
five-paragraph essays, 12, 17
flashbacks, 96, 114
footnotes, 211–212

Index

form, of poetry, 109
formal English, 135
forms. *see* reader response and review
free writing, 5

General Rubric for Papers, Scale of 1-5, 199
General Rubric for Projects, Scale of 1-5 (for evaluating capstone portfolio and project), 200–202
genre, 95
glossary of literary terms, 113–116
Grading Sheet, 203–207
grammar. *see* mechanics
graphs, 128

Hawthorne, Nathaniel, 92–95, 101–103
historical interpretation, 100
Huckleberry Finn (Twain), 98
Hughes, Langston, 100–101
hyperbole, 114
hyphens, 151–152, 160

illiterate language usage, 135
images, 98, 114
inclusive page numbers, 62–63
incomplete sentences, 136–137
indexes
    business indexes, 133
    periodical indexes, 132
informal English, 135
informative writing, 9
initials, 145
initiation, 115
interlibrary loan, 132
Internet
    assessing sources from, 71–72
    online style resource for, 211
    as source for research, 60, 134
interpretation, literary criticism and, 91–92, 100–101, 115
interviews, 117–118
introduction
    introductory paragraphs, in essays, 12
    revision of, 37
    in three-section essays, 11–12
italicizing, 154

job interviews, 117–118
journalists' questions, 8
journals, 4

laboratory reports, 127
letter writing
    business letters, 118–120
    job acceptance letters, 124
    letters of recommendation, 124–125
    memoranda, 126
    thank you letters, 118
libraries, 129
    card catalogs, 129–132
    computer and Internet sources, 134
    interlibrary loan, 132
    librarians, 134
    non-print sources, 132
    periodical indexes, 132
    special help from, 133–134
Library of Congress
    card catalog system, 129, 131
    Library of Congress Subject Headings index, 132
lighting, 104
literal interpretation, 100
literary criticism, 91–95
    analysis and, 91–92, 95–100
    criticism, defined, 91–92, 101–103
    film analysis and, 103–108
    interpretation and, 91–92, 100–101
    literary terms and, 113–116
    poetry analysis and, 108–112
literary works, citing, 82–83
London, Jack, 98
long quotations, 86–87. *see also* quotations

magazines, 60
main ideas
    comparison development and, 31–32
    in formal essay organization, 11
    topic sentences and, 21–22
Manual for Writers, A (Turabian), 211
manuscript preparation, 38–40
mapping, 7
*M*A*S*H* (television series), 96
mechanics

abbreviations/symbols used in grading of papers, 162
agreement, 138–141
brackets, 155
capitalization, 141–143
common mistakes, 161
dashes, 156
ellipsis, 155–156
numbers, 144–145
parallel construction, 137–138
parentheses, 155
of poetry, 110
punctuation, 145–154
punctuation, spacing marks, 159–160
sentence structure, 136–137
spelling, 157–159
style and, 13
underlining/italicizing, 154
usage, 135–136
memoranda, 126
metaphor, 115
meter, 115
Miller, Arthur M., 9
Mitford, Jessica, 9
MLA (Modern Language Association), 47
citation for quotations, 80–82, 86–87
model student papers, MLA style, 163, 164–165, 165–167, 168–171, 172–174, 175–176, 176–178, 178–183
Works Cited, 60–67
model student papers, 163
APA style, 184
essays, MLA style, 164–165, 165–167, 168–171, 172–174, 175–176, 176–178, 178–183
montage, 105

narration
development, 27
point of view and, 99–100
netiquette, 58
newspapers, 60
nonfiction, 11, 96
non-idiomatic English, 135
non-standard language usage, 135

notes
assessing sources for research papers and, 71–72
note cards, 76–77
note taking, 2–3
numbers, 144–145

obsolete words/phrases, 136
occupational dialects, 136
Oedipus the King (Sophocles), 97, 100
Olds, Sharon, 111–112
online sources. *see* Internet
onomatopoeia, 115
"On the Road" (Hughes), 100–101
order of importance, 14–15, 23, 25
organization
for college essays, 11–12
organization plan page, 14–18
outlines and, 19–20
for paragraphs, 21–26
writing hints for, 13–14
outlines
note taking and, 3
organization of, 3, 19–20
for research papers, 78

paradox, 115
paragraphs
coherence and unity of, 23–25
development of, 21–23
essay organization and, 11–12
organization of, 21–26
patterns of development for, 27–37
topic sentences, 16–18
transitions for, 25, 26
parallel construction, 137–138
paraphrasing, 86
parentheses, 155
"pearls of wisdom" method, 3
periodicals
indexes of, 132
as source for research papers, 60
periods, 145–146
persona, 99–100
person against God (fate) conflict, 97
person against person conflict, 97

Index

person against self conflict, 98
person against society conflict, 97
personification, 115
persuasive writing, 9, 36–37
plagiarism, 72–77
planning process
    for research papers, 78
    writing for an audience and, 10
    writing for a purpose and, 9
plot, 96, 115
Poe, Edgar Allen, 98
poetic word usage, 136
poetry, 108–112
point of view, 99–100, 115–116
points. *see* main ideas; point of view
précis, 47, 48, 51
pre-writing, 4
    brainstorming, 6
    free writing, 5
    journalists' questions, 8
    mapping, 7
    reading for writing, 8
process development, 30
producers, 103
professional dialects, 136
pronoun/antecedent noun agreement, 138, 140–141
Psycho (film), 104
punctuation, 13, 145
    apostrophes, 149–151
    colons, 148
    commas, 146–148
    end marks, 145–146
    for quotations, 83–87
    semicolons, 149
    spacing and, 159–160
purposeful writing, planning for, 9

question marks, 145–146
quotations, 79. *see also* mechanics
    APA citations and, 87
    citing literary works and, 82–83
    long, 86–87
    MLA citation and, 80–82, 86–87
    quotation marks, 152–154
    reference books for, 134

    special punctuation for, 83–85
    summarizing and paraphrasing, 86

reader response and review, 185
    Essay Response Forms, 185–186, 187, 189
    General Rubric for Papers, Scale of 1-5, 199
    General Rubric for Projects, Scale of 1-5 (for evaluating capstone portfolio and project), 200–202
    Grading Sheet, 203–207
    Reader Response Forms, 195–196
    Recognizing Logical Fallacies, 209–210
    Response Sheet for Essays, 191
    Response Sheet for Paragraphs, 193
    Response Sheet for Reports, 193
    Writer Reflection Forms, 197, 198
Reader Response Forms, 195–196
reading
    for content, 41–45
    for writing, 8
Recognizing Logical Fallacies, 209–210
recommendation, letters of, 124–125
reference books, 133
References, 61, 62, 68–70
regionalisms, 135
religious interpretation, 100–101
repetition, 25, 27
reports (reviews), 50–51, 52, 90–91. *see also* literary criticism; reader response and review
research papers, 59–60. *see also* libraries
    bibliographies for, 60–71, 78
    checklist for, 89–90
    choosing topics for, 60
    final drafts, 88
    first drafts, 79–87
    notes and resources for, 71–78
    reviewing, 90–91
    revision of, 88
response log, 3
Response Sheet for Essays, 191
Response Sheet for Paragraphs, 193
Response Sheet for Reports, 193
response to literature. *see* literary criticism
résumés, 121–125
reviews. *see* reports (reviews)

revision, 37. *see also* reader response and review
    manuscript preparation and, 38–40
    of research papers, 88
    writing as recursive process and, 40
rhetorical précis, 48, 51
rhyme (rime), 116
"Rose for Emily, A" (Faulkner), 98

science writing
    ACS Style Guide for chemistry, 211
    graphs, 128
    laboratory reports, 127
    Scientific Style and Format: The CBE Manual for Authors, Editors, and Publishers for biological sciences, 211
scriptwriters, 103
search engines, 60
"Self-Defense: Can You Protect Yourself and Avoid the Slammer?" (Miller), 9
semicolons, 149
sentence structure, 136–137
setting, 116
"Sex without Love" (Olds), 111–112
similarity, grouping by, 31–32
simile, 116
slang, 135
slashes, 160
sociological interpretation, 101
Sophocles, 97, 100
sound, 104
spatial order, 14–15, 23–24
special help, from libraries, 133–134
specialized writing. *see also* business writing; science writing
    evaluations, 51–52
    reports and reviews, 50–51
    summarizing, 47
spelling, 157–159
Spielberg, Steven, 105
stacks, 129, 131
Straight Time (film), 97
style, 13–14
    defined, 116
    of works, 99
subject elements
    grouping by, 31–32

    organization and, 14–15
summarizing, 47, 86
supporting statements, 22–23
symbols, 116
    symbolism, 98
    used on graded papers, 162

technical writing, 47
"Tell-Tale Heart, The" (Poe), 98
tense, 14
thank you letters, 118
theme, 100, 110, 116
thesis statements, 15, 16–18
    in formal essay organization, 11
    purpose of, 21–22
    revision of, 37
    support for, 22–23
third person limited account, 99–100, 116
third person objective, 99, 116
third person omniscient narration, 100, 116
three-section essays, 11–12
titles
    of poetry, 109
    style for, 13
    underlining/italicizing for, 154
    using library catalog systems and, 129
    working titles, 15
"To Build a Fire" (London), 98
tone, 99, 116
topics
    choosing, 60
    organization and, 14
topic sentences. *see* thesis statements
transition words, 25, 26
Turabian, Kate L., 211
Twain, Mark, 98

underlining, 154
unity, 23–25
usage
    mechanics of word usage, 135–136
    transition words, 25, 26
    word choice for résumés, 121

verb/subject agreement, 138, 139–140
video cassettes, 132

Index

Williams, Tennessee, 100
Works Cited, 60–67, 211–212
World Wide Web. *see* Internet
Writer Reflection Forms, 197, 198
writing process
    essays, 11–12
    learning about, 2–4
    organization plan page, 14–18
    outline alternatives, 20
    outlines, 19–20
    paragraphs, 21–26
    paragraphs/essays, patterns of development for, 27–37
    planning, 9–10
    pre-writing, 4–8
    writing as recursive process, 40
    writing hints, 13–14

"Young Goodman Brown" (Hawthorne), 92–95, 101–103
"you," writing style and, 13